Thinking in Education

Second Edition

MATTHEW LIPMAN
Montclair State University

CAMBRIDGE
UNIVERSITY PRESS

PUBLISHED BY THE PRESS SYNDICATE OF THE UNIVERSITY OF CAMBRIDGE
The Pitt Building, Trumpington Street, Cambridge, United Kingdom

CAMBRIDGE UNIVERSITY PRESS
The Edinburgh Building, Cambridge CB2 2RU, UK
40 West 20th Street, New York, NY 10011-4211, USA
477 Williamstown Road, Port Melbourne, VIC 3207, Australia
Ruiz de Alarcón 13, 28014 Madrid, Spain
Dock House, The Waterfront, Cape Town 8001, South Africa

http://www.cambridge.org

Cover: Pre-Columbian, Mexico, Guerrero, Xochipala, Ceramic
Figures *Seated Shaman* and *Seated Youth*. Early Formative,
red-brown micaceous clay; H. 13.5 cm. and H. 11.0 cm.
Courtesy: Princeton University Art Museum

First published 2003

Printed in the United Kingdom at the University Press, Cambridge

Typeface Palatino 10/13.5 pt.   *System* LATEX 2$_\varepsilon$ [TB]

A catalog record for this book is available from the British Library.

Library of Congress Cataloging in Publication Data
Lipman, Matthew.
Thinking in education / Matthew S. Lipman. – 2nd ed.
    p.   cm.
Includes bibliographical references and index.
ISBN 0-521-81282-8 (HB) – ISBN 0-521-01225-2 (PB)
1. Thought and thinking – Study and teaching.   2. Critical thinking – Study and
teaching.   3. Creative thinking – Study and teaching.   4. Judgment in education.
I. Title.
LB1590.3 .L57   2003   2002023089
371.3 – dc21

ISBN 0 521 81282 8 hardback
ISBN 0 521 01225 2 paperback

Contents

Preface

I am grateful to the students and visiting scholars who have read and commented on various sections of this work at a number of stages of its development. Their criticisms were very helpful and resulted in numerous improvements in what was, in my opinion, a manuscript with many difficulties. I want to express my appreciation to Samantha Spitaletta, from the Office of Publications at Montclair State University, for her contribution to the preparation of the artwork. I also want to express my gratitude to Manuela Gómez for her help in developing this manuscript so as to fit the enlarged outlook of the second edition onto the foundation represented by the first edition. If the result turns out to be successful, no small part of the credit should be given to her; I am alone responsible for the shortcomings that remain. Likewise, I am indebted to Joanne Matkowski, who lavished care on the manuscript through each of its various incarnations.

I am also grateful for permission to reprint my following articles:

To Venant Cauchy, "Educating for Violence Reduction and Peace Development," in Venant Cauchy (ed.), *Violence and Human Coexistence*, vol. 2 (Montréal: Éditions Montmorency, 1994), pp. 363–78.

To Thea Jelcich Zanfabro, "Thinking Skills Fostered by Philosophy for Children," in Judith W. Segal, Susan F. Chipman, and Robert Glaser (eds.), *Thinking and Learning Skills*, vol. 1, *Relating Instruction to Research* (Mahwah, N.J.: Lawrence Erlbaum Associates, 1985), pp. 83–7.

To Armen Marsoobian, "On Children's Philosophical Style," *Metaphilosophy* 15 (1984), pp. 318–30.

To Oxford University Press for permission to reprint Edwin Muir, "The Question," in *Collected Poems* (New York: Oxford University Press, 1965).

Introduction to the Second Edition

If there is any institution that can legitimately claim to be world-wide, it is probably the school. However different the cultures may be, the schools resemble one another remarkably. The system of education they provide is founded on the presupposition that children go to school to learn. They learn basic skills, like reading, writing, and arithmetic proficiencies. And they learn content, like geography, history, and literature.

A cynical commentator once observed that human beings invented speech in order to conceal their thoughts. The same observer might have added that they send their children to school to learn in order to keep them from thinking. If so, it is a tactic that has had only limited success. Children are not easily prevented from thinking. Indeed, it is often the case that our most cherished recollections of our school years are of those moments when we thought for ourselves – not, of course, because of the educational system, but in spite of it.

Yet there has always been a strand of educational thought that held that the strengthening of the child's thinking should be the chief business of the schools and not just an incidental outcome – if it happened at all. Some have argued in this way because they thought that the schooling of future citizens in democracy entailed getting them to be reasonable and that this could be done by fostering children's reasoning and judgment. Others have argued in this way because they saw their social systems – particularly the economic, bureaucratic, and legal systems – congealing into rationality, and it was by fostering children's rationality that the schools could best prepare children for the world they would face when they grew up. And still others have contended that helping children to think well and think for themselves is required not just for reasons of social utility but because children have the right to receive nothing less.

Since the mid-1970s, the proponents of thinking in the schools (and colleges) have become distinctly more numerous and more vocal. The banner they have unfurled is emblazoned with the phrase "critical thinking," and although neither they nor those who oppose them are very clear about just what critical thinking entails, the hue and cry continues to mount. This awareness among educators that something has to be done to improve the quality of thinking in the classroom has prevailed until now.

What constitutes thinking? To this expert, good thinking is accurate, consistent, and coherent thinking; to that one, it is ampliative, imaginative, creative thinking. This scholar points to examples of good thinking in literature; that one points to instances of it in the history of science or conceives of it as the employment of scientific methodology. One philosopher hails it for its embodying logic and rationality; another, because it embodies deliberation and judgment. One educator acclaims it for helping us decide what to believe; another argues that belief decisions are out of place in a school context and that the teacher should aim at helping students discover only what they have sufficient evidence for asserting.

Amid the confusion, school administrators have to make decisions about how they are going to upgrade the educational offerings in their schools, about whether or not teachers should be retrained and, if so, about what approach should be employed. To make such decisions, they will need to be guided by definitions that clearly indicate just what a significant improvement of thinking is and how it can be made operational. They need to determine by what criteria teachers and researchers can decide whether or not such operationalization has been successful.

Thinking in Education has been proposed as a step in this direction. It does not claim to be definitive, but it does try to raise a few of the questions that need to be raised and to supply some of the answers that can be provided at this very early stage in the development of a thinking-oriented educational process.

Thinking in Education makes no claim to being a work of specialized scholarship. Nor does it claim to be impartial and nonjudgmental. It regards the capacity of philosophy, *when properly reconstructed and properly taught*, to bring about a significant improvement of thinking in education. The case for this claim has not yet been made; the present study can be regarded as a kind of prologue to the making of such a case.

There is a second important (though not final) claim to be made in *Thinking in Education*, which is that the pedagogy of the "community of inquiry" should be the methodology for the teaching of critical thinking, whether or not a philosophical version of it is being employed. A third claim is that it is no accident that critical thinking is affiliated with such cognate terms as "criticism" and "criteria." These terms have to do with reasoning, evaluation, and judgment, and these in turn have to do with the improvement of thinking in which students are being encouraged to engage. Insofar as judgment is an art, the community of inquiry provides an environment in which it can be practiced and acquired. Spinoza was being unduly grim when he remarked that everything excellent is as difficult as it is rare. We have to create a society in which excellence flourishes in diversity and abundance. Upgrading the reflective element in education is a reasonable place to begin.

Throughout the past decade, efforts were made to introduce "thinking skills" into schools in which the acquisition of education had hitherto been equated with the acquisition of information. According to the earlier rhetoric prevailing in state departments of education and local boards of education, these efforts were making progress, and students could be said to be acquiring "knowledge," or, to use an even headier term, "understanding." But these were traditional conceptions of the aims of education, and what we were now told was happening was that the schools everywhere were engaged in equipping their students with "critical thinking." The arrival of the millennium seemed to be right on schedule. "Critical thinking" was the watchword for what the better teachers supposedly taught in the better schools. So ran one account. According to another, "critical thinking" was characteristic of the sharper students, whether or not as a result of their having been taught to think that way. Some students are just naturally clear thinkers, it was said. What was to be done with the others was not quite evident.

In some respects the situation was a puzzling one. The last decade of the twentieth century was expected to be one of a gathering of momentum by the critical thinking movement. There would be more textbooks devoted to the topic, to be used by college undergraduates as well as by teachers-in-preparation. There would be more national and international conferences devoted to critical thinking, argumentation, informal logic, and "cooperative learning." There would be more degree programs in critical thinking, more minicourses in the subject for teachers looking for in-service credits, more philosophers and educational psychologists devoting themselves to expanding the scholarly side of critical thinking by strengthening its claims to be a discipline. The fact is that some of these things have been happening but others have not. The great conferences on thinking and its educational possibilities are no longer prevalent. The journals that once flourished by exploring the many facets of this latest of educational paradigms were now struggling, in what had been the most prosperous of decades, to keep from going under. The university-based academics, whose fledgling interest in matters of educational significance had been expected to grow stronger year by year, were instead, in increasing numbers, turning their backs on opportunities to contribute to the strengthening of the theoretical framework of the critical thinking movement. Not even the historical scholars were now devoting time to examining the undoubtedly genuine credentials of the important history of that movement, and without such an examination, critical thinking's claims to be a discipline can hardly be persuasive.

Still, this bleak account fails to give the whole picture. Publishers *are* putting out more and more textbooks in critical thinking. Teachers *are* being required to devote a portion of their time to in-service enrichment courses, and among these, critical thinking courses appear to be very popular. The trendy educational newspapers and periodicals, like *Educational Leadership*, which devoted much space to teaching for thinking in the 1970s and 1980s, but then pulled back in the 1990s, are now beginning to show signs of renewed interest in the topic and perhaps even of a renewed sense of responsibility for the outcome. Everywhere there seem to be signs – no doubt feeble in many cases – of a certain degree of *institutionalization* of critical thinking in the schools. Perhaps this is all we could have hoped for, given the circumstances. This is what happens to educational fads that are considered successful: They come to be taken for granted, although at a fairly low level of efficiency.

For the vast majority of elementary school students, critical thinking has not fulfilled its promise. To be sure, more promises were made for it than it could possibly keep. But there were a number of deficiencies that doomed it from the start:

1. The critical thinking approach was, by itself, narrow and skimpy. It needed to be based much more solidly on informal logic, formal logic, educational psychology, developmental psychology, and philosophy, but this was seldom done.
2. Even where some instruction in these areas was provided, teacher preparation was insufficient.
3. Little effort was made to devise, as part of the approach, a creative thinking component that would engage students in imaginative thinking, and in thinking about the imagination.
4. Likewise, no serious effort was mounted to construct a valuational component, in which students would be able to talk together freely about the different sorts of values, and how they were to be appreciated.
5. Not only was there little teaching for judgment, there was seldom a clear identification of what was meant by "teaching for judgment," possibly because educators did not recognize judgment as an important educational goal or because they thought it incapable of being taught.
6. It was not recognized that most pedagogies of the "thinking in education" movement were inappropriate. The only fully appropriate pedagogy was the one called "the community of inquiry approach," and relatively few teachers had been effectively prepared to use that approach.
7. No effort was made to connect the various dimensions of thinking (critical, creative, and caring) into a whole, both conceptually and developmentally. Critical thinking by itself came to be

seen as a disconnected, discontinuous fragment, shouldered with responsibility for upgrading the whole of education.

Some parts of the second edition of *Thinking in Education* are retained from the first edition; Parts Three and Four are almost completely new. What these new parts offer is a view of education at a more comprehensive level of effectiveness than critical thinking by itself could ever hope to achieve. Some components new to the elementary school level of education have been introduced: emotions, caring thinking, mental acts, and informal fallacies. I have tried to merge both new and old elements into an integrated developmental sequence that will offer at least a glimpse of the direction in which we are to go. It is my hope that we can thus achieve an education that enriches, enlightens, and liberates, that fosters understanding, strengthens judgment, improves reasoning, and imparts a clear sense of the relevance of inquiry to the enlargement of humanity. Fortunately, there are already in existence approaches to education that demonstrate unequivocally that these goals are feasible.

PART ONE

EDUCATION FOR THINKING

1

The Reflective Model of Educational Practice

There are three key models of private and public institutions in our
society. The family represents institutionalized private values. The
state represents institutionalized public values. And the school epit-
omizes the fusion of the two. As an amalgam of private and public
interests, the school is no less important than the distinctively private
or the distinctively public. In some ways it is the most important of
all, because through it past and present generations deliberately and
consciously attempt to stamp a design upon the future. Yet in all three
institutions – family, government, and school – practice and policy
conflicts abound, for each family and each government administration would like to shape succeeding generations in its own image,
but the facts of social change – growth, regression, aimless or orderly
drift – conspire to defeat such aspirations.

The school is a battleground because it, more than any other social institution, is the manufacturer of the society of the future, and
virtually every social group or faction therefore aspires to control the
school for its own ends. Not that this is generally acknowledged. The
received opinion has it that the schools reflect the accepted values of
their time; they are not to challenge such values or suggest alternatives to them. Many parents shudder at the notion that the schools
will take it upon themselves to become initiators of social change, because they fear that this will merely mean that the schools will have
been captured by this or that social faction seeking to impress its will
upon the world.

If, then, the school is looked upon as the representative of all social factions rather than of any one in particular, it is able to retain its claim to legitimacy in a democratic society, because it will not have surrendered its claim to impartiality. On the other hand, it will tend to be under these circumstances a very conservative – even traditionalist – institution.

And this is, in fact, what the school is in our present society. As for the schools of education that prepare future teachers, they probably do not see themselves as suppliers of technical personnel to school districts that constitute the market for such personnel. Yet school districts specify what textbooks they want taught and how they want them taught, and it would be unlikely that they would hire prospective teachers who have been trained to teach very different books in very different ways. So schools of education justify their resistance to change on the ground that it would be a disservice to their students to prepare them any differently, despite the fact that few professors of education have full confidence in the methods of teacher preparation they employ. But schools of education are not alone in this; school districts excuse themselves on the ground that textbook and test publishers provide them with no feasible alternatives, and the publishers in turn point out that they are circumscribed by state departments of education and defended by the research that emerges from the schools of education in these same states. And so each factor sees itself as fixed in its position and helpless to change. For all practical purposes, therefore, critics from the outside are wasting their breath. Considerations like tests and texts and turfs – in short, economic and bureaucratic considerations – have locked the system in place so that, like a boat with a jammed rudder, it is only free to move about in circles.

Were these the only considerations, the situation would be much more dismal than it actually is. The allegiances that keep the members of the family cemented together are kinship, child-rearing necessities, the economic division of labor, and sexual interdependence. The primary governmental allegiance is to consensus, in the name of which virtually any military or economic policy can be justified. (The courts represent a partial exception to this generalization, since constitutionality and precedent must also be taken into account. But the laws followed by the courts are consensus-generated.) The schools, on the other hand, have a very different criterion to which they can appeal, and that is *rationality*.

RATIONALITY AS AN ORGANIZING PRINCIPLE

There are, of course, many kinds of rationality. There is means–end rationality. An example is the corporation that sees its ultimate objective as profit and its various policies as means of maximizing profits. Another type of rationality has to do with the distribution of authority in a hierarchical organization. Examples are the military, the church, and the government. These may also be seen as mixed types. The army, for instance, is hierarchically organized yet is always prepared to seek military victory. The schools too are bureaucracies, with a rationalized distribution of authority, but their goal is the production of educated persons – persons who are as knowledgeable as they need to be and as reasonable as they can be helped to be.

Reasonableness is not pure rationality; it is rationality tempered by judgment. The schools, like the courts, are under a mandate of rationality, but in a democratic society we need reasonable citizens above all. How are we to educate for reasonableness?

It is not simply that the schools must themselves be rationally organized so that they can justify their organization and procedures to lay boards of education. It is not simply that they operate for the good of those they serve (in contrast to businesses, which operate for the profit of those who own or who manage them). It is that the students who pass through the schools must be reasonably treated in an effort to make them more reasonable beings. This means that every aspect of schooling must be, in principle at any rate, rationally defensible. There must be better reasons for using this curriculum, these texts, these tests, these teaching methods than for using alternatives to them. In every instance, the rationale is the same: Children brought up in reasonable institutions are more likely to be reasonable than children raised under irrational circumstances. The latter, as we know, are more likely to be those who grow up irrational and raise their own children irrationally. More reasonable schools mean more reasonable future parents, more reasonable citizens, and more reasonable values all around.

Can we educate for reasonableness without educating for thinking? This is the dilemma Kant was faced with. He sincerely wanted people to think for themselves, and he was ready to contemplate teaching them to do so while they were still children. But the thinking for oneself Kant had in mind was not the full-fledged engagement in inquiry that we advocate today; it was rather the voluntary obedience of each individual to universally generalizable principles.[1] Rationality for Kant was therefore very different from rationality for Socrates or Aristotle or Locke or Dewey.

SCHOOLING WITHOUT THINKING

It is a fact often noted and commented on with regard to very young children as they begin their formal education in kindergarten that they are lively, curious, imaginative, and inquisitive. For a while, they retain these wonderful traits. But then gradually a decline sets in, and they become passive. For many a child, the social aspect of schooling – being together with one's peers – is its one saving grace. The educational aspect is a dreaded ordeal.

Since the child's first five or six years were spent at home, and since this did not seem to impair the child's intellectual energies, it seems strange to condemn the child's background for a subsequent loss of curiosity and imagination. It is more likely due to the nature of schooling. How are we to explain why the child's intellectual alertness is not extinguished in the often adverse circumstances of family or childcare life, while it is all too frequently damped down in the often congenial circumstances of the classroom?

One hypothesis that seems worth considering is that children learning to speak are in a situation even more mystifying and enigmatic than that of an immigrant in a foreign culture. The immigrant still has the use of his or her native tongue; the toddler has no language at all. But the child is surrounded by a world that is problematic through and through, a world in which everything invites inquiry

---

[1] Kant's 1784 essay *What Is Enlightenment?* begins with a powerful statement of the need for a society in which we each think for ourselves instead of having guardians who do our thinking for us. But as the essay proceeds it is apparent that Kant has not grasped the necessity, in democratic institutions, of internal self-criticism. His later *Foundations of the Metaphysic of Morals* continues and systematizes this approach.

and reflective questioning, a world as provocative of thought as it is of wonder and action. And of all the puzzling things in this world, none is more puzzling than one's own family and the bewildering regimen that its members follow and seek to impose upon the new-comer. The child finds this world extraordinary, but the uncanniness is evocative; it draws speech and thought out of the child. This devel-opment is further abetted by the prospect that the child's acquisition of speech will lead to a fuller integration into the life and practices of the family and the home.

What the child probably expects from the school is a surrogate home and a surrogate family – a surrounding that constantly stim-ulates thought and speech. Even when it is uncaring, as it often is, the home environment contains so much to be learned, so much to be experienced, that it represents a constant challenge to the very young child. What the child discovers in early elementary school, on the other hand, is a completely structured environment. Instead of events that flow into other events, there is now a schedule that things must conform to. Instead of statements that can be understood only by gleaning their significance from the entire context in which they occur, there is a classroom language that is uniform and rather indif-ferent to context and therefore fairly devoid of enigmatic intimations. The natural mysteriousness of the home and family environment is replaced by a stable, structured environment in which all is regular and explicit. Children gradually discover that such an environment is seldom an invigorating or challenging one. Indeed, it drains them of the capital fund of initiative and inventiveness and thoughtfulness that they brought with them to school. It exploits their energies and gives them back little in return. Before long, children become aware that schooling is enervating and dispiriting rather than animating or intellectually provocative. In short, schooling provides few natural incentives to thinking in the way that the home environment does. A drop-off in student interest is the natural consequence.

To teachers who have worked long and hard to become profes-sionals in charge of primary school classrooms, these remarks may be hard to take. But they are not intended as accusations. Teachers do what they are taught to do, and by and large they do it well. What they are taught to do is likely to be where the problem lies, yet this is an area of education that is most taken for granted and most unlikely to be subject to reappraisal. Taking one's professional preparation pretty much for granted is normal academic practice.

Indeed, many teachers nowadays are aware that the constant insistence upon order and discipline can be stultifying and can destroy the very spontaneity that they would most like to cultivate and cherish. The solution does not lie in alternating periods of rigor and randomness: now paper-and-pencil exercises and now free play. The solution lies rather in the discovery of procedures that encourage both organization and creativity, such as having children invent stories and tell them to their classmates. As John Dewey puts it, "The problem of *method* in forming habits of reflective thought is the problem of establishing *conditions* that will arouse and guide *curiosity*; of setting up the connections in things experienced that will on later occasions promote the *flow of suggestions*, create problems and purposes that will favor *consecutiveness* in the succession of ideas."[2] A curriculum that itself lacks consecutiveness can hardly be a model for the child in his or her struggle to develop a sense of sequence. Children have a keen sense of what is going on, but they do not necessarily have a keen understanding of how things can be sequenced so that they will begin to build and grow on their own. This is why children need as textbooks narratives instead of sourcebooks of information, so that growth and development, with recurrent themes and variations, can be constantly before their eyes. Children need models both of reasonableness and of growth. The model of growth may be better provided by the curriculum and by the community of one's peers than by those who are already adult.

NORMAL VERSUS CRITICAL ACADEMIC PRACTICE

A distinction can be drawn between "normal" and "critical" academic practice. Let me say first, however, that by "practice" I mean any methodical activity. It can also be described as customary, habitual,

---

[2] *How We Think* (New York: Heath, 1933), pp. 56–7 (italics in original). Dewey's most important educational works are *The Child and the Curriculum* (Chicago: University of Chicago Press, 1902), *Democracy and Education* (New York: Macmillan, 1916), and *Experience and Education* (New York: Macmillan, 1938). However, there are important statements in out-of-the-way places, like his critique of the avant-garde education of his day, to be found in Joseph Ratner (ed.), *Intelligence in the Modern World: John Dewey's Philosophy* (New York: Random House, 1939), pp. 616–26.

traditional, and unreflective, but these do not convey as well as the term *methodical* the fact that practice is not random, unsystematic, or disorganized. Moreover, there is generally a sense of conviction about our attitude toward our own practice, just as we have a sense of conviction about our own opinions that is lacking regarding the opinions of others. It would not be indulging in caricature to say that *practice is to action as belief is to thought.* Beliefs are thoughts we are convinced of despite the fact that we do not continually question them; practice is what we do methodically and with conviction but without a conspicuous degree of inquiry or reflection.

It is often assumed that unreflective practice is irrational and even downright dangerous, but this need not be so and is generally not the case. Unreflective practices, like customs and traditions that prevail successfully in a given cultural context, are likely to continue to prevail as long as that context does not change. And even if the context does change – and drastically – it may be that it is only the survival of those customs and traditions that holds the community together, as Durkheim has noted.[3]

In other cases, traditional practice may be unsuccessful but is continued anyway, either because no alternatives exist or because the viable alternatives have been decreed out of bounds and are therefore not even contemplated. Still another option is token examination of practice, which is what often takes place in educational contexts. This permits the practitioner to espouse the lofty notion that unexamined practices are not worth performing while hewing in actuality to the maxim that performed practices are not worth examining.

A society that expends vast sums on research into certain modes of practice is generally considered to be dedicated to the improvement of such practice; again, this is not necessarily the case. For example, much educational research is engaged in for the explicit purpose of justifying or solidifying existing educational practice, and a good deal more has this consequence even though not carried out with this intent.[4] Nevertheless, the converse is also true. It is normal for a certain amount of educational research not aimed at improvement in educational practice to have the consequence of producing such

[3] Emile Durkheim, *The Division of Labor in Society* (New York: Macmillan, 1933).
[4] Cf. Donald Schön, *The Reflective Practitioner* (New York: Basic, 1983).

improvement, just as it is normal for much research explicitly aimed at educational improvement to have only negligible consequences of a beneficial nature.

Despite the fact that instructional behaviors involve a fairly broad zone of discretion, the practice of teaching is normally institutional-ized and tradition-bound. Teachers do make use of these areas of dis-cretion and are very proud of their ability to do so. Nevertheless, such creative endeavors on the fringe of normal academic practice are insufficient to bring about large-scale changes in teacher behavior. This is partly owing to what Veblen has called the "trained incapacity" of teachers to reconstruct the role definitions impressed upon them in schools of education.[5] Even more so, it is a result of the isolation of the teacher in the classroom and the specious solidarity of the teacher corps. Innovation by a particular teacher is applauded and even wel-comed by the principal in a particular school building, but it is taken for granted that such inventiveness is not likely to spread, and the chance that it might affect academic practice generally is considered highly remote.

No doubt teachers resent the way they seem to be disregarded when it comes to curricular innovations, and they come to recog-nize the enormous power wielded by the large textbook houses and the purchasing agreements of the larger states. On the other hand, the textbook publishers do not ignore teachers and their experience when it comes to the construction of new texts; it is simply that the publishers look for the best representatives they can find of normal academic practice, with the result that texts are generally written by professors with a limited command of practice, by teachers with a limited command of theory, or by huge crews of freelance writers. In any event, the result is the reinforcement of normal academic prac-tice.[6] (The same pattern prevails with respect to the production and publication of tests.)

This brings us at last to steps to be taken to make normal prac-tice critical. Four steps can be specified as stages of reflection on practice. They are (1) criticism of the practice of one's colleagues,

---

[5] See Thorstein Veblen, *The Higher Learning in America* (New York: Sagamore, 1957).

[6] Cf. Thomas Kuhn's trenchant analysis of the way texts are constructed and used in science education, in *The Essential Tension* (Chicago: University of Chicago Press, 1977), pp. 228–39.

(2) self-criticism, (3) correction of the practice of others, and (4) self-correction. The degree to which normal academic practice has become critical depends upon the extent to which any or all of these factors are involved.

Reflection on practice may therefore involve the clarification of prevailing assumptions and criteria as well as of the consistency between such principles and prevailing practice. It may involve challenging these matters and not merely clarifying them. It may furthermore involve the active institution of changes and not merely the proposal of such changes. After all, reflection upon practice constitutes inquiry into practice, and effective inquiry includes appropriate interventions.

As an academic practitioner, you are pressed to think critically on occasions such as these (in no particular order):

- When the work of a colleague is being read or reviewed
- When you serve on a committee that must make a judgment regarding a proposal from a colleague
- When a grievance is filed or must be acted on
- When students challenge (1) the criteria by which courses are graded, (2) the materials being taught, or (3) the pedagogy being used
- When a grant proposal is being written or reviewed
- When judgments are made regarding school or campus conflicts, such as students vs. administration, administration vs. faculty, or faculty vs. students
- When you contrast your actual professional conduct with what you think it ought to be, or your school or profession with what you think it ought to be
- When you detect bias or prejudice in yourself or others
- When you search for alternatives to established but unsatisfactory practice
- When you find to be problematic that which others regard as non-problematic
- When you evaluate theory by means of practice and practice by means of theory
- When you acknowledge the implications for others of your professional conduct

The list could obviously be greatly elaborated. It tends to spell out some of the particular reasons we have for insisting that critical thinking must be self-corrective thinking, even if the attempted self-correction is unsuccessful.

RESTRUCTURING EDUCATIONAL PRACTICE

In what follows, I shall assume that there are two sharply contrasting paradigms of educational practice – the standard paradigm of normal practice and the reflective paradigm of critical practice. The dominating assumptions of the standard paradigm are

1. Education consists in the transmission of knowledge from those who know to those who don't know
2. Knowledge is about the world, and our knowledge of the world is unambiguous, unequivocal, and unmysterious
3. Knowledge is distributed among disciplines that are nonoverlapping and together are exhaustive of the world to be known
4. The teacher plays an authoritative role in the educational process, for only if teachers know can students learn what they know
5. Students acquire knowledge by absorbing information, i.e., data about specifics; an educated mind is a well-stocked mind

In contrast, the dominant assumptions of the reflective paradigm are

1. Education is the outcome of participation in a teacher-guided community of inquiry, among whose goals are the achievement of understanding and good judgment
2. Students are stirred to think about the world when *our* knowledge of it is revealed to them to be ambiguous, equivocal, and mysterious
3. The disciplines in which inquiry occurs are assumed to be neither nonoverlapping nor exhaustive; hence their relationships to their subject matters are quite problematic
4. The teacher's stance is fallibilistic (one that is ready to concede error) rather than authoritative

5. Students are expected to be thoughtful and reflective, and increasingly reasonable and judicious
6. The focus of the educational process is not on the acquisition of information but on the grasp of relationships within and among the subject matters under investigation

It should now be clear that the reflective paradigm assumes education to be inquiry, whereas the standard paradigm does not. Hence there is disagreement about the conditions under which the process must take place, and there is disagreement about the goals to be targeted. There are differences in what is done and in how it is done. For example, in the standard paradigm, teachers question students; in the reflective paradigm, students and teachers query each other. In the standard paradigm, students are considered to be thinking if they learn what they have been taught; in the reflective paradigm, students are considered to be thinking if they participate in the community of inquiry.

I have been contrasting in very general terms the standard paradigm of normal practice with the reflective paradigm of critical practice. At this point I want to consider a number of cardinal features of the reflective paradigm. This brief outline will be done in very broad strokes; in a sense, the remainder of the book will be occupied with filling in the details. The key concepts with which I will be working are not precise, clear-cut, and technical; instead, they are rather diffuse and contestable. They include such redoubtable stalwarts as inquiry, community, rationality, judgment, creativity, and autonomy, all of which have about them more than a whiff of traditional philosophy. These are, nevertheless, important concepts for any theory of education, and we had better confront them head on rather than risk becoming even more confused by trying to steer around them.

At the same time, I want to emphasize that concepts such as these, the principles that connect them, and the implications that flow from them are merely the abstract, theoretical side of critical practice. If we fail to come to grips with the practice – the ways in which reflective education can actually take place in the classroom – we will be just as likely to fall prey to misunderstanding as those whose lives are filled with practice and devoid of theory.

Education as inquiry

John Dewey was convinced that education had failed because it was guilty of a stupendous category mistake: It confused the refined, finished end products of inquiry with the raw, crude initial subject matter of inquiry and tried to get students to learn the solutions rather than investigate the problems and engage in inquiry for themselves. Just as scientists apply scientific method to the exploration of problematic situations so students should do the same if they are ever to learn to think for themselves. Instead, we ask them to study the end results of what the scientists have discovered; we neglect the process and fixate upon the product. When problems are not explored at first hand, no interest or motivation is engendered, and what we continue to call education is a charade and a mockery. Dewey had no doubt that what should be happening in the classroom is thinking – and independent, imaginative, resourceful thinking at that. The route he proposed – and here some of his followers part company with him – is that the educational process in the classroom should take as its model the process of scientific inquiry.

Community of inquiry

This phrase, presumably coined by Charles Sanders Peirce, was originally restricted to the practitioners of scientific inquiry, all of whom could be considered to form a community in that they were similarly dedicated to the use of like procedures in pursuit of identical goals.[7] Since Peirce, however, the phrase has been broadened to include any kind of inquiry, whether scientific or nonscientific. Thus, we can now speak of "converting the classroom into a community of inquiry" in which students listen to one another with respect, build on one another's ideas, challenge one another to supply reasons for otherwise unsupported opinions, assist each other in drawing inferences from what has been said, and seek to identify one another's assumptions. A community of inquiry attempts to follow the inquiry where it leads rather than be penned in by the boundary lines of existing disciplines.

---

7 C. S. Peirce, "The Fixation of Belief," in Justus Buchler (ed.), *Philosophical Writings of Peirce* (New York: Dover, 1955), pp. 5–22.

A dialogue that tries to conform to logic, it moves forward indirectly like a boat tacking into the wind, but in the process its progress comes to resemble that of thinking itself. Consequently, when this process is internalized or introjected by the participants, they come to think in *moves* that resemble its *procedures*. They come to think as the process thinks.

Sensitivity to what is problematic

Teachers may ask questions and students may answer them without either party feeling the least twinge of doubt or puzzlement and with hardly any real thinking taking place, because the process is mechanical and contrived. On the other hand, there are times when inquiry begins because what has been encountered – some aberration, some discrepancy, something that defies being taken for granted – captures our interest and demands our reflection and investigation. If, then, thinking in the classroom is considered desirable, the curriculum cannot present itself as clear and settled, for this paralyzes thought. The curriculum should bring out aspects of the subject matter that are unsettled and problematic in order to capture the laggard attention of the students and to stimulate them to form a community of inquiry.

Reasonableness

Insofar as it can, science attempts to be a model of rationality. It seeks to predict what will occur and formulate laws to account for what does occur. It may even recognize a moral role for itself and attempt to make transformations where they are called for in order to make things better than they would have been without such intervention. But many aspects of the world – particularly those that deal with human conduct – cannot be dealt with or formulated with the precision characteristic of science. Approximations are needed, and we have to develop a sense of the appropriate rather than expect our thought and the shape of things to correspond exactly. We must be content to reach an equitable solution, not necessarily one that is right in all details. We must be satisfied with a sensible or reasonable outcome even if it is not strictly speaking a "rational" one. This is particularly true in ethical disputes, for more and more we discover that the contested issues in these cases cannot be justly resolved and that we must make compromises and employ trade-offs that allow each of the parties to save face and retain self-respect. Education can be seen as the great laboratory for rationality, but it is more realistic to see it as a context in which young people learn to be reasonable so that they can grow up to be reasonable citizens, reasonable companions, and reasonable parents.

Relationship and judgment

To judge is to judge relationships, either by discovering relationships or by inventing them. Few readers will have forgotten those essay-type examinations that sought to elicit judgment by formulating an assignment beginning with the magic words "Compare and contrast." "Compare and contrast the historical impact of the American and French revolutions." "Compare and contrast the psychological theories of Piaget and Vygotsky." "Compare and contrast the artistic styles of Renaissance and Baroque painting." Obviously, the criteria in such cases are *similarity* and *difference*, but similarities and differences are kinds of relationships, just as are part–whole, means–end, cause–effect, and countless others. Every classification scheme establishes formal relationships for empirical entities. Every law, every principle, bears a relationship, or more precisely a set of relationships, to the events to which it applies. Disciplines are only trivially the information they contain; more important, they are the structures of relationships into which such information is organized. They are our understandings.

Thinking in the disciplines

According to Hirst, Dewey has it wrong when he talks about the logic of the inquiry process as having educational preeminence. He thinks that what education should take from science is not the process but the product. Scientific knowledge is a model of rationality. All scientific knowledge is contingent and must be justified by means of evidence or reasons. It is just such knowledge that students should be taught to aspire to. The knowledge that is the finished product of the inquiry process is logically organized, and the student must be educated to seek that organization so that no claims of fact will be made without

Characterizations

Judgments are settlements or determinations of what was previously unsettled, indeterminate, or in some way or other problematic. We can say that *inquiry* and *judgment* are generally related to one another as process and product, but the connection is not an exclusive one; some inquiries do not terminate in judgments, and some judgments are not the products of inquiry. Typically, however, the products of inquiry sum up and express the appraisive character of the inquiry process: Estimating produces estimates, portraying produces portraits, and analyzing produces analyses. As for *good* judgments, we often attempt to explain these as a happy admixture of critical and creative judgings. Such retrospective accounts can be useful and have their place, but it is likely that, in the long run, what makes good judgments good is their role in the shaping of *future* experience: They are judgments we can live with, the kind that enrich the lives we have yet to live.

Relationships. Thinking is a process of finding or making connections and disjunctions. The world is made up of complexes (evidently there are no simples) such as molecules and chairs and people and ideas, and these complexes have connections with some things and not with others. The generic term for connections and disjunctions is *relationships*. Since the meaning of a complex lies in the relationships it has with other complexes, each relationship, when discovered or invented, is a meaning, and great orders or systems of relationships constitute great bodies of meaning.

evidence, no opinions will be proffered without accompanying reasons, and no judgments will be made without appropriately relevant criteria.[8]

---

[8] Paul H. Hirst, "The Logical and Psychological Aspects of Teaching a Subject," in R. S. Peters (ed.), *The Concept of Education* (New York: Humanities Press, 1967), pp. 44–60.

What Hirst does acknowledge, however, is that, just as the student of foreign languages must aspire to think in those languages (and not merely be able to translate mechanically from one language to the next while thinking only in his or her own), so the recipient of a liberal education must aspire to think in the different languages that the disciplines represent. It is not enough to learn what happened in history; we must be able to think historically. "What we want is that pupils shall begin, however embryonically, to think historically, scientifically or mathematically; to think in the way distinctive of the particular subject involved."[9] But this is apparently as far as Hirst will permit himself to go in the direction of "effective thinking," and when confronted by the 1946 Harvard Committee report *General Education in a Free Society*,[10] which identifies the essential attributes of general education as the ability to think effectively, to communicate thought, to make relevant judgments, and to discriminate among values, he gives up on thinking and retreats to an invocation of "the public features of the forms of knowledge."[11]

Conversational apprenticeship

The infant growing up in the family is intrigued by the adventure of family conversation and learns to "recognize the voices" and to "distinguish the proper occasions of utterance" so as gradually to be initiated into the "skill and partnership" of this ongoing dialogue. When it is time for formal education, there is once again, as Michael Oakeshott puts it, "an initiation into the skill and partnership of this conversation in which we learn to recognize the voices, to distinguish the proper occasions of utterance, and . . . acquire the intellectual and moral habits appropriate to conversation. And it is this conversation which, in the end, gives place and character to every human activity and utterance."[12] Martin Buber, on the other hand, extols dialogue

9 Ibid., p. 45.
10 London: Oxford University Press, 1946.
11 Paul H. Hirst, "Liberal Education and the Nature of Knowledge," in R. F. Dearden, P. H. Hirst, and R. S. Peters (eds.), *Education and the Development of Reason* (London: Routledge and Kegan Paul, 1972), p. 397.
12 "The Voice of Poetry in the Conversation of Mankind," *Rationalism in Politics* (New York: Basic, 1962), p. 199.

rather than conversation. (He classifies conversation, along with debate, friendly chat, and lovers' talk, as a mere spectre of dialogue.) Genuine dialogue occurs only where each of the participants "really has in mind the other or others in their present and particular being and turns to them with the intention of establishing a living mutual relationship between himself and them."[13] Ideally, the relationship between teacher and students has this character of face-to-face dialogue. It is at once a community exhibiting both apprenticeship and mutual respect and a workshop in which traditional skills are passed on from one generation to the other. Despite the obviously traditionalist emphasis in both Oakeshott and Buber, their outlooks on education have had considerable influence on educational reforms in the final quarter of the twentieth century.

Autonomy

Not uncommonly, the reflective model of education is distinguished from the standard model on the ground that the primary objective of the reflective model is the autonomy of the learner. There is a sense in which this is correct: the sense in which autonomous thinkers are those who "think for themselves," who do not merely parrot what others say or think but make their own judgments of the evidence, form their own understanding of the world, and develop their own conceptions of the sorts of persons they want to be and the sort of world they would like it to be. Unfortunately, autonomy has often been associated with a kind of rugged individualism: the independent critical thinker as a self-sufficient cognitive macho type, protected by an umbrella of invincibly powerful arguments. In reality, the reflective model is thoroughly social and communal. Its aim is to articulate the friction-causing differences in the community, develop arguments in support of the competing claims, and then, through deliberation, achieve an understanding of the larger picture that will permit a more objective judgment.

This may suggest to some that the aim of the reflective model is achieved with production of the judgments just referred to. But this would be a misreading of the situation. The aim of the educational

---

[13] Martin Buber, *Between Man and Man* (London: Kegan Paul, 1947).

process is to help us form better judgments so that we can proceed to modify our lives more judiciously. Judgments are not ends in themselves. We do not experience works of art in order to judge them; we judge them in order to be able to have enriched aesthetic experiences. Making moral judgments is not an end in itself; it is a means for improving the quality of life.

Reflective thinking

The improvement of thinking involves reflection. Virtually everyone is familiar with the distinction between holding sound convictions without knowing the reasons or grounds on which such convictions rest and holding such convictions while being aware of the reasons and grounds that support them. The second way is more reflective, and in the long run it is the more excellent form of thinking. *Reflective* thinking is thinking that is aware of its own assumptions and implications as well as being conscious of the reasons and evidence that support this or that conclusion. Reflective thinking takes into account its own methodology, its own procedures, its own perspective and point of view. Reflective thinking is prepared to recognize the factors that make for bias, prejudice, and self-deception. It involves *thinking about its procedures* at the same time as it involves *thinking about its subject matter*. In a discussion that takes place in a legislature there must be constant awareness of parliamentary procedure all the while that there is consideration of matters of substance. Likewise, in deliberative inquiry in the classroom there must be continual awareness of the importance of the methodology of such inquiry all the while that matters of substance are being discussed. It is because this is so seldom the case that bias and self-deception so frequently have free rein in classroom argumentation. The conversation is a ventilation of prejudices rather than a deliberative inquiry.

In its simple form, then, thinking may be solely procedural or solely substantive. Thinking about logic or mathematics – or better, thinking logically about logic or mathematically about mathematics – is an instance of purely procedural or methodological thinking. Thinking solely about content, taking procedure wholly for granted, is wholly substantive thinking. The mixed mode created by the overlapping of these two simple forms is reflective thinking. What is here called reflective thinking includes recursive thinking, metacognitive thinking, self-corrective thinking, and all those other forms of thinking that involve reflection on their own methodology at the same time as they examine their subject matter.

The improvement of thinking involves the cultivation of its caring, critical, and creative dimensions, as well as of its reflective aspect. This brings us back to the question of what can be done to produce such thinking. What can be done to make education more critical, more creative, more caring, and more appraisive of its own procedures? My recommendation is that, as a start, we add philosophy to the elementary and secondary school curriculum. Of course, such an addition will not be sufficient. More has to be done to strengthen the thinking that must occur within and among all the disciplines. And of course, when I speak of philosophy at the grade-school level, I do not mean the dry, academic philosophy traditionally taught in the universities.

There will no doubt be some who will say that the cure sounds worse than the disease. One can only wonder if they have looked lately at the patient. To be sure, schools everywhere stand accused because student knowledge is so scanty, but what is worse is that what little students know they hold so uncritically and what little they reflect upon they reflect upon so unimaginatively. Students like these will not become the thoughtful citizens that robust democracies require, nor can they look forward to the productivity and self-respect that they themselves require as individuals. We unquestionably have the capacity to make such changes as need to be made. Whether we have the will to do so is far from clear. What is clear enough is that we must more thoroughly reexamine what we are doing. Such reflection upon practice is the basis for inventing improved practices that will invite, in turn, further reflection.

2

Approaches in Teaching for Thinking

ENTER THE CRITICAL THINKING MOVEMENT

During the 1980s there was a constant drumbeat of criticism of the educational process from such persons as Secretary of Education William Bennett, his assistant Chester Finn, and the director of the National Endowment for the Humanities, Lynne Cheney. Bennett even came to office vowing to preside over the demolition of the very department he headed, so deplorable did he consider its activities.

These were not, of course, voices from the left crying out against social and economic injustice. They were conservatives critical of existing institutions – a rather different breed from the usual run of conservatives. One might even speak of them as educational fundamentalists.

Their complaint, in a nutshell, was that Americans were poorly served by the educational system, because those emerging from the system knew little, or nothing worth knowing. Consequently, they concluded, the entire system of schooling was in crisis.

The response of those in the lower echelons of education – teachers and administrators alike – was to draw up their wagons in a circle and exchange volley for volley with their attackers. They ridiculed the naive lists of items that every educated person should know (as drawn up by E. D. Hirsch of cultural literacy fame) and cited mountains of educational research in defense of what they were doing. In brief, they behaved the way members of most professions behave when attacked: They found little amiss in their practice but much to be desired in the circumstances under which that practice had to be carried out.

The schools sought to exonerate themselves, in other words, by contending that the crisis, if indeed there was one, lay not in them but in the society of which they were a part. Students were being taught the right things in the right ways, but they just weren't learning. They were too distracted by television, drugs, sex, family discord, and peer pressures. Textbook writers worked hard to compress the essentials of a vast subject between the covers of a book, and teachers worked hard to convey those essentials to their students. Unfortunately, many teachers seemed to be saying, we live at a time in which the factors keep multiplying that tend to make such knowledge seem irrelevant. We no longer live in a time in which education is valued for its own sake. It has value today, most students seem to feel, only as a ticket to enter the job market with a few acceptable credentials. Consequently, education is disposable, like a paper cup – something you acquire for only as long as you need it and throw away when you are done with it. The knowledge one gets in the schools, students feel, is not relevant to life; it is relevant only to the tests that bar one from entering or permit one to enter life. Once a test has been taken, the knowledge needed for it can be forgotten with no more regret than one has in throwing away the paper cup.

Such, at any rate, is the defense many teachers offer when confronted with the accusations of the educational fundamentalists. When the fundamentalists charge, "You don't teach well because you don't know your own subjects well enough! All you know is what you got from those wretched methods courses in the schools of education!" the teachers summon up their dignity and reply haughtily, "We know our subjects quite well enough, thank you. But we are today in the position of the teachers of Latin and Greek a hundred years ago. The times are passing us by. Who needs to read for meaning or write grammatically in an era of MTV? How can the histories of Rome and Greece seem relevant to our students when their parents don't bother to vote? It is not we who have lost our way but the world we live in."

The underlying assumption of both the defenders of the schools and their critics is that the purpose of education is to instill knowledge. It is taken for granted that great bodies of knowledge exist and that these can be summarized and transmitted to students. The controversial issue as both educational fundamentalists and teachers see it has to do with how well the job of transmission is being accomplished. And if it is not being done well, why not? In a sense, then, the combatants share similar assumptions and indeed belong to the same educational tradition. But meanwhile, in that same decade of the 1980s, something else was happening.

How we got to where we are

During the Carter administration and before, back to the Kennedy administration, a great deal of money was allocated to the National Institute of Education (NIE) for research. For a while in the 1970s, there had been a hold on these funds, but then there was a brief period of clear sailing until the weather closed in once again in the early 1980s. In the Teaching and Learning Division of the NIE in the late 1970s and early 1980s, there was a sense of an era coming to an end and a desire to make an important gesture, to do something significant before it was too late. Dissatisfaction with Piagetian orthodoxy was beginning to emerge. The most stirring influences seemed to be Vygotsky and Bruner, and the magic words were *thinking, cognitive skills*, and *metacognition*.

And so, under the leadership of Susan Chipman, Judith Segal, and Robert Glaser, all of the NIE, a conference was called to take place at the Learning Research and Development Center of the University of Pittsburgh. Its ostensible goal was "to examine educational practices and scientific investigation concerned with students' abilities to understand, reason, solve problems, and to learn. The plan for the conference was to bring together cognitive researchers, program developers, and teachers of cognitive skills to provide mutual advice and to discuss their theories, findings, and recommendations."[1] Among the program developers present were Reuven Feuerstein, Jack Lochhead, Edward de Bono, Martin Covington, and myself. Among the

---

[1] Robert Glaser, preface to Judith W. Segal, Susan F. Chipman, and Robert Glaser (eds.), *Thinking and Learning Skills*, vol. 1 (Hillsdale, N.J.: Erlbaum, 1985), p. x.

cognitive psychologists were Philip Johnson-Laird, John Bransford, Robert Siegler, James Greeno, Robert Sternberg, Jonathan Baron, Susan Carey, and Jerome Bruner. Still others came from educational psychology and related fields: Carl Bereiter, Beau Fly Jones, David Perkins, Donald Meichenbaum, and Allan Collins. It would be a groundbreaking, exhilarating experience for all participants, and it would set the stage, it was hoped, for a new era in which thinking would play a leading role in the educational process.

The conference did usher in a new era, but it also ended one. It was a smashing coda for a certain phase of the NIE's activities, and then the NIE lapsed into silence.

But enough had been done to send a responsive shiver through the educational research community. People began talking about teaching for thinking. At first, many of them saw it as merely ancillary to teaching for learning. Before long, however, there were those, such as Lauren Resnick, who identified thinking as the very heart of the educational enterprise, even though they were reluctant to assign learning a less important role.

One place where the idea of teaching for thinking did have a special impact was in the editorial offices of *Educational Leadership*, a powerful opinion-shaping journal published by the Association for Supervision and Curriculum Development and aimed at educational administrators. The journal's managing editor, Ron Brandt, together with his colleagues, began to welcome articles on the teaching of thinking skills, and by 1984 they were able to devote the first of several issues to that theme.[2] Before long, hardly an educational periodical remained that had not recognized and welcomed the sexy newcomer to the educational scene. And soon teachers and professors alike were insisting that all along they had been teaching for thinking; nothing new was really required of them.

Some educators perceived, however, that the problem was bigger than this. Of course traditional education involved thinking, they acknowledged. But the *quality* of such thinking was deficient. What was needed was not merely teaching for thinking, but teaching for *critical* thinking.

[2] "Thinking Skills in the Curriculum," *Educational Leadership* 42:1 (September 1984).

Some more recent origins of critical thinking

Critical thinking? What in the world was that?

No one seemed to know where the term had originated, nor did anyone seem to care very much. Some guessed that it was connected with a textbook, *Critical Thinking*, by Max Black, published in 1952.[3] Black's book obviously represented a genuine effort on the part of a logician to make logic more accessible to students. Others guessed it was related to the work of an equally respected logician in Great Britain, Susan Stebbing, whose *Thinking to Some Purpose* was another attempt to demonstrate the practical value of logical thinking.[4]

But there was another work published in this period that may have lent an even greater impetus: Monroe Beardsley's *Practical Logic*.[5] Beardsley was a philosopher with great sensitivity to literary values, and at the same time he was quite taken by the language-oriented approaches to logic of Frege and Wittgenstein. He had also been an English teacher at one time. Not surprisingly, therefore, Beardsley's book was an ingenious interweaving of logic, grammar, rhetoric, and writing. His work had widespread educational implications, as might have been expected from someone who greatly admired the work of John Dewey. To students who might otherwise have been paralyzed by the logical exercises and examples that had descended from ancient times, Beardsley brought a breath of fresh air: sparkling new exercises that made logical practice a pleasant challenge rather than a dreary task. So Beardsley's work was relevant: to the interests of students, to the language they spoke, and to the world they lived in.

Other authors of logic textbooks often made a fetish of the truth values of propositions and seemed to be fascinated with truth tables, whose function seemed to many students to be at times quite counterintuitive. Beardsley was more concerned with meaning than with truth, as befits someone immersed in the problems of aesthetic criticism. For this reason, he gave considerable attention to matters of translation, which were meaning-oriented, and not just to matters of

---

[3] 2d ed., Englewood Cliffs, N.J.: Prentice-Hall, 1952. Also worthy of mention is a still earlier milestone: Edward Glaser's *Experiment in the Development of Critical Thinking* (New York: Columbia University Press, 1941).

[4] Harmondsworth: Penguin, 1939.

[5] Englewood Cliffs, N.J.: Prentice-Hall, 1950.

inference, which were truth-oriented. (You could say that the conclusion of a deductive inference preserves the *truth* of the premises from
which it is derived, while a good translation preserves the *meaning*
of the original text from which it is derived.) It is hardly necessary
to point out that the translation skills and procedures emphasized
by Beardsley held great promise for those attempting to improve
reading comprehension, since reading involves translation from the
thought and language of the writer into the thought and language of
the reader.

I do not mean to give the impression that Beardsley and Black were
the first American logicians to be associated with the development of
critical thinking. That honor may very well belong to Josiah Royce, an
eminent philosopher in his own right, an idealist, and, late in his life, a
pragmatist. Royce's *Primer of Logical Analysis for the Use of Composition
Students*, which apparently fell stillborn from the press in 1881, was
admirable in its mastery of formal logic, but its exercises were stuffy
and musty, and it could hardly have been of much help to composition
students. Like most in the critical thinking field, however, Royce had
a strong sense of social accountability, and he wanted to show that
logic was educationally useful. In this he was drawing on the earlier
work of the German logician Sigwart and the British logician Venn
(the latter the inventor of the famed Venn diagrams, so helpful to
beginning students of class logic who are visually oriented and so
puzzling to those who are not). Moreover, Royce's philosophy of
community, in part derived from Plato and Hegel and in part from
Charles Sanders Peirce, had powerful implications for education. For
Royce, the community is a community of interpretation – a meaning-
sharing, meaning-creating community – just as for Peirce it had been
a community of inquiry in which even logic itself was seen as an
essntially social enterprise. It was G. H. Mead who, a generation later,
picked up these threads of social origins and social responsibility and
wove them into a communal theory of communication and of the self.
Mead's social interpretation of behaviorism still influences those in
the critical thinking and informal logic movements who recognize in
the social impulses of the child perhaps the most powerful motives
for education and for becoming reasonable.[6]

---

[6] *Mind, Self and Society* (Chicago: University of Chicago Press, 1934).

Dewey and the Deweyans

Dewey had been a student of Peirce's at Johns Hopkins University in the 1870s, and there can be no doubt that the concept of pragmatism invented by Peirce became the guiding force for Dewey's sweeping philosophical endeavors up until the middle of the twentieth century. Peirce was a man of enormous originality. Indeed, he was too continuously creative ever to have time to construct a system or to spell out the practical implications of his ideas (even while maintaining that the meaning of his ideas lay precisely in their practical implications). What Dewey took from Peirce was not a doctrine but a method, and that method he proceeded to apply to science, to art, to logic, to education, and to many another area of learning.

Dewey's interest in education began early, in the last two decades of the nineteenth century. Historians of philosophy have tended to make much of his original attachment to Hegel, but his early monographs on Leibniz and Darwin display his immense excitement as a result of encountering their writings. The mid-nineteenth-century educational scene focused on the decline of the classics and the vigorous bid of science for a place in the curriculum. To Dewey, this was a triumph of the flexible, adaptable method of inquiry over the adapted but inflexible deference to classical humanism. He never thereafter rescinded his allegiance to science as "the method of intelligence," his equation of scientific inquiry with inquiry in general, or his conviction that the reconstruction of education along the lines of inquiry was the desirable way to proceed. Our society could not be fully civilized and our schools could not be fully satisfactory, Dewey thought, until students were converted to inquiry and thereby prepared to be participants in a society likewise committed to inquiry as the sovereign method of dealing with its problems.

But it must be remembered that Dewey was also a psychologist, and when he addresses himself to educational matters there is always a subtle blending of his approaches to education as a psychologist and as a philosopher. His psychological approach is presented most straightforwardly in *How We Think*, first published in 1903. Here Dewey traces the natural history of scientific inquiry back to its origins in everyday problem solving. He attempts to show that early peoples, when they discovered their conduct to be blocked in some way or other, were able to evolve an algorithm for problem solving based on a history of success in the use of that algorithm. On sensing a difficulty, they would note that something they had been taking for granted, some belief they had assumed to be true, could no longer be counted on as reliable. It would be necessary to define the problem, convert wishes into possibly desirable outcomes, form hypotheses as possible ways of achieving ends-in-view, imaginatively consider possible consequences of acting on these hypotheses, and then experiment with them until the problem was resolved. The blockage would be removed, and a new belief could be taken for granted. This algorithm for problem solving, drawn from *descriptions* of everyday human behavior, when combined with scientific inquiry, becomes *prescriptive*, and we glide, by imperceptible steps, from what *is* (or *was*) to what *ought to be*. Little wonder the contemporary cognitive psychologists, in their desperate quest for a problem-solving paradigm, fastened on Dewey's model with the alacrity with which medieval Christianity fastened upon the naturalistic philosophy of Aristotle!

And yet the very same book, *How We Think*, set out the distinction Dewey made between ordinary thinking and something called reflective thinking, by which Dewey meant thinking that is aware of its causes and consequences. To know the causes of ideas – the conditions under which they are thought – is to liberate ourselves from intellectual rigidity and to bestow upon ourselves that power of choosing among and acting upon alternatives that is the source of intellectual freedom. To know the consequences of ideas is to know their meaning, for as Dewey, pragmatist and follower of Peirce, was convinced, their meaning lies in their practical bearings, the effects they have upon our practice and upon the world. To many in the critical thinking movement today, it was Dewey's emphasis on reflective thinking that was the true harbinger of critical thinking in this century.

Scarcely more than a decade later, Dewey's major work in education appeared. *Democracy and Education* continues the appeal for education fashioned on the model of scientific inquiry, but the emphasis upon thinking *in* education is strengthened. We have got to learn how to teach children to think for themselves if we are to have a democracy worth having. The thinking individual is as important as the inquiring society. It is as if Dewey had begun to suspect that democracy and inquiry were not natural allies, although with effort they could be made compatible with one another.

To many a contemporary reader, Dewey's vision of the relationship between democracy and education is a powerfully persuasive one. There are hints aplenty that community is the middle term or link between scientific method and democratic practice. But there is a difficulty lurking in Dewey's approach that did not become apparent until much later. The problem is that thinking may be no more a natural ally of science than democracy is. The differences are papered over in *How We Think*, but the fact is that for many students of the matter, reaching all the way back to Plato, excellent thinking is conceived of as philosophical thinking, and philosophy and science are independent ventures in no way reducible to one another. Therefore, if good thinking is to become a prime objective of the classroom, is it to be along the lines of scientific inquiry or philosophical inquiry?

This is a question Dewey never takes up. His love of philosophy is utterly beyond question, but he seldom addresses himself to the problem of what it is, aside from an occasional essay or the throwaway remark that it is "the general theory of education." Consequently, some of those who have been inspired by Dewey's vision have argued that philosophy in the schools is the route to the improvement of student thinking. But many, including a good number of those who also consider themselves Deweyans, have rejected that approach and have adopted other routes of implementation.

Most ill-starred of these ventures was "progressive education," which appeared over the horizon in the 1920s and in a decade had so disappointed Dewey that he wrote *Experience and Education* in denunciation of it. Another effort to keep faith with Dewey was the "reflective education" movement of the 1950s under the leadership of Ernest Bayles, H. Gordon Hullfish, Lawrence Metcalf, and others. In one sense it was an unsuccessful movement. It failed to provide curricula that would pass the teacher's thinking along to the student. But in another sense it can be considered successful, in that schools of education that are concerned only with reflective teachers and are indifferent to whether the thinking proces is instilled in the student have adopted this approach and proclaim that they are now "teaching for critical thinking." A prime example was the sound educator Louis Raths, who attempted, reasonably enough, to use the Deweyan problem-solving algorithm as a format for "teaching for thinking."[7] For Dewey – and for Raths – such an approach could be helpful in distinguishing better values from worse. But when Raths was unable, for reasons of health, to continue with his work, his followers took over and transformed his approach into "values clarification," in which no value was to be considered better or worse than any other. So what began as a model of critical thinking had before long become a model of uncritical thinking.

Another contribution, of considerably greater substance, came from B. Othanel Smith and Robert Ennis, whose edition *Language and Concepts of Education*,[8] supplemented by Israel Scheffler's *The Language of Education*,[9] was among the earlier efforts in the United States to examine the linguistic and logical aspects of education. In 1963, Ennis published in the *Harvard Educational Review* "A Definition of Critical Thinking,"[10] an article that was destined to have widespread influence on the developing concept of education for thinking. With his strong background in logic (he was the author of *Logic for Teachers*,[11] a fine logic text, but one that said little about how logic might best be taught), he has continued to tinker with his definition of critical thinking in order to give it the logical power and educational relevance it undoubtedly requires. He now defines the term as "reasonable, rational thinking that helps us decide what to believe and do." This formulation continues to have great popularity, more so than any of its competitors. To nonphilosophers especially it seems to hit the nail square on the head.

In searching for the distinctive Deweyan contributions to the critical thinking movement, we cannot limit those contributions to his ideas concerning reflective thinking. It should not be forgotten that Dewey makes a strong case in *Experience and Nature*[12] for a conception of philosophy as criticism. (It is this conception of philosophy that Beardsley continues in his major work, *Aesthetics: Problems in the*

---

7 Louis E. Raths, Selma Wassermann, Arthur Jones, and Arnold Rothstein, *Teaching for Thinking* (1967), 2d ed. (New York: Teachers College Press, 1986).
8 Chicago: Rand McNally, 1961.
9 Springfield, Ill.: C. C. Thomas, 1978.
10 32:1 (1962), 81–111.
11 Englewood Cliffs, N.J.: Prentice-Hall, 1969.
12 2d ed., La Salle, Ill.: Open Court, 1929.

Philosophy of Criticism [1958].) Dewey locates philosophy as a special
nonscientific form of cognition that is concerned with the judgment
of value as a unique form of inquiry – a judgment of judgment, a
"criticism of criticism" (p. 398). Those who see little connection between critical thinking and philosophy would do well to reread the
final chapter of Dewey's major work in metaphysics to which I have
just referred.

Analytic skills and cognitive objectives

The British, meanwhile, must have seen little connection between
the emergence of critical thinking in the United States and their own
interest in developing an analytical philosophy of education. They
were unaware of the practical implications that their philosophical
work would have: The first British text in critical thinking did not appear until 1988. (It was Alec Fisher's edited volume *Critical Thinking:
Proceedings of the First British Conference on Informal Logic and Critical
Thinking.*)[13]

Nevertheless, a series of public lectures given at the University of
London in early 1965 had devoted itself to the conceptual and logical
aspects of teaching and learning, and the lecturers were the foremost
figures in the area of philosophical reflection on the educational process: R. S. Peters, D. W. Hamlyn, Gilbert Ryle, and Michael Oakeshott.
Two years later, Peters edited a collection, *The Concept of Education*,[14]
of which these talks formed the core. Additional articles were sup-
plied by, among others, Paul Hirst and R. F. Dearden, the Americans
Israel Scheffler and Max Black, and the Australian John Passmore.
Passmore's article, "On Teaching to Be Critical," was the last in the
collection but the first to recognize the need to operationalize the theoretical discourse that prevailed in the other contributions. His article
remains to this day a sparkling exemplar of critical thinking theory. It
deals effectively with the question of cognitive skills and even more
effectively with the dispositions that critical thinkers need to have or
to develop.

Mention of cognitive skills brings us to another highly relevant
portion of the academic background out of which the critical thinking

[13] Norwich: University of East Anglia, 1988.
[14] New York: Humanities Press, 1967.

movement emerged. In the 1950s, educational discussions and practice were filled with references to "behavioral objectives" in the classroom. At the University of Chicago, Benjamin Bloom and his colleagues asked themselves, "What about cognitive objectives?" and "What about the skills needed to achieve those objectives?" Thus was born *Taxonomy of Educational Objectives*, vol. 1: *Cognitive Domain*, edited by Bloom and others,[15] which to many a professor of education and many a teacher was to be the last word in education in the last half of the twentieth century. The book was and remains useful despite the glaring absence (one might even say the critical absence) of the objectives of logical reasoning. But one of its most influential aspects was the hierarchy it proposed. Mere memory (of inert knowledge) was consigned to the lowest status. Ascending, one found comprehension, analysis, synthesis, and, at the apex of the pyramid, evaluation. To many an observer of the educational scene, this appeared to be a landmark move toward critical thinking; knowledge had been downgraded and evaluative thinking upgraded, and this may well be what Bloom and his cohort had intended. One could carp at the details of the hierarchy (Nelson Goodman was to argue, much later, that evaluation was a developmental, instrumental process, not a summative one).[16] But the way seemed much clearer than before to the installation of critical thinking as a major objective of the educational system.

In education, the twists and turns of fate are especially chancy, however, and what happened to Bloom was something like what had happened to Dewey a half-century before with the advent of progressive education. Dewey discovered that his ideas, when dropped suddenly into an educational context unprepared for them, were interpreted as and transformed into something quite contrary to his intentions. The context into which Bloom's ideas were dropped was that of sovereign Piagetianism, the dominant force in child psychology from the 1930s through the 1970s. For most of his life (his views relaxed some in his final years), Piaget had maintained that the mental existence of young children was "concrete" – perceptual and affective. Children could not be entrusted with abstract ideas, which, in

---

[15] New York: McKay, 1956.
[16] *Languages of Art* (Indianapolis: Bobbs-Merrill, 1968), p. 262.

their ignorance, they distorted and misunderstood. Education was a matter of getting time to shuck off their childish ways of thinking and acquiesce in the truth – that is, the way adults understood things. It might have to be late secondary school or even college before students could be expected to handle ideas.

When Bloom's concepts penetrated the Piagetian empire in education, they were accorded an interpretation that allowed them to blend in perfectly with Piaget: The hierarchy was to be understood as a theory of developmental stages. Children's concrete throught processes in their early years allowed them to perform little more than memory tasks, but they could ascend, stage by stage, until finally they would arrive at the adult level, the pinnacle of the entire process, the evaluational stage.

The net effect was to preclude teaching critical thinking to children. Given the longitudinal, developmental interpretation, young children were not capable of monitoring their own thought, of giving reasons for their opinions, or of putting logical operations into practice. It was only in the late 1970s, with the exhaustion of the "back to basics" movement, that educators were prepared to reexamine their assumptions about knowledge and thinking and that psychologists could reexamine theirs about Piaget and Vygotsky. And it was only in the 1970s that educators began to suspect that students were in fact abstraction-deprived and that this might be remedied by teaching them reasoning through philosophy and philosophy through reasoning.

The emergence of informal logic

The critical thinking movement's momentum was increased considerably in the late 1970s with the formation of the enterprise known as informal logic. For some time, a dissident group of logicians had been calling for a logic that was more attuned to natural language and that would be better adapted than classical logic or symbolic logic to help students reason more effectively. Toward this end, a conference was held at the University of Windsor in Canada in 1978, and this in turn produced the *Newsletter of Informal Logic* (later to become the *Journal of Informal Logic*). The very first issue of the *Newsletter* announced the credo of the group: "Our conception is very broad and liberal, and covers everything from theoretical issues (theory of fallacy and argument) to practical ones (such as how best to display the structure of ordinary arguments) to pedagogical questions (how to design critical thinking courses; what sorts of material to use)."[17] Among those who participated in the Windsor conferce were scholars who remain in the forefront of informal logicians: Ralph Johnson and J. Anthony Blair (coeditors of the *Newsletter*), Howard Kahane, Michael Scriven, Douglas Walton, Robert Ennis, and Alex Michalos. Indeed, Scriven's role in the formation of the informal logic movement was virtually that of a founding father, and in his contribution to the conference he contended that the movement would "save philosophy" and "would manifest itsself in the improved teaching of basic skills."[18]

The phrase "informal logic" may well have commenced with Gilbert Ryle's use of it in his article "Formal and Informal Logic,"[19] and there can be no doubt that the analysis of natural language by Wittgenstein, Austin, and Ryle had done much to prepare the way for an informal logic movement. The contributors to this movement are too numerous to mention, but among those who sought to build bridges between linguistic analysis and critical thinking by way of informal logic one would have to mention Paul Grice, Stephen Toulmin, Robert Fogelin, C. L. Hamblin, and Rupert Crawshay-Williams, in addition to Michael Scriven. Informal logic is now in a very productive phase, with a considerable number of textbooks being published every year and with a continuing affirmation of its kinship to critical thinking.

While in some ways informal logic was very new, in other ways it was very ancient. We will put aside for the moment its roots in ancient philosophy, particularly in Aristotle (just as we leave aside, for the time being, the roots of critical thinking in Socrates and the Sophists). Nevertheless, the study of rhetoric did not terminate with antiquity but has been a living tradition through to the present day, and many of those in the critical thinking and informal logic movements owe more than a little of their inspiration and skill to the tradition. Indeed, if Continental philosophy is to be linked to the rise of critical

---

[17] Ralph Johnson and J. Anthony Blair, in *Informal Logic* 1:1 (July 1978), 1.

[18] In ibid., p. 5.

[19] Gilbert Ryle, "Formal and Informal Logic," in *Dilemmas* (Cambridge University Press, 1966), pp. 111–29.

thinking, one of the firmest of connections is the work on rhetoric and argumentation of such writers as Chaim Perelman, Paul Ricoeur, Arne Naess, Hans Blumenberg, Hans-Georg Gadamer, and Jacques Derrida.

In a sense, informal logicians and rhetoricians attack the same problem from different directions and in the best of all worlds could be expected to meet somewhere in the middle, like the crews building a tunnel by starting at either side of a river. Both are examining claims to reasonableness (and therefore are concerned with the theory of rationality). But the informal logicians move toward a new conception of reasonableness by broadening and refining the concept of logic, while the rhetoricians do so by examining writing that is not or does not appear to be formally logical, in an effort to determine what justification such prose may claim to have to being reasonable. Moreover, both are inclined to focus on argumentation, but the one group emphasizes the persuasive force of argument while the other emphasizes its logical force.

Other conversations, other voices

Just as rhetoricians and informal logicians support critical thinking from different directions, so philosophers tend to emphasize the reasoning component in critical thinking, while nonphilosophers (particularly scientists) tend to emphasize the problem-solving (or "decision-making") component. The "problem-solving approach" in scientific, professional, and technical education is not particularly new; it has been used for decades, especially in schools of engineering but also in mathematics, physics, chemistry, biology, and medicine. Of more recent vintage are generalized rather than specialized problem-solving courses and theories. A conference, "Problem-Solving and Education," held at Carnegie-Mellon University in 1978 gathered many cognitive researchers together to compare their approaches to the theory and methods of problem solving. Some were more optimistic than others about the possibility of finding generalized problem-solving processes by going beyond the memorization of specific heuristics based on knowledge in specific domains. Among the more hopeful have been those cognitive psychologists, like Raymond Nickerson and Allan Collins, who have been using computers to test theories of problem solving and who as a result are now developing educational theories of "cognitive apprenticeship."

Still another connection can be traced, although it may be more tenuous: one between critical thinking and applied philosophy. The applied philosophy movement did not organize itself until the mid-1980s. In Britain it has attracted such luminaries as Richard Hare and A. J. Ayer, but in the United States there appears to be somewhat greater reluctance by those in so-called pure philosophy to cross over in support of a branch of philosophy prepared to get its hands dirty by dealing with the practical issues of life. There are now several journals dealing with applied philosophy and publishing papers exhibiting the impact of philosophical thinking upon problems in education, business, law, health care, ecology, and government.

Some versions of critical thinking may seem to be best placed under the rubric of applied philosophy. This could be the case of the educational approach known as "Philosophy for Children." It is a clear example of philosophy applied to education for the purpose of producing students with improved proficiency in reasoning and judgment. There are, however, some significant differences, not the least of which is that the usual forms of applied philosophy represent an intervention by philosophers with the aim of clarifying or resolving problems faced by nonphilosophers, whereas Philosophy for Children is an intervention that aims to get students to do philosophy themselves.

Finally, there are those in the field of education itself who were among the first to champion critical thinking. Hilda Taba, James Shaver, Philip Phenix, Freeman Butts, and Thomas Greene come to mind, as well as, more recently, Arthur Costa, Ron Brandt, and Barry Beyer.

I have concentrated on those who have contributed positively to the development and promotion of critical thinking in education, with the result that I have not dealt with those whose concern has been more adversarial. This is something that a comprehensive history of the critical thinking movement will have to do. However, it would be useful to take note, in passing, of John McPeck's *Critical Thinking and Education*, which takes critical thinking to task for attempting to teach thinking as a separate subject instead of conceding that thinking is completely discipline-specific and can be fostered only within the context of individual disciplines. A running debate has taken place, in consequence, between McPeck and those, such as Robert Ennis and Richard Paul, who defend the notion of teaching generic skills in separate, free-standing courses.[20] While many points made by McPeck against critical thinking have some validity, he seems to be clearly in the wrong in his contention that all teaching of thinking must be discipline-specific, for he ignores the flagrant counterinstance of philosophy. That philosophy and logic do exist and that they are normative disciplines concerned with specifying what excellence in thinking ought to be – these facts are in themselves a refutation of McPeck's rejection of the notion that there is a discipline specifically devoted to the teaching of thinking as an autonomous activity.

The educational assimilation of critical thinking

Efforts to publicize the emergence of critical thinking reached their peak in the later 1980s and the earlier 1990s. In 1992 alone, there were conferences in Critical Literacy and Critical Thinking (Chicago), Thinking (North Queensland), Critical Thinking and Educational Reform (Sonoma, Calif.), and Critical Thinking and Education (Montclair, N.J.). Up to 1992, the annual number of such conferences had increased; after 1992, they seem to have decreased. The same is true of conferences in Informal Logic (an important theoretical arm of critical thinking), many of which were held in Canada, and featured Canadian researchers. The two major axes of the movement in the United States during this period were Sonoma, which held well-attended conferences annually but which was faced with serious attrition in the last half of the 1990s, and Montclair, which established a well-endowed Institute for Critical Thinking that concentrated on improving the quality of critical thinking on the college campus and in the schools of surrounding school districts. The Montclair institute had held a conference in 1989, the proceedings of which were published as *Critical Thinking: Focus on Social and Cultural Inquiry* (1991). The proceedings of the 1992 conference were entitled *Critical*

---

[20] See John E. McPeck, *Critical Thinking and Education* (New York: St. Martin's, 1981); Richard W. Paul, "McPeck's Mistakes," *Informal Logic* 7:1 (Winter 1985), 35–43; John E. McPeck, "Paul's Critique of *Critical Thinking and Education*," ibid., pp. 45–54.

Thinking as an Educational Ideal (1993). And *Critical Thinking and Learning* was the title of a collection of papers on education published in 1992. The editors of these three publications were Wendy Oxman, Mark Weinstien, Nicholas Michelli, and Lesley Coia. During this period, the institute began publishing the periodical called *Inquiry: Critical Thinking Across the Disciplines*.

But this was the high point of the movement to publicize critical thinking; just a few years afterward, the Montclair institute suspended operations, and the Sonoma center refocused itself on teacher education workshops. The public visibility of critical thinking had been successfully established. Critical thinking was assimilated into all levels of education.

However, a closer look at what was happening yielded far fewer grounds for optimism. It was now standard for publishers to offer one or several textbooks in critical thinking in their annual or seasonal catalogs, but these books differed little among themselves and evidently were to be used chiefly as a source of critical thinking exercises. A curriculum in which all disciplines were to be taught critically and learned communally was as far off as ever. Critical thinking had been assimilated – few educators would go on record *against* it – but only by first making it a toothless tiger.

Still, there were some hopeful signs. The journal *Informal Logic*, always a paragon of integrity, now devoted a portion of each issue to questions of teaching. And Montclair State University moved to give a critical thinking spin to all its courses in teacher preparation, as well as to offer graduate education programs leading to masters and doctoral degrees with a specialization in Philosophy for Children. It also embarked, under the sponsorship of the U.S. Department of State, on a joint venture with Kirovograd State Normal University (Ukraine) to bring critical thinking to the university's higher education courses and elementary school philosophy to its lower level courses. American education's flirtation with critical thinking will become a more substantial and meaningful relationship when other colleges of education begin to infuse their teacher education courses with multidimensional thinking.

This has been no more than a thumbnail sketch of the recent sources of the critical thinking movement. It is a movement that has had some difficulty in deciding on its own identity – for example, its relationship to philosophy on the one hand and to creative thinking on the other. But its attempt to overcome this difficulty is a major reason for its value to us.

CRITICAL THINKING AND THE INCULCATION OF BELIEF

No one has labored more strenuously than Robert Ennis to advance critical thinking. We should therefore give him our attention when he tells us that critical thinking is aimed at helping us decide "what to believe and do." His choice of *believing* and *doing* is revealing, because believing and doing happen to be the targets of normal academic practice. School (so the thinking goes) is one of the places where we learn the presumably right things to believe and where we learn to act appropriately. Actually, the maxim is not couched in such blunt terms. It is said, rather, that school is a place where we learn the right things to know. But the inference is clear: If we have somehow been made to know something, then we have been compelled to believe it. And we can be counted on to act in accordance with our beliefs. In reading Ennis's definition of critical thinking, one has the uncomfortable feeling that this is precisely the language a late-twentieth-century society would employ if it wanted to ensure the acceptance by students of the more or less official ideologies of that society: It would do so under the guise of helping students think for themselves, helping them be more rational, and so on.

If we turn from normal academic practice to the inquiry paradigm of academic practice, we note that there is no longer a need to inculcate a set of substantive beliefs disguised as "knowledge." Instead, students are asked to accept in a tentative, provisional way the methodology of inquiry. This is the procedure that has been adopted by the inquiring community of which they are members. There are innumerable situations to be inquired into, and from countless ongoing inquiries there emerges a variety of settlements or verdicts, some fairly firm, representing what is "warrantedly assertible." For schoolchildren, what is in doubt may be friends and grades; for adult citizens, it may be inflation and the environment. It is because of the highly problematic nature of these issues that the general populace is said to need critical thinking. People are said to need it to help them assess knowledge claims by distinguishing the stronger from the weaker; that however is a far cry from employing critical thinking to decide "what to believe." Critical thinking simply helps us avoid thinking uncritically and acting unreflectively.

Indeed, critical thinking is, if anything, even more valuable with respect to essentially contestable concepts and perennial arguments than it is with respect to matters for which there are acceptable decision procedures. When it comes to such questions as whether what has just been conceived is a human being, what the attitude of human beings toward animals and the rest of nature should be, and whether one can rightfully terminate one's own life, it is obvious that, although the debates may move as slowly as glaciers so that progress is imperceptible, they nevertheless do move.

If the purpose of critical thinking is not to help us decide what to believe, what can that purpose be? Insofar as the question of knowledge and belief is concerned, I would say that the role of critical thinking is defensive: to protect us from being coerced or brainwashed into believing what others want us to believe without our having an opportunity to inquire for ourselves. There are great and powerful forces ranged against the individual in every society – the political, the military, and the economic are the most obvious examples – and their aim is often to get us to acquiesce without reflection in the views they want us to have. The armor of skepticism that critical thinking can provide is not an impervious one as far as any given individual is concerned, but in a populace so armored it could be decisive. *I think we are much better off construing critical thinking as nurturing in students a tentative skepticism than as nurturing in them a set of beliefs of dubious long-term reliability.* Critical thinking can help us decide what claims *not* to believe.

Ennis's twin targets – belief and action – represent a misreading of the nature of education characteristic of the popular confusion between education and schooling. It is schooling, not education, that insists that we be conventional and conform in our thought as well as in our behavior. What education insists upon, in contrast, is that we be reasonable and exercise good judgment while remaining cautious and open-minded with regard to beliefs.

It will be said, no doubt, that there is no basis for claiming that inquiry and belief are mutually incompatible (except, of course, for the belief in inquiry itself). But we cannot continue to believe that which is the subject of inquiry. When inquiry begins, it is because evidence has surfaced that constitutes grounds for suspension of belief, and until the inquiry is concluded, skepticism is the order of the day. The progressive self-correction that inquiry entails and the numerous settlements that are reached along the way progressively reduce the grounds for such skepticism. With the conclusion of an inquiry episode, when the problem has been resolved, there will be a renewed opportunity for belief, but it will be a reconstructed and chastened belief as a consequence of the inquiry that has just taken place.

Some will be quick to dismiss reasonableness and judgment as "mere process" or "mere method" and will decry the lack of attention to "content." It must be acknowledged that content is indispensable for the fostering of good judgment. Thus, if we want students to have good historical judgment, we will have to expose them to history; if we want them to have good literary judgment, we will have to expose them to literature; and if we want them to have good ecological judgment, we will have to expose them to ecology. But here precisely is where the mode of teaching – the mode of critical educational intervention – makes such a difference. If *all* we want is for the students to learn history or literature or ecology, little improvement in judgment can be expected. But if we understand that we are teaching them history critically *in order to* improve their historical judgment and not merely to provide them with grounds for patriotism, then content assumes its rightful place alongside method, neither inferior to it nor superior to it.

In point of fact, there is no way around teaching specific disciplinary contents (unless it is teaching *among* the disciplines as well as *within* them). If critical thinking essentially involves *sensitivity to context,* then it is only by direct encounters with particular contents that we can discover the contexts to which we should be sensitive. Unless we come up against the specificity of particular contents, their undeniable, inescapable *thisness,* we have little to become sensitive *to.* It is the irreducible particularity or individuality of specific disciplinary contents that demands scrupulous student attention. And to such encounters students must be taught to bring the self-correcting method of inquiry.

Finally, it is no less important that students engaged in academic practice come to understand the criterion dependency of all judgments and the judgment dependency of all inquiry. We tend to think of criteria as esoteric logical devices thinly populating some remote epistemological Olympus. We forget that criteria are applicable to every mental act, even where such acts do not themselves involve the conscious employment of criteria in their making. The person who exclaims "Shakespeare's poetry is glorious" may or may not be aware of taking into account the differences between Shakespeare and Bacon, between poetry and prose, between "is" and "was," or between "glorious" and "flamboyant," but subsidiary judgment such as these undergird the judgment expressed in the proposition, and these subsidiary judgments are guided by their own proper criteria. Nouns may be primarily classification devices, adjectives and adverbs evaluation devices, and verbs both, but in any case, whether it is a matter of classification or of evaluation, such usages are judgments and are therefore criterion-dependent.

ALTERNATIVE APPROACHES TO TEACHING
PRACTICAL REASONING

Mere practice ranges from dull, mindless, habitual routine to dull, mechanical competence. When, however, practice comes to be permeated with critical thinking, so that we reflect critically on what we do before, while, and after we do it, mere practice becomes self-correcting practice and self-correcting practice is inquiry.

Different purposes express themselves in different types of programs. There are programs devoted to cognitive improvement through the enhancement of logicality and rationality. There are programs that aim at improved levels of skilled performance – academic achievement, athletic achievement, artistic achievement, moral achievement, and so on. And there are programs that attempt to strengthen the student's ability to recognize and resolve problems. It is not, of course, that these three purposes are so different that the programs follow strictly separate paths: there is a great deal of overlap. Nevertheless, the emphasis of the first group is upon sound reasoning, the second emphasizes adroit performances that satisfy explicit criteria, and the third stresses the rapprochement of ends and means. Another way of putting this would be to say that some programs put their emphasis on the guidance of practice by reasons, others on the guidance of practice by criteria, and others on the guidance of practice by hypotheses and consequences.

The guidance of practice by reasons

Children are very much aware that certain acts are generally disapproved of and others are given social approval. They are also aware that the teacher carries moral authority, and they generally do not feel in a position to question that authority. This means that ethical inquiry, which involves a certain amount of thinking for oneself about moral issues, is very difficult to bring about in the classroom setting. If, for example, one child hits another, students are fully aware that hitting is considered wrong and that the teacher will condemn the act. Therefore, the children have no opportunity for inquiry into the situation that prompted the act. Let us, however, consider an alternative scenario in which the teacher is concerned to decenter both the act and his or her authority in order to invite the class to think about what happened and therefore to assume some responsibility for the decision that must be made with regard to it. Thus, instead of immediately condemning the act, the teacher might inquire in an impartial manner what reasons the child might have had for hitting the other. Suppose the child says, "I didn't like his looks." The teacher may then turn to the class and ask, "Is that a good reason?" The members of the class may now proceed to weigh *the reason rather than the act*. They may very well chorus, "No, *that's* not a good reason." Alternatively, the child may say, "He pulled a knife on me!" and the class will have to deliberate about *that* reason. The point is that the children will learn that all ethical acts must have reasons and that it is well to think of the reason before one engages in the act, because if one does not, one must face the moral censure of one's peers. This is not decision making by mere consensus. The guidance we receive is from a critical community that weighs the reasons for actions and not just the actions in isolation.

The normal objection to this approach is that it shifts the basis of moral authority from the strong position of the teacher to the weak position of the class. In a sense, this is certainly true. The aim is to decenter the burden of moral responsibility by removing at least some of it from the teacher. But the teacher's position is not as strong, in the eyes of the students, as it appears to be to us. The teacher's moral authority rests on his or her being an adult and not on being an expert in ethical decision making. The students may respect the teacher for being able to offer a rational justification for praise of this action or condemnation of that one.

As a matter of fact, the teacher's situation is intimately familiar to each of us, because we are in it every day. We may reiterate to ourselves over and over again that overeating is wrong, smoking is wrong, drinking is wrong, and so on, yet we persist in doing the very things we condemn. So with children. They are as aware as the teacher is that lying, stealing, and hitting are condemned by adults as wrong, and they may not disagree with the judgment. Their problem is to avoid *doing* what they consider to be wrong.

Merely to prohibit certain behaviors is insufficient. Merely to explain them causally is insufficient. Children must be encouraged to discuss and deliberate about the reasons such conduct is problematic – to us and to themselves – so that they can proceed to determine what they deem right or wrong based on reasoned justifications.

Criterion-based performance

Now consider a different situation: A member of the school swimming team has entered a national competition for diving. She has been practicing for months and reviewing her practice with her coach. She has also been prepping herself about the criteria that the judges will employ, and she recognizes the need to set very high standards for each criterion. In many ways her performance will be responsive to and guided by these criteria. This is again an inquiry approach, especially if the whole team and the coach have, as a community, discussed the relationship of relevant criteria and standards to their swimming and diving practice.

The guidance of practice by hypotheses and consequences

The approach to practice guided by hypotheses and consequences is a descendant of Dewey's "problem-solving" procedure, first outlined in *How We Think*. Here is a contemporary version of it:

Eight steps to solutions
1. Encourage your child to look for signs of different feelings and to express them. Example: "I feel upset."

2. Help your child encapsulate the problem into a statement: "I feel upset *because Todd is teasing me.*"

3. Assist your child in deciding on a goal, such as "I want Todd to stop picking on me."

4. Don't provide answers. Help your child list multiple solutions of his or her own, such as "I could hit Todd or yell at him."

5. Enable your child to anticipate possible consequences of each approach: Q: "What would happen if you hit Todd?" A: "I'd get into more trouble or Todd could get hurt."

6. Help your child decide on the best solution. "I'll yell at Todd." Should an inappropriate approach begin to emerge, offer an opinion without squashing the child's creativity. Don't wait until after a decision has been made to express your opposition.

7. Assist your child in planning when or how the decision might be executed. Help anticipate obstacles that could occur: "What might happen that could make yelling at Todd not work?" A child who can foresee possible problems is less discouraged by any roadblock that might occur.

8. Have your child try out the solution and evaluate its effect. End by inviting your child to "Let me know how it worked out."[21]

Note what is involved in each of these steps:

1. Expression of *feeling* that there is a problem
2. Identification of *cause* of feeling (*formulation* of problem)
3. Choice of desired *end*-state or goal (formulation of *purpose*)
4. Identification of *means* (devising of *hypothesis*)
5. Anticipation of *consequences*
6. Selection among *alternatives*
7. Devising *plan* of operations
8. *Evaluation* of effects

This strikes me as being a sensible algorithm: an eight-step sequence of procedures that need to be employed in dealing with problematic situations. Putting such an algorithm into operation would likely be an effective demonstration of rational conduct.

To many people, thinking like this seems to come naturally. But

---

[21] This eight-step procedure is quoted from "How to Teach Decision-Making to Kids," *U.S. News and World Report*, April 21, 1986, p. 64, a discussion of the problem-solving approach of Maurice J. Elias and John F. Clabby. See also Elias and Clabby, "Teaching Social Decision Making," *Educational Leadership* (March 1988), 52–5, and George Spivack and Myrna Shure, *The Social Adjustment of Young Children* (San Francisco: Jossey-Bass, 1974).

in fact to many others it is much more difficult than it looks. Each of the eight procedures requires considerable skill; combining them properly requires even more skill. And although the algorithm looks reasonable and commonsensical, whether we do in fact utilize it in daily life is hardly self-evident. Certainly an impulsive, unreflective child might be expected to have some difficulty with it. It is therefore useful to learn from Elias and Clabby, the proponents of this approach, that experimental testing has shown it it be significantly successful.

In general, with regard to cognitive algorithms of this type, whether designed for therapeutic or for educational purposes, we would do well to integrate them into broad-gauge efforts to enhance reflection, raise consciousness, and sharpen thinking skills, rather than use them all by themselves. Some of the stages of the algorithm specifically involve reasoning, and virtually all involve judgment. As we will see in the last part of this book, without continued practice in critical, creative, and caring thinking, the algorithm could be of far less value than it otherwise promises to be.

It seems to me that these problem-solving, decision-making approaches are more likely to be successful when they are part of a comprehensive pedagogical approach aimed at improving children's inquiry, reasoning, information organizing, and communication skills. It is precisely this overarching approach that philosophy provides. Other programs emphasizing problem solving can be made to fit very well into philosophy, although philosophy is too extensive to serve as a component of any one of them. Some skeptics are apt to see this as a kind of "curricular imperialism." Raising spectres of this kind, however, is not likely to be very profitable. We have seen what education *without* philosophy is like. It is time to see what it is like *with* philosophy.

The approaches we have seen are rather cognitive in contrast to a more or less "Gestalt" approach, which is more focused on the appropriateness of the act rather than on the reasons for the act. "Self-correction" and "sensitivity to context" are features to be found in virtually all instances of practical reasoning. Insofar as we are considering ethical inquiry, we can understand "self-correction" as that aspect of inquiry that looks for reasons, as well as for better reasons. Hence the stress on reasonableness – on the vindication of the act rather than on the act itself. Self-correction as a search for better reasons represents, in a manner of speaking, a syntactical approach to ethical judgment, while sensitivity to context represents a more semantical approach, one grounded in the actual circumstances and their meanings. Sensitivity to context calls for an act to be appropriate to the situation that evokes it. This is illustrated by a Gestalt approach in which the pronouncedness of the character of the incomplete or deficient situation calls forth the act that is appropriate to the situation. (A Gestalt psychologist would offer the example of a triangle minus its apex, or the example of a traveler who, adrift in Rome and puzzled by the local mores, might find appropriate guidance in doing as the Romans do.) In ethical inquiry, a *self-realization ethics* is an example of the Gestalt approach, in the sense that one projects an ideal of oneself and then judges alternative modes of conduct insofar as they promise to realize that ideal. The emphasis upon self-correction represents a kind of *good-reasons ethics*. In moral education, students should be given practice in both approaches, so that they can understand their options when dealing with the practical, particular, or unique aspects of actual life situations.

TEACHING FOR BRIDGING, TRANSFER, AND TRANSLATION

One of the problems of present-day education is that students acquire bits of knowledge that, like ice cubes frozen in their trays, remain inert and incapable of interacting with one another. Consequently, educational reformers have placed a premium on helping children construct bridges from one knowledge domain to another, such as by discovering intervening variables, middle terms, missing links, and the like by means of which disparate domains can be connected. Emphasis has also been placed on the development of generic skills that are not specific content areas but are transferrable from one domain to another. Finally, there has been a search for ways of treating various domains as symbolic systems, languages, or communities, so that translation procedures that would enable students to translate the contents of one domain into another can be learned.

An example of bridging can be taken from classificatory reasoning. If we present students with a completion exercise such as "All Londoners are _____ ; all _____ are British; therefore, all Londoners are British," they are not limited to a single answer, but the students are of course required to find a middle term that will link those who are residents of London with those who are British. Alternatively, one might give students bridging practice by offering them a term such as "residents of England" and asking them what domains it connects. It is then possible to move to other concepts, asking such questions as "What do sunspot activity and precipitation have in common?" and "What domains does barter connect?"

Examples of transfer are amply provided by David N. Perkins and Gavriel Salomon, who distinguish between "low road" and "high road" transfer.[22] We are engaged in low-road transfer when, being already proficient in driving an automobile, we find it relatively easy to learn to drive a truck. The skills needed to drive the truck are sufficiently congruent to those needed to drive the car that we can readily extrapolate from the one situation to the other. In the case of high-road transfer, the two domains are not closely related but far apart. It may take a metaphor to establish a connection between them. When Shakespeare uses the phrase "summer's lease," we are forced to connect the brief tenancy that summer has during the course of a year with the tenancy one has in the apartment one rents or in the brevity of the life one lives. The carryover from such disparate domains is of course far richer (if more tenuous) than that linking the world of cars and the world of trucks.

With translation, the paradigm case is translating from one natural language to another. We find that knowledge of a root language like Latin makes it easier for people to learn French or Spanish than it would be if they had no such preparation. Or there is Aristotelian logic, which aims to furnish us with a highly simplified but universal language. Or there are parallel constructions, as in the arts, where musical and poetic structures can be compared, or painterly and photographic treatments of nature, or architectural and sculptural treatments of masses in space.

No doubt all three of these strategies – bridging, transfer, and translation – require of students facility in analogical reasoning. The connections that have to be established may be readily evident or they may be far-fetched, but whatever the degree of difficulty they present, preparation for making them requires intense immersion in analogical practice. This is a skill developed in the arts and humanities

[22] "Teaching for Transfer,"*Educational Leadership* (September 1988), 22–32.

as well as in the sciences. It is the most generic of the creative skills and the most imaginative of the analytic skills. The intellectual flexibility and resourcefulness needed to engage in successful translation and transfer will occur only when analogical practice is cultivated with the same feverish intensity we now reserve for the learning of, say, arithmetic.

SOME CHARACTERIZATIONS OF CRITICAL THINKING

The last decade of the twentieth century saw the triumphant spread and virtual institutionalization of "critical thinking" in many of the nooks and crannies of the world of education. The general idea of the approach was that one's thinking could be improved by one's thinking carefully and constructively about it. Hence the term "metacognition" employed by many psychologists. Those who think critically have been often described as "keenly analytical," "scrupulously accurate," " clear-headed," and a host of other such terms. In recent years, critical thinking has come to denote *any* thinking that, when applied to an instance of thinking, could make it more efficient and more reliable. A slew of characterizations of critical thinking have been proposed, of which some examples follow.

Most of these represent specific authors' positions:

1. Reasonable reflective thinking that is focused on deciding what to believe or do (Ennis)
2. Thinking that helps us solve problems and make decisions (Sternberg)
3. Thinking that enables critical skills to be transferred to educational subjects (McPeck)
4. Thinking that contains enabling skills (e.g., principles of reasoning, skills of logic) as well as skills shared across fields of expertise (Resnick)
5. Thinking that comes in or may come in when we suspect something to be amiss (McPeck)
6. Thinking that *represents* the philosophy of x, for the philosophy of x should ideally be an integral part of what it means to learn x (McPeck)

7. Thinking that helps students understand the logical connectives of English (Adler)
8. Attentiveness to the formal aspects of thinking (Garver)
9. Discussion of argumentative literature drawn from traditional works of the humanities (Garver, Adler)
10. Thinking performed by those who are appropriately moved by reasons (Siegel)
11. Thinking that aims to overcome bias, prejudice, and stereotyping (Paul)
12. Thinking that aims to protect us from deceptions by others and from self-deception (Paul)
13. Reflective skepticism (McPeck)
14. Literacy (David Olson)
15. The correct assessing of statements (Ennis)
16. Becoming conscious of one's own thinking so as to be able to transfer it from familiar to unfamiliar contexts (Arons)
17. Thinking aimed at the integration of thought and action (J. R. Martin)
18. Thinking about thinking
19. Thinking appraisively about any human product, whether said, made, or done
20. The ability of thinkers to take charge, to develop intellectual standards and apply them to their own thinking (Paul)
21. Thinking explicatively and interpretively, as critics do
22. The application of theoretical thinking to practical, problematic situations
23. Reflections upon the causes and consequences of what happens
24. The reflective assessment of practice
25. Thinking that considers how to facilitate communication between experts and the world
26. A systematic search for the reasons by which one's thinking can be justified
27. Thinking that seeks to disclose the persuasive aspects of all explanation, while holding that all explanation is argument
28. Thinking that examines differences of interpretation resulting from differences in contexts, conceptual schemes, and points of view

29. A light version of philosophy
30. The testing of claims
31. Thinking that attempts to arrive at a judgment only after hon-
    estly evaluating alternatives with respect to available evidence
    and arguments (Hatcher)

No doubt there are dozens more of such characterizations that
are equally worthy of mention. From most of them one gets the impression that critical thinking is thinking that strives to be *impartial,
accurate, careful, clear, truthful, abstract, coherent,* and *practical.* Critical
thinking is practical in the sense that it is *applied,* and one can apply
very abstract thinking to very abstract issues or to very concrete ones.

This is one way to approach critical thinking: Consider it as it
appears from a number of different (but mostly authoritative) points
of view. The problem is that we lack an organizing principle that
will enable us to put these random characterizations together in a
consistent and coherent way. Some of the characterizations just listed
overlap with others, some contradict others, some are subordinate to
others. We wonder if there is not a better approach.

One thing we can do is make sure that we are dealing with items
that reflect a single organizing principle from the start. We can then
sift through them, screening in and screening out but confident always that we are dealing with characterizations that stem from a
single, authoritative point of view. We must first, of course, choose a
particular perspective as that of a recognized authority. Let us choose,
for this purpose, the highly respected work in critical thinking of
Raymond S. Nickerson.[23] We can be sure that Nickerson would be
high on any list of *reliable* writers treating the topic of what constitutes
good thinking. We can feel fairly well assured that each characterization on the following list that Nickerson offers us is likely to be
considered *acceptable* by other authorities in the domain under study.
But rather than repeat these characterizations in the order Nickerson
offers them to us, I would like to separate them into two groups:
The first group will be those that I think are standard or familiar; the
second are those that are less commonplace and more likely to be a

---

[23] I am referring in particular to Nickerson's article "Why Teach Thinking?"in J. B.
Baron, and R. J. Sternberg (eds.), *Teaching Thinking Skills: Theory and Practice* (New
York: W. H. Freeman and Co., 1986), pp. 29–30.

product of Nickerson's ingenuity or thoroughness. In other words, I propose dividing the list up into those that are more or less conventional (but nevertheless important) and those that are more or less unconventional and evidence of cognitive creativity.

First I shall list the more familiar characterizations in the column on the left, and the more specialized, less familiar ones in the column on the right:

1. uses evidence skillfully and impartially;
2. organizes thoughts and articulates them concisely and coherently;
3. distinguishes between logically valid and invalid inferences;
4. suspends judgment in the absence of sufficient evidence to support a decision;
5. attempts to anticipate the probable consequences of alternative actions before choosing among them;
6. applies problem-solving techniques appropriately in domains other than those in which they were learned;
7. listens carefully to other people's ideas;
8. looks for unusual approaches to complex problems;
9. understands the differences among conclusions, assumptions, and hypotheses;

1. understands the difference between reasoning and rationalizing;
2. understands the idea of degrees of belief;
3. has a sense of the value and cost of information, knows how to seek information, and does so when it makes sense;
4. sees similarities and analogies that are not superficially apparent;
5. can learn independently and, at least equally important, has an abiding interest in doing so;
6. can structure informally represented problems in such a way that formal techniques (e.g., mathematics) can be used to solve them;
7. understands the difference between winning an argument and being right;
8. recognizes that most real-world problems have more than one possible solution and that those solutions

10. habitually questions one's own views and attempts to understand both the assumptions that are critical to those views and the implications of the views; and
11. recognizes the fallibility of one's own opinions, the probability of bias in those opinions, and the danger of differentially weighting evidence according to personal preferences.

may differ in numerous respects and may be difficult to compare using a single figure of merit;
9. can strip a verbal argument of irrelevancies and phrase it in terms of its essentials;
10. is sensitive to the difference between the validity of a belief and the intensity with which it is held;
11. can represent differing viewpoints without distortion, exaggeration, or characterization; and
12. is aware that one's understanding is always limited, often much more so than would be apparent to one with a noninquiring attitude.

If it is agreed that the list on the right is less routine than the one on the left, how are we to explain that difference? Obviously it will not do to hide behind the word "creativity." What we can say, instead, is that the right-hand list gives evidence that Nickerson is unusually scrupulous in examining his own *experience* when in inquiry situations and that he has the *imagination* to recognize that these findings may be as important as the more familiar characterizations.

I think that, later on, when we take a more leisurely look at the nature of creative thinking, we will see once again how much such thinking represents the interpenetration of experience and imagination. Without experience, imagination is likely to become quickly irrelevant, and without imagination, experience readily becomes tedious and pedestrian. In combination, however, as they are in metaphors and analogies, they can open up unsuspected ranges of alternative possibilities.

Nickerson's characterization of critical thinking is a relatively extensive one. Let us consider a very different one: the brief and elegant definition offered by another stalwart of the critical thinking movement: Harvey Siegel. Siegel's entry uses only four words to touch some of the major aspects of the topic. What he says, with admirable simplicity, is that critical thinking is thinking that is "appropriately moved by reasons." Let's reflect a bit on this:

a. By insisting that critical thinking be appropriate, Siegel makes sure that what one thinks is right when contextual considerations are taken into account.
b. By appealing to the motivating force of reasons, Siegel guarantees that critical thinking is rational.
c. And by affirming that such thinking is the result of being moved by reasons, Siegel boldly acknowledges the crucial role of emotions: Critical thinking, for him, involves the passionate pursuit of rationality.

If brevity is indeed the soul of wit, then Siegel's definition is quite obviously a witty one, although some would question whether it is sufficiently exhaustive of the domain of critical thinking to which it refers. I have introduced it here, however, for a different reason: to point up the vacillation we engage in between speaking of critical *thinking* in contrast to critical *thinkers*. Whereas Ennis, Sternberg, McPeck, and many others resolutely insist they are talking about a manner of thought, Siegel, Garver, and Arons seem to be referring to a type of thinker.

There are strong differences between what the critical thinker does and what critical thinking is, just as there are strong similarities between them. The similarities may be so strong that we lose any sense we had of the thinker and the thinking being two separate things. Thus Emerson proclaimed that he was both "the doubter and the doubt," and Yeats complained that "we cannot tell the dancer from the dance." We hear a momentary snatch of music, and we assert, not "That's by Schubert," but "That's Schubert." And we can be perfectly serious. It is as if the producer and the product share a common quality. And how about Spinoza's declaration that "the mind is the form of the body" – how can we imagine this, except that the mind and the body have in common the same form?

That brings us to the question of what the connection may be between the person herself and the way she thinks. The self-effacing Shakespeare seems to be worlds apart from his works, and he and his works are very different. But what about his distinctive way of thinking: Isn't that of a piece with Shakespeare the man?

Obviously, this is a matter of some controversy. (Should we take seriously the claim that a dog and its master, after spending many years together, come to resemble one another?) In any event, some things can be predicated of human beings that cannot be predicated of works of art, and vice versa. When Siegel says that critical thinking is "appropriately moved by reasons," he means that the thinker is moved, not the thought. It is the thinker who is compelled by reasons, emotionally moved by them, touched by them, stirred by them. The critical thinker enjoys and appreciates the cogency, the reasonableness of what she reads, and she incorporates this cogency into her critical thought.

The four defining features I once attributed to critical thinking I now perceive as belonging to the critical thinker. It is the thinker, not the thinking necessarily, that is productive of judgments, guided by criteria and standards, sensitive to context, and self-corrective.

Strictly speaking, then, the composer's creative skills result in compositions that have qualitative musical values, and the critical thinker's cognitive skills result in qualities of thinking such as logical, grammatical, rhetorical, expository, narrative, and so on. Nevertheless, we understand the difference and take it into account as we speak. Just as we understand "Vivaldi is rhythmic" to refer to Vivaldi's music and not to him, so we understand "appropriately moved by reasons" to mean either the thinking produced by the critical thinker or the critical thinker herself, depending on the context. At one extreme we have the painterly qualities of a painting – say, the agitated, almost hysterical qualities of a painting by Munch, qualities that are precipitates of such behavior on the part of Munch himself – and at the other extreme we have painterly qualities that bear little resemblance to the qualities of the artist's personal conduct. On the one hand, there is the philosophical or literary quality of a person's thought, which is composed of an idiosyncratic distribution of mental acts, while on the other hand there is the psychological quality of that person's thought – a certain calm or a certain anxiety – that may not show itself in her thinking. As we read Shakespeare's *Sonnets*, the literary and philosophical qualities of his style are readily apparent, but we may be dissatisfied with these, and try to reconstruct from the poems his personal, psychological qualities, which are maddeningly unavailable to us.

In Part Four of this book, I shall offer a characterization of critical thinking that could be understood to apply to either the thinking or the thinker. Insofar as it applies to the thinker, it is a "functional characterization"; insofar as it applies to the thinker's thought, it can be understood to consist of cognitive/affective qualities or values analogous to musical values, painterly values, or the spatial values to be found in architecture.

3

Obstacles and Misconceptions in Teaching for Thinking

CONCEPTUAL OBSTACLES TO THE STRENGTHENING OF THINKING

I take up first the conceptual obstacles to the improvement of thinking in schools and colleges. Later I will deal with some of the more practical aspects of the problem.

Disagreements over the nature of thinking

We are not sure what thinking is, just as we are not sure what life is, or experience, or being human. When problems like the abortion issue come to the surface, the general public discovers that matters like these have to be confronted and deliberated upon by everyone. But we must first make provision in the schools for installing thinking as a fundamental aspect of education; and to do this, we need clues as to just what arguments we are dealing with. Following are some of the disagreements that emerge when we begin to consider what we must do to focus on education for thinking.

1. The conception of thinking primarily entails *problem solving*
   versus
   The conception of thinking primarily entails *problem seeking*

Comment. By and large, this difference exemplifies the radical difference between education in the sciences and education in the humanities. Science textbooks tend to treat scientific knowledge as *settled.* Students learn standard methods of problem solving and then are assigned problems that vary somewhat from the paradigm to see if they can extrapolate from the established approach. In the humanities, in contrast, the subject matter is treated as intrinsically *problematic,* and students are encouraged to look for new problems of interpretation or conceptualization.

2. Seeing a major objective of thinking as the production of beliefs
versus
Emphasizing the *process* of inquiry, so that beliefs are seen as merely psychological end-states of no special cognitive value

Comment. Inquiry commences when beliefs we had counted on are found to be unreliable, and it ceases with the acquisition of convictions that are more reliable. So belief is a state that precedes and also follows inquiry but is not a part of inquiry itself (unless one considers the fact that those who inquire believe in the process of inquiry). Obviously, we employ critical thinking to erode our biases and prejudices: that is, to straighten out our cockeyed beliefs. But believing as such is not part of critical thinking in the way that assuming, hypothesizing, deducing, explaining, and the like are parts of it. It is a psychological state that adds no further warrant to what is assertable.

3. Conceiving of critical, creative, and caring thinking as three dimensions, like length, breadth, and depth
versus
Conceiving of critical, creative, and caring thinking as discontinuous, discrete, or even opposed to one another

Comment. There are various conceptions of the creative/critical/caring thinking rubric, ranging from those that see the three as mutually reinforcing to those that see them as merely compatible to those that envisage a fundamental opposition among them. A promising approach, I believe, is to consider the three as forms of inquiry that merge and interact with the improved understanding of thinking.

4. Formulating the problem as one of getting students to think
versus
Conceding that students already think but need to learn to think better

Comment. We very often congratulate ourselves on having gotten students to think better when in fact all we have done is gotten them to think about the same things we are thinking about in the same way we think about them. This is a shift in the content of what is thought about, not an improvement in the quality of thinking. The students may not be thinking either more or better, and they need to be doing both.

5. Ranking various thinking operations hierarchically
   versus
   Avoiding overall rankings and insisting that taxonomies be purely descriptive

Comment. The compromise that suggests itself here is that there are functional hierarchies within particular situations but no overall hierarchies. Thus, in a situation calling for justification, giving reasons may be a more important skill than defining terms, but in a different situation the reverse could be true.

6. Giving the concrete priority over the abstract in teaching for thinking
   versus
   Giving the abstract priority over the concrete

Comment. This debate has to be understood with regard to the presuppositions of current educational practice. Recent assumptions have been that the concrete should predominate in early childhood education (because young children "cannot handle abstractions" and that the abstract should predominate in higher education (because college students need only to "have knowledge"; they don't need to "make judgments"). Both presuppositions are obviously unwarranted.

Disagreements over the proper psychological approach

Obviously, among psychologists there are a great many disputes, such as those over the nature of learning, the role of memory and concept formation, and the nature of intelligence and of affective factors, that have been followed keenly by educators because of the bearing these issues can be expected to have on education. Much hangs, therefore, upon the psychological approach that educators suppose to be correct when they begin the planning that will make their schools more reflective. We must not confuse

1. Attempting to understand children's cognitive development by studying what children *can't do without intervention*

with

    Attempting to understand the cognitive development of children by studying what children *can do with intervention*

Comment. This is, in part, the issue between Piaget and Vygotsky. Since virtually all educational situations involve adult mediation between the culture and the child, and since such mediation comes in a variety of styles, each has its own impact on children's learning. It is hazardous to accept the Piagetian approach as a norm for curriculum construction or for the devising of pedagogies. Piaget is so interested in showing what children cannot do unaided at a given stage that he is unable to focus on how they can be helped to do it.

2. Stressing all the varieties of human intelligence (mathematical, musical, linguistic, etc.) so as to aim at the cultivation of all varieties

versus

    Emphasizing only certain varieties of human intelligence

Comment. In the long run, Howard Gardner's emphasis on the variety of human intelligence is both correct and just, for it provides a fair and humane goal for the educational process. But it is of little consolation to those who are language-deficient and who discover that language and mathematics, rightly or wrongly, are the established currencies of the classroom. All of the child's potential modes of intelligence deserve to be developed, and the schools should develop literacy in each of these modes, but this will not begin to happen until the entire curriculum undergoes an agonizing reappraisal that is long overdue.

Disagreements over the role of philosophy

Among educators who favor allowing philosophy a role in education, there are disagreements that replicate some of the disagreements
philosophers have among themselves. There may be few disputes
among teachers and administrators as to whether children should be
encouraged to learn philosophy or actually do it; the preference for
the latter is near-unanimous. But it is still not clear to many whether
teachers should be encouraged to do either or both. To me, the hand-
writing on the wall is legible enough: Until teachers have learned
philosophy *and can do it,* prospects of thinking in education will not
be very bright.

1. Emphasizing *either* formal logic *or* informal logic *or* rhetoric
   versus
   Attempting to induce critical thinking in the classroom without
   recourse to formal logic, informal logic, or rhetoric

Comment. Insofar as critical thinking necessarily involves facility in
the employment of criteria, and insofar as philosophy is the discipline
that is, among other things, concerned with the establishment of
criteria, it is difficult to see how we could responsibly engage in
critical thinking without to some extent internalizing this aspect of
philosophical practice. It is difficult to conceive of overcoming uncritical thinking without recourse to at least a moderate amount of logic.

2. Conceiving of philosophy as having a special connection with
   good thinking
   versus
   Conceiving of philosophy as having no special connection
   with good thinking

Comment. One tradition in philosophy (regarded by others as ar-
rogant and imperialistic) sees philosophy as identical with excellent
thinking. Another tradition, more moderate, holds that philosophical reflections on thinking have a directness and immediacy that
psychological inquiry necessarily lacks. Insofar as philosophy claims
to have an exclusive competence in thinking critically about thinking,
the disagreement may be incapable of resolution.

3. Approaching thinking descriptively
versus
Approaching thinking normatively

Comment. In one sense, this is a fallacious dichotomy. All norms presuppose descriptions, and all descriptions presuppose norms or criteria. Even in the case of formal logic, it is unclear whether its principles are to be taken as exclusively descriptive or exclusively normative. Nevertheless, to the extent that education involves the making of recommendations and not merely the retailing of descriptive information, it is unlikely that students can be encouraged to think more critically without becoming acquainted with the criteria by means of which critical and uncritical thinking are to be distinguished from one another. Both formal and empirical recommendations can be of value.

4. Contending that the only good model for good thinking is the scientific model
versus
Contending that, just as literature is the discipline that is the appropriate aegis for instruction in writing, so philosophy is the appropriate aegis for instruction in thinking

Comment. Science, philosophy, and literature are all disciplines from which humanistic values can be extracted and formulated as recommendations for practice. But literature is too diffuse and diversified to serve as the primary aegis for thinking instruction, and science is too narrow and unified. Philosophy, with its tough insistence on logical rigor and its emphasis on flexibility, is a much more likely candidate.

Disagreements over the preferred educational approaches

In addition to their disagreements over philosophical and psychological approaches, educators disagree among themselves concerning matters that are purely educational or that connect educational quandaries with philosophical or psychological quandaries.

1. Claiming that all thinking is discipline-specific

   versus

   Claiming that there are generic thinking skills that overarch
   the disciplines

Comment. Those who claim that all thinking is discipline-specific
do so to bolster their case that critical thinking can be taught only
in the context of each particular discipline: They contend that it cannot be taught per se. Their opponents contend that there are generic
thinking skills (e.g., some skills of formal logic, like *modus tollens*)
that are not modified from one disciplinary context to the other
and that it would therefore be more efficient to teach such generic
skills in an autonomous critical thinking course. I might add that
the entire discipline of philosophy bears a unique relationship to
the other disciplines, in that philosophy prepares students to think
in those other disciplines. The reasoning, concept-formation, and
judgment-shaping skills that philosophy strengthens in early elementary school are indispensable for the child's middle-school years.
What philosophy provides throughout elementary school – a reser-
voir of fundamental humanistic ideas for classroom deliberation – is
indispensable for secondary school, college, and citizenship, to say
nothing of parenthood. The legend that philosophy is solely for the
old is most unfortunate. It is essentially *preparatory*, and the sooner
other disciplines acknowledge this the better it will be for thinking
in education generally.

2. Attempting to make the separate disciplines more reflective
   by adding critical thinking exercises to each chapter of their
   curricula

   versus

   Incorporating all cognitive exercises in an autonomous course
   in critical thinking

Comment. The first approach runs the danger of being superficial
and the second of being irrelevant. There is, however, a middle path.
We need both an independent course in critical thinking and infusion
and reinforcement of critical thinking in the separate disciplines. The
middle path is to direct the skills learned in the independent course
to the "basic" skills of reading and writing. If reading and writing can

be made more critical, students themselves will transfer this added reflectiveness to the particular disciplines.

3. Attempting to teach critical thinking by teaching *about* it

versus

Attempting to teach critical thinking by stressing practice rather than theory

Comment. There is little or no evidence that teachers in preparation who have studied critical thinking research have thereby become better critical thinkers. The alternative, to stress the practice rather than the theory, is all right when dealing with teachers whose training is just beginning, but teachers whose training is well under way should be increasingly involved in inquiries that require that theory and practice be acquired together.

4. Approaches that center the acquisition of cognitive skills on the teacher on the assumption that they will rub off on the students

versus

Approaches that use the teacher as a conduit to the students but in addition provide students with curricular models of thinking to supplement the teacher's modeling

Comment. The second alternative seems definitely preferable, especially if the "curricular model of thinking" is a children's story about a group of children forming their own community of thinking inquiry. This is a powerful motivating device, and it is sad to say that most critical thinking approaches fail to provide anything of the kind to motivate students who feel no initial attraction to activities aimed at improving their reasoning and judgment.

5. Approaches that utilize didactic methods of instruction, such as lecturing

versus

Approaches that seek to convert the classroom into a community of shared and cooperative inquiry

Comment. Only the second alternative recognizes the vital role of conversation and dialogue in the strengthening of reasoning and judgment. And only the second is consistent with the broader goal of a democratic and participatory society, even if the first need not be incompatible with such a goal. It is desirable, however, that we employ means that are consistent with the ends we are trying to attain.

Faced with an epidemic of some unusual ailment, investigators will often begin by trying to establish the *criteria* by means of which they can distinguish cases of the specific illness from noncases. In effect, they begin with a working *definition* that is subject to modification.

Now, teaching for the improvement of thinking is, rather, a wholesome educational development. But it does have its perplexing aspects. We need careful examination of the *assumptions* we are likely to make about teaching, thinking, skills, content, and standards. Let us consider some mistaken assumptions, keeping in mind that each may not be unsound by itself but that they may be ineffectual when taken collectively.

Misconception 1: Teaching for thinking is equivalent to teaching for critical thinking

If teaching for thinking and teaching for critical thinking were the same, then those who teach for thinking would be right when they reply, "Teach for critical thinking? Why, we're already doing it!" But are they? And if they are not, why not?

Let us invent the case of Mr. A. As a teacher, Mr. A is alert, forceful, and energetic. His mind is constantly on his subject and constantly awhirl with thoughts. He wants his pupils to think about the subject as he does, with the same interest and care and excitement he feels in himself. Consequently, he refrains from lecturing. Instead, he shoots questions, in rapid fire, at his students, because he knows that questions will make them think. Likewise, his homework assignments challenge the students to reflect. If asked about the intellectual behavior of his students, he will say that sudents tend to be thoughtless and indolent; they need to have their attention galvanized by a dramatic teacher who compels them to think more and more about the issues at hand rather than permit then to drift into aimless but pleasant reveries.

Comment. Perhaps Mr. A wants to increase the quantity of his students' thinking and assumes that he will thereby improve its quality. Perhaps he assumes that it is unrealistic to expect students to think *better*; one can only try to get them to think more. And to some extent, of course, he's right – more thinking in the classroom *is* better than less.

But is Mr. A correct in assuming that students, when not being taught, are simply thoughtless, mindless? Perhaps what he means is that their thoughts are unfocused and that he succeeds in focusing them. Or perhaps he believes that their thoughts are focused elsewhere and that he succeeds in focusing them on the topic at hand.

Mr. A is rightly suspicious of lecturing as a means of getting students to think critically, although it has its merits as a means of getting them to think. However, he monopolizes the questioning process instead of encouraging the students to think up the questions themselves. In so doing, he gets them thinking but not thinking for themselves – this being, in part, what the difference between answering questions and asking them comes down to. And even if he were to get them to ask questions, this would be no great advance if they were to believe that only he could provide the answers or if questioning were all they could do.

Misconception 2: Reflective teaching will necessarily result in reflective learning

When genuine teaching occurs, both teachers and learners are involved in thinking, just as buyers and sellers are together involved in commercial transactions. But it does not follow that reflective teachers will necessarily produce reflective learners, just as it does not follow that rapid teachers will produce rapid learners.

Consider the case of Ms. B. Ms. B is justly proud of her reputation for knowing her subject and for demanding that her students acquire as much as possible of that knowledge for themselves before they depart from her course. Many students find her courses difficult; there seems to be so much material to cover, retain, and master. Some students feel that their previous courses have not prepared them with the skills needed for dealing with these complex and specialized topics. With this opinion the teacher will likely concur, adding that it is up to previous teachers to do their job better rather than that she herself should water down her course content by teaching skills.

Comment. There can be little doubt that Ms. B's knowledge of her subject is authoritative. Moreover, she has carefully examined the assumptions generally made by her colleagues (as well as her own), and it would be hard to deny that her grasp of her subject is the product of a great deal of critical thinking.

Now, thinking in general is the conscious processing of experience – or at least so I take it to be. And I assume that critical thinking begins with reflections on practical activity and eventuates in judgment. All of this is what Ms. B has done. She has processed the "raw, crude, macroscopic experience" (to use Dewey's terminology) of her professional life and converted it into the refined end products called knowledge. In the process, *she* has been compelled to think critically. It does not follow, however, that the students who learn those end products will be thereby empowered to think critically. For this to be possible, *they* must have access to at least some of the crude, raw, problematic material with which she herself began so that they can work their way through it as she did.

A further comment about Ms. B pertains to her attitude that students who enter her classroom must be prepared with the skills necessary for mastering the content she will provide and that she cannot be expected to take time out rehearsing them in such skills. But this is not the only way in which skill deficiencies can be made up. For example, if she were willing to conceive of her subject matter as problematic rather than as settled, as a starting point rather than as a terminus of inquiry, she might find that her students' cognitive proficiencies would improve concurrently with the progress of the inquiry.

While I have great respect for the importance of the teacher as a model of good thinking, I doubt there is much evidence to show that this alone is sufficient to bring about significant improvement in the way students think. There is a persistent conviction among those who educate teachers that if teachers think more critically, it will trickle down somehow to the students. I suspect that, short of a drastic overhaul of texts and tests and classroom methodologies, we may well see the phenomenon of teachers thinking more critically but students nowhere getting the benefit of it.

Misconception 3: Teaching about critical thinking is equivalent to teaching for critical thinking

Of all the faulty assumptions we might refer to in this matter, that teaching about critical thinking and teaching for critical thinking are equivalent is perhaps the most insidious and the most important, because it itself rests upon still deeper mistaken assumptions about the role of values in education. I cannot examine these underlying assumptions here in any detail; perhaps it will be sufficient to say that, in my opinion, *we will not be able to get students to engage in better thinking unless we teach them to employ criteria and standards by means of which they can assess their thinking for themselves*. I do not see this coming about through teaching *about* critical thinking as it is now understood and practiced.

For example, we can consider the case of Ms. C. Ms. C is quite fascinated by the question of how we think and is eager to make her students equally fascinated with it. Consequently, she is frequently to be found relating to other teachers, to students, and to parents the latest research findings concerning the thinking process and its underlying conditions or basing her teaching on these findings. She distinguishes among her students according to their cognitive styles or their right-brain/left-brain dominance or their stages of moral development or their sex or their body types – there are many ways of setting students apart. Having categorized and characterized students in accordance with the empirical differences noted by and reported by experimenters, her next job is to address each student as appropriately as possible, on the assumption that individual attention is needed in order to deal effectively with individual differences.

Comment. There can be no doubt that empirical research about teaching and learning can be useful to teachers, just as there can be no doubt that individual attention is often desirable because of the special characteristics of particular students. Nevertheless, these differences should not be construed as an excuse for fragmenting the class into a mere collection of isolated individuals. Teachers should pursue the creation of a classroom community of inquiry *in spite of* individual differences rather than settle for a rag-tag aggregation of individuals *because of* such differences. We can hardly hope to build an equitable pluralistic society if at the first sign of diversity we attempt to disband and segregate the classroom community.

Teaching students about critical thinking is about as likely to create a nation of critical thinkers as having students learn the results of research into bicycle riding is likely to create a nation of bicycle riders. (This is not to say that elementary school courses in psychology or in the psychology of cognition would be inappropriate in terms of the knowledge students would acquire from them. It is simply to say that critical thinking involves participating in *practical* reasoning, and teaching *about* critical thinking has little to contribute in this regard.)

In short, knowing more is not equivalent to thinking better. Critical thinking, like education generally, is an intervention whose aim is not simply to bring children's thinking into line with everyone else's thinking but to get them to be more reflective, more reasonable, and more judicious. Paradoxical as it may seem, teaching the facts about a subject cultivates a distanced, theoretical attitude toward that subject rather than a practical one.

Misconception 4: Teaching for critical thinking requires drill in thinking skills

As a child learns her first language in the midst of the life of the family, she is rarely drilled or rehearsed in grammar or usage. She finds herself immersed in a series of situations, each of which has its unique quality and in each of which there are utterances that have their unique meaning. Each context prescribes its meaning, and these meanings accrue to the speech acts and language utilized in those contexts. To divorce such acts from their contexts is to divorce them from their meaning, which is not salvaged by monotonous repetition. Now, where meaning is minimal (as, for example, in memorizing the multiplication table), drill may be justifiable, but where the meaning component is significant – and this is, one would hope, the desired state of affairs – drill is counterproductive because it involves a disso-ciation of the thinking process from the meanings we might otherwise have to think about. The intelligence produced by drills is likely to be an alienated intelligence.

Consider the arguments produced by Mr. D. He is an experienced teacher, quite aware of the powerful role that practice has in education. Very often, he reasons, we learn to do something by going out and doing it. This is the way we learn to swim, dance, and skate. Skills are matters of "knowing how"; contents are matters of "knowing that." Contents can be passed from one mind to another by teaching, but skills have to be acquired by practice. Consequently, Mr. D contends, since the quality of our thinking is a matter of skill, of knowing how to think, and since skills emerge out of practice, what better approach can there be to teaching for improved thinking than to give students lots of drill in performing specific thinking operations? Besides, according to Mr. D, if previous teachers have failed to provide the students with the skills necessary for coping with the contents of his course, then he has a responsibility for providing them himself.

Comment. Mr. D is making a number of assumptions that are frequently made by educators. The first is that, if students are lacking in the skills needed to master the content of a course, one can simply implant or infuse the skills into the curriculum. Second, he assumes that the best way of teaching skills is by drill. And third, he assumes that skills are all that is needed.

With regard to the first question, one might inquire what the evidence is that the infusion approach works. And if it does work, is it because of its own merits or because it reinforces what has been acquired by the students in a separate course in critical thinking?

The response to the "building skills by thinking drills" approach is much the same. One can, first, ask if it works. And one can, second, ask how it compares with less artificial methods, such as logically disciplined dialogue in the classroom.

As for the third assumption, we may respond by pointing out that a good critical thinker is a good craftsperson and craft is never a mere aggregation of skills. We may be ever so skilled in drilling, filing, cutting, grinding metals, and so on, but if we lack such criteria as utility, serviceability, and beauty, or if we have such criteria but have low standards for satisfying them, we cannot be other than poor artisans, if artisans at all. So with critical thinking: It is essential that critical thinkers recognize, work with, and be prepared to appeal to the criteria that are relevant to the matters under investigation. It is also essential that they have high standards of performance, so that they do not permit themselves to engage in thinking that is shoddy: illogical or uncritical. And it is essential that they become adept at handling more than one skill at a time, for at any one moment numerous skills may be clustered together, while at the next moment they may have to be reorganized into a contrapuntal arrangement.

Mr. D needs to reflect much more thoroughly on his practice, so as to discover the kinds of situations in which drill is profitable and the kinds in which it is not. He also needs to ask himself how one can aim at going beyond mere skills to cultivation of the *art* of thinking well.

Misconception 5: Teaching for logical thinking is equivalent to teaching for critical thinking

If critical thinkers aim to avoid (among other things) being illogical, it is tempting to assume that critical thinking *is* being logical. If this were the case, it might follow that nothing more is needed than a good course in logic.

Ms. E, for example, has for a long time been fed up with the slovenly reasoning of her students. It is not enough, she argues, to teach them grammar and vocabulary or arithmetic and geometry; they have to learn how to reason logically. She therefore obtains permission to give a course in formal logic.

Comment. Ms. E is probably correct in her suspicion that the failure of the schools to insist upon elementary logical competence among students, while demanding an arithmetical competence perhaps even beyond what is needed for a balanced approach, represents a serious flaw in the educational process. But while Ms. E may be right that logical competence is necessary, it does not follow that logic, if added to the curriculum, would be sufficient to set matters right.

For one thing, teaching logic in isolation in no way shows students how to *apply* that logic to the subject matters of the various disciplines. Unless students are taught how to marry logical skills and course content, they will generally be helpless to do so on their own.

Our failure to integrate skills and content in the schools reflects our taking the model of the university too seriously in this regard. (There are ample other respects in which we do not take it seriously enough.) It is in the university that undergraduates are given, in each course, a paradigm of overspecialization. (The high schools eagerly ape the colleges on this point.) If I had my way, instead of giving undergraduates a course in logic or critical thinking and a course in biology or anthropology or philosophy, I would see to it that they got an introductory course in biological reasoning or anthropological reasoning or philosophical reasoning, so that the logical skills and the course content would be presented to the students as integrated with one another from the very start. (For majors, a senior course called "The Study of _____ " would also be mandatory.)

Misconception 6: Teaching for learning is just as effective as teaching for critical thinking

Some educators would apparently like to defuse the demand for critical thinking by maintaining that teaching for learning is just as good and probably better. This can be settled only by asking, "Good for what?" It depends on the goals of education. Are we trying to produce people who will grow up to be informed and knowledgeable citizens or people who will be reasonable and reflective citizens or both?

Ms. F's case is a case in point. Ms. F is, by the standards prevailing in her district, an exceptionally good teacher. But she is troubled and dissatisfied nevertheless. She knows her subject, and she teaches it the way she was taught to teach it. Why, then, when her students are tested, do they not seem to know all she expects them to know?

Comment. We may want students to grow up to be reasonable and reflective, but we test them on what they know – on what they have learned. There is a serious discrepancy here. Students and their parents expect that the education provided by schools will be relevant and applicable to life and the world in which we live. We cannot be expected to develop good judgment if we cannot see the applicability of what we are taught to our daily practice and daily experience.

The result is general dissatisfaction – among parents, among teachers, and among students – because the conception of education prevailing among those who make the tests is generally knowledge-based rather than judgment-based. And even when concessions are made by the test makers in the form of "reflective items," such concessions are likely to be grudging and inadequate. It is not that tests in pure abstract-reasoning abilities are needed, but that we should be trying to find out if students *can make judgments based on what they know* and not merely on whether or not they know it.

There are, I suspect, a great many teachers in Ms. F's situation. They can't figure out what's wrong. Some days they blame the students; some days they blame themselves. Until educators get their priorities straight – until, in other words, they agree upon a consistent and coherent set of criteria and standards applicable to the educational process – serious, well-intentioned teachers like the ones we have been considering here are going to continue to sense that something, somewhere, is wrong with the system while continuing to blame themselves for shortcomings.

PART TWO

COMMUNITIES OF INQUIRY

4

Thinking in Community

All inquiry is self-critical practice, and all of it is exploratory and in-quisitive. Some aspects of inquiry are more experimental than others. And inquiry is generally social or communal in nature because it rests on a foundation of language, of scientific operations, of symbolic systems, of measurements and so on, all of which are uncompromisingly social.

But while all inquiry may be predicated upon community, it does not follow that all community is predicated upon inquiry. There is nothing self-contradictory in the notion of a fixated, tradition-bound community. The glue that holds a community together is practice, but it does not have to be self-critical practice.

Thus, there is something paradoxical, something faintly startling, about the notion of a community of inquiry; it unites two concepts that are not ordinarily found together or juxtaposed. This makes it all the more surprising that so unconventional a notion should be proposed as a master educational paradigm.

Consider at this point some of its features. First I think we need to see that the community of inquiry is not aimless. It is a process that aims at producing a *product* – at some kind of settlement or judgment, however partial and tentative this may be. Second, the process has a sense of direction; it moves where the argument takes it. Third, the process is not merely conversation or discussion; it is dialogical. This means it has a structure. Just as a parliamentary debate is governed by parliamentary rules of order, so inquiry has its procedural rules, which are largely logical in nature. Fourth, we need to consider a bit more closely how reasonableness, creativity, and care apply to the community of inquiry. Finally, there is the matter of using the community of inquiry to operationalize and implement the definitions of critical, creative, and caring thinking. We will look at these points in this and in the following chapters of this book.

FOLLOWING THE ARGUMENT WHERE IT LEADS

It is often assumed that children are born as little savages and that they must learn to become civilized. Education is thought to have a decent influence upon them. As a result of its benign influence, they become social beings. It was this doctrine that George Herbert Mead stood on its head when he wrote that "the child does not become social by learning. He must be social in order to learn."[1] It was Mead, therefore, who first grasped the profound educational implications of fusing together, as Peirce had, the two independently powerful notions of *inquiry* and *community* into the single transformative concept of the *community of inquiry*. Dewey had already seen, Mead acknowledges, that the role of the teacher is to mediate rather than dominate: "To use Professor Dewey's phrase, instruction should be an interchange of experience in which the child brings his experience to be interpreted by the parent or teacher. This recognizes that education is interchange of ideas, is conversation – belongs to a universe of discourse."[2] Mead then addresses the question of what the topic of such conversation should be, and he gives us the unequivocal answer that it must be the subject matter of instruction:

Just insofar as the subject-matter of instruction can be brought into the form of problems arising in the experience of the child – just so far will the relation of the child to the instructor become a part of the natural solution of the

---

[1] "The Psychology of Social Consciousness Implied in Instruction," *Science* 31 (1910), 688–93, reprinted under the title "Language as Thinking" in *Thinking: The Journal of Philosophy for Children* 1:2 (n.d.), 23–6.
[2] Ibid., p. 25.

problem – actual success of a teacher depends in large measure upon this capacity to state the subject-matter of instruction in terms of the experience of the children.[3]

Nor does Mead flinch when it comes to stating how a lesson or a textbook should be organized – they should be conducive to inquiry by being modeled on the way we think when we inquire. Thus, the ideal textbook "is so organized that the development of the subject-matter is in reality the action and reaction of one mind upon another mind. The dictum of the Platonic Socrates, that one must follow the argument where it leads in the dialogue, should be the motto of the writer of textbooks."[4] Mead all but says outright that the ideal text-book should be direct and fresh in its impact rather than something warmed over and secondhand; it should be brimful of the child's experience rather than being a desiccated version of the adult's experience; it should resound to the clash of ideas and the clash of minds; it should dramatically depict the encounter of the minds of the children with the subject matter of instruction; and it should follow the argument where it leads.

Now, the notion of following an argument where it leads has been a perplexing one ever since Socrates announced it as the guiding maxim of his own philosophical practice. If we think of the matter in more general terms, how *is* inquiry guided? If nature were everywhere equally enigmatic, we would not know where first to turn. But we do seem to know where first to turn; something establishes our priorities and gives us a sense of direction. What is it?

I find Dewey's answer a compelling one. Inquiry takes place in situations – in contextual wholes or fields. A situation is a whole by virtue of its "immediately pervasive quality."[5] This quality is not only what binds all constituents in the situation into a whole but is also unique and indivisible. No two situations have the same permeating quality. The distinctions and relations we institute within them are recurrent and repeatable, but not their unique qualities. These qualities are not to be confused with what is "red" or "hard" or "sweet," for these are what we distinguish *within* a situation. Rather, they are akin

3 Ibid.
4 Ibid.
5 *Logic: The Theory of Inquiry* (New York: Holt, 1938), p. 68.

to what we designate by such terms as "perplexing," "cheerful," and "disconsolate." These are the tertiary qualities that guide the artist and that are precipitated in created works of art. What George Yoos calls the primary aspects are analogous to these qualities.[6] All inquiries are guided by such qualities, including Socratic inquiry. Every community of inquiry has about it a requiredness or *Prägnanz* that lends it a sense of direction, and every participant in such a community partakes of that qualitative presence, which is the tertiary quality of which Dewey speaks. It is a quality more readily possessed than described, but were it not present and acknowledged, the participants would lack any standard of *relevance* or *irrelevance*.

We learn from Dewey, then, that the progress of a community of inquiry is guided by the Gestalt quality of the unique, immediately experienced inquiry situation, and we learn from Mead that the educational community of inquiry actively discusses the subject matter under investigation. We need to know more, however, about the nature of this discussion. For example, must every discussion come to closure? Justus Buchler warns us not to confuse the product that discussions produce with the conclusions or closures that some people expect them to produce:

Where we can speak of a conclusion at all, it may be developed only after many hours, and then with qualifications befitting the circumstances. But, regardless of this, a product is inevitably established in any given hour of discussion. For the product need not take the form of an assertive conclusion. It may be an enumeration of possible views, or a fuller definition of a problem, or a growth of appreciative awareness. It may be more of an exhibiting than of an affirming. . . . Students may have no right to demand final answers, but they certainly have a right to expect some sense of intellectual motion or some feeling of discernment.[7]

Some feeling of discernment – right. Seldom have I seen children dissatisfied with the product they took from a philosophical discussion, even if it is only some modest philosophical distinction, for they recognize how before that acquisition they had even less. Children, unlike adults, do not look insistently for answers or conclusions. They

[6] George Yoos, "A Work of Art as a Standard of Itself," *Journal of Aesthetics and Art Criticism* 26 (Fall 1967), 81–9. See pp. 243–4 in this book.
[7] "What Is a Discussion?" *Journal of General Education* 7:1 (October 1954), 7–17.

look rather for the kind of transformation that philosophy provides –
not giving a new answer to an old question, but transforming all the
questions.[8]

For example, when Socrates poses Euthyphro the powerful question whether something is right because the gods command it or
whether the gods command it because it is right, it is clear that nothing thereafter can be the same. To ask the question is to compel people
to think differently about the world.

THE LOGIC OF CONVERSATIONAL DISCOURSE

When we speak of a community of inquiry, we cannot help noticing
the contrast between the emphasis on the personal in the concept of
community and the emphasis on inquiry on a logic that transcends
the personal. So in contrasting conversation and dialogue we cannot
help seeing in conversation a process in which the personal note is
strong but the logical thread is weak, whereas in dialogue just the
reverse is the case.

In contrasting conversation with dialogue, one of the things that
are striking is the way in which conversation involves stability while
dialogue involves instability. In conversation, first one person has
the ascendancy and then the other. There is reciprocity, but with the
understanding that nothing is to move. A conversation seesaws between the protagonists; it contains moves, but the conversation itself
does not move.

In a dialogue, on the other hand, disequilibrium is enforced in
order to compel forward movement. One cannot help thinking of
the analogy with walking, where you move forward by constantly
throwing yourself off balance. When you walk, you never have both
feet solidly on the ground at the same time. Each step forward makes
possible a further step forward; in a dialogue, each argument evokes
a counterargument that pushes itself beyond the other and pushes
the other beyond itself.

A conversation is an exchange: of feelings, of thoughts, of information, of understandings. A dialogue is a mutual exploration, an

---

[8] This is a paraphrase of a remark by Gilbert Ryle in his essay "Hume," *Collected Papers*,
vol. 1 (New York: Barnes and Noble, 1971), p. 160.

investigation, an inquiry. Those who converse with one another do so cooperatively, like tennis players volleying genially and interminably as they practice. Those who engage in dialogue do so collaboratively, like law enforcement officers working together on the same case. The aim of those who volley is to extend the rally for as long as possible. The aim of the officers is to resolve the case in as short a time as possible.

The logic of dialogue has its roots in the logic of conversation. If we briefly consider here the discussions of conversation by Paul Grice and Ruth Saw, we will be able to discern the outlines of a logic that becomes progressively more pronounced as it moves from conversation to dialogue.

Grice proposes to examine "the conditions governing conversation"[9] and thus to be able to formulate the maxims we take for granted and endeavor to conform to whenever we engage in conversational discourse. He recognizes that our conversing resembles our thinking in that both are characterized by what William James called "flights and perchings." Conversations are not smoothly continuous; there are gaps and seams everywhere. We blurt something out and then we back off. We allude and intimate; our partners gather and surmise. The work of conversation, of putting together what is meant from the bits and pieces that have merely been said, involves what Grice calls *implicature*. And implicature is made possible because conversation is a shared experience with shared values and shared meanings. Our conversational cooperation conforms to certain shared expectations. When we converse, our comments are elliptical, but we fill in the gaps voluntarily so as to achieve a single seamless skein of meaning that we each grasp at one end. In so doing, the maxim we conform to is what Grice calls the Cooperative Principle: "Make your conversational contribution such as is required, at the stage at which it occurs, by the accepted purpose or direction of the talk exchange in which you are engaged." In other words, Grice advises us to allow the requiredness that we sense in the conversation to dictate to us just how and when we are to make our contribution.

[9] "Logic and Conversation," in *Studies in the Way of Words* (Cambridge, Mass.: Harvard University Press, 1989), p. 26.

THE ART OF CONVERSATION

Ruth L. Saw offers us an interpretation of the conditions that make for conversation.[10] She begins with some questions. What is a conversation? Could we properly describe a tenant and a landlord as having a conversation with regard to overdue rent? Does the judge call lawyers from both sides into his chambers for a conversation? Do we have a conversation with our children when we find they have not shown up in school for several days? How do conversations differ (if they do) from discussions? From dialogues? From arguments? What is the connection between conversation and communication?

The essence of conversation, Saw contends, is its disinterestedness, its innocence of any ulterior purpose. A conversation cannot be guided or directed, nor can we in any way attempt to manipulate the persons with whom we converse. Conversations are carried on for their own sake, very much as if they were pure art forms. "Whenever people speak in order to impress, to exhibit their wit, their wealth, their learning, or to bring about some advantage to themselves, they are failing to treat their hearer as a person, as an end in himself, and conversation with him as carried on for its own sake."[11]

Saw says it does not matter if the purpose of our manipulations is a commendable one; the end result still cannot be a conversation. If we are engaged in drawing out a child so that she may better display her intelligence, conversation cannot be said to take place. Or if we are devious in disclosing our attitudes, the interaction cannot be a conversational one.

Conversation is predicated upon there being a rational partnership of those who converse, a partnership of free and equal individuals. The direction the conversation takes will be determined not so much by the laws of consistency as by the developing needs of the conversation itself, much as a writer, halfway through a book, begins to find it dictating what must be written. The author may still introduce some surprises, just as those who engage in conversation may introduce revelations by which they surprise and delight one another.

[10] "Conversation and Communication," inaugural lecture at Birkbeck College, 1962, as reprinted in *Thinking: The Journal of Philosophy for Children* 2:1 (n.d.), 55–64.

[11] Ibid., p. 64.

Indeed, so guileless is a conversation that in the course of it you listen to yourself in ways you previously had been unable to do. You listen to yourself talk and remark, "I must be jealous," thereby witnessing a disclosure about yourself no less objective than it would have been if you had inferred from the other person's remarks, "He must be jealous." For in a conversation you are capable of stepping back and listening to what you say, just as an artist can in the act of painting step back and take stock of what he or she has been doing.

For Saw, conversation is a symmetrical relationship. "A cannot converse with B if B does not converse with A."[12] It is a mutual exploration of one another's individualities. One cannot exact disclosures from the other without being prepared to make similar disclosures about oneself. Perhaps this stipulation can be better understood if we go back to Saw's distinction between "communicating something to someone" and "being in communication with someone." The first suggests conveying a content of some kind from one person to another. The second suggests that sort of interpersonal experience in which each participant causes the other to think; it is when we are truly in communication with others, Saw insists, that we are provoked to think independently.

THE STRUCTURE OF DIALOGUE

Unfortunately, Saw's treatment of dialogue is something of a caricature, since she lumps engaging in dialogue together with other forms of asymmetrical behavior such as giving orders to, taking instructions from, making suggestions to, vetoing the suggestions of, and countless other manipulative moves characteristic of hierarchical organizations. Her illustrations of dialogue are mostly of the edifying kind, such as can be found in Victorian children's books:

HARRY: Papa, you promised to tell us something of the habits of bees on our next walk in the country.
FATHER: I am glad you reminded me, my boy, for we can all learn from these busy little creatures . . .[13]

---

[12] Ibid., p. 60.
[13] Ibid.

While discourse such as this may be considered dialogical, it is not of such ludicrous dialogues that communities of inquiry are constituted.

If Saw is correct, that the essence of conversation lies in its being nonpurposive, nonmanipulative discourse, then the other end of the discourse spectrum would be occupied by the persuasive arts that are the subject matter of rhetoric. Dialogue evidently lies somewhere between the two, for it is not wholly free from purpose, and it may well involve arguments whose purpose is to persuade. Dialogue, unlike conversation, is a form of inquiry, and since we follow inquiry wherever it leads, our dialogical behavior cannot be said to be nonpurposive. Nor do the participants in dialogue necessarily refrain from fashioning arguments to persuade other participants of the rightness of their convictions. Even here, however, there is room for disagreement. J. M. Bochenski, for example, maintains that persuasion of others is alien to all philosophical dialogue:

If a philosopher engages in a discussion, as he often does, this will not be in order to convince his adversary. The only thing he desires to achieve is *his own* conviction. He hopes either that he might learn from his opponent that his views are wrong and so gain a new and better grasp of reality, or that the arguments of his adversary may help him to formulate better, improve and strengthen his views.[14]

Bochenski seems to be ruling out only persuasion of others, not of oneself. Whether or not this interpretation is compatible with the community of inquiry concept will continue to be a topic for discussion, as it has been since the time of Socrates.

DIALOGUE AND COMMUNITY

Martin Buber's espousal of dialogue is well known. He conceives of it as discourse in which "each of the participants really has in mind the other or others in their present and particular being, and turns to them with the intention of establishing a living mutual relation between himself and them." He contrasts such dialogue with monologue, which is self-serving; debates, in which each treats the other as a position rather than as a person; conversations, in which one

[14] "On Philosophical Dialogue," *Boston College Studies in Philosophy* 3 (1974), 56–85.

is primarily concerned to make an impression on the other; friendly chats, in which each considers himself absolute and legitimate and the other relativized and questionable; and lovers' talk, in which each is concerned with enjoying his or her own private and precious experience. Buber proceeds to show the connection of dialogue with thinking on the one hand and community on the other.[15]

No doubt there are similarities between the ethical requirements Ruth Saw lays down for conversation and those Buber sets forth for dialogue. These normative considerations are useful for helping to distinguish between what is and what merely purports to be a community of inquiry. But while they are relevant, and perhaps even necessary, they are not sufficient. For one thing, communities of inquiry are characterized by dialogue that is disciplined by logic. One must reason in order to follow what is going on in them. For example, how could anyone lacking in logical understanding appreciate this story by Thackeray:

An old abbé, talking among a party of intimate friends, happened to say, "A priest has strange experiences; why, ladies, my first penitent was a murderer." Upon this, the principal nobleman of the neighborhood enters the room. "Ah, Abbé, here you are; do you know ladies, I was the Abbé's first penitent, and I promise you my confession astonished him."[16]

When the classroom has been converted into a community of inquiry, the moves that are made to follow the argument where it leads are logical moves, and it is for this reason that Dewey correctly identifies logic with the methodology of inquiry.[17] As a community of inquiry proceeds with its deliberations, every move engenders some new requiredness. The discovery of a piece of evidence throws light on the nature of the further evidence that is now needed. The disclosure of a claim makes it necessary to discover the reasons for that claim. The making of an inference compels the participants to explore what was being assumed or taken for granted that led to the selection of that particular inference. A contention that several things are different demands that the question be raised of how they are to be

---

[15] *Between Man and Man* (London: Kegan Paul, 1947), sect. II.
[16] The story is related by Morris R. Cohen and Ernest Nagel in *An Introduction to Logic and Scientific Method* (New York: Harcourt Brace, 1934), p. 174.
[17] *Logic*, p. 5.

distinguished. Each move sets up a train of countering or supporting moves. As subsidiary issues are settled, the community's sense of direction is confirmed and clarified, and the inquiry proceeds with renewed vigor.

Of course, we should not delude ourselves about these occasional settlements. They are perches or resting places, without finality. As Dewey puts it:

> The "settlement" of a particular situation by a particular inquiry is no guarantee that *that* settled conclusion will always remain settled. The attainment of settled beliefs is a progressive matter; there is no belief so settled as not to be exposed to further inquiry.... In scientific inquiry, the criterion of what is taken to be settled, or to be knowledge, is being *so* settled that it is available as a resource in further inquiry; not being settled in such a way as not to be subject to revision in further inquiry.[18]

Settlements provide us with grounds for assuming, warrants for asserting. They represent *provisional judgments* rather than firm bases for absolute convictions.[19]

LEARNING FROM THE EXPERIENCE OF OTHERS

The community of inquiry is in one sense a learning together, and it is therefore an example of the value of shared experience. But in another sense it represents a magnification of the efficiency of the learning process, since students who thought that all learning had to be learning by oneself come to discover that they can also use and profit from the learning experiences of others.

This seems so obvious as to be hardly worth noting, except that actual classroom experience reveals how little it is understood. It is

---

[18] Ibid., pp. 8–9.
[19] Kant is very helpful with regard to provisional judgments, and it is worth quoting him here at some length:

> As concerns, however, *suspension* or *reservation* of our judgment, it consists in the resolve not to let a merely *provisional* judgment become a *determinate* one. A provisional judgment is one by which I suppose that there are more grounds *for* the truth of something than against it that these grounds, however, do not suffice for a *determinate* or *definite* judgment by which I decide straightway for the truth. Provisional judging is therefore a consciously problematic judging. (Kant's *Logic*, trans. Robert S. Hartman and Wolfgang Schwartz [Indianapolis, Ind.: Bobbs-Merrill, 1974], pp. 82–3)

not unusual to find college students who stop listening when one of their classmates begins to speak. They cannot conceive that their peers might have experience that complements their own (in which case they have much to gain by hearing it out), corroborates their own (in which case they might be prepared to hold their own convictions more firmly), or disagrees with their own (in which case they might have to reexamine their own positions).

Often the degree to which students think they can learn from each other's experience is inversely proportional to what they think they can learn from the instructor's experience. Nor are students mistaken in thinking they can benefit from adults who can mediate between children and the world. The adult often serves to translate the society's experience, its culture, to the student and to translate the student's experience to the society. The community of inquiry embeds that translation in everyday school practice.

THE ROLE OF THE COMMUNITY OF INQUIRY IN EDUCATION

Having education revolve around inquiry requires that the classroom be converted into a community in which friendship and cooperation would be welcomed as positive contributions to a learning atmosphere, rather than be the semiadversarial and competitive conditions that prevail in too many early childhood classrooms. Communities of inquiry are characterized by nonadversarial deliberations, shared cognitions, the cultivation of literacy and philosophical imagination, the encouragement of a deep reading, and the enjoyment of dialogical texts.

There are, however, communities and communities – thinking communities and unthinking communities, communities that are reflective and self-corrective and communities that are not. What education requires, obviously, are *communities of inquiry*, often grouped with, but not the same as, "communities of scholars," "communities of learning," and the like. Not all schooling is inquiry – far from it. For there to be inquiry, there must be some doubt that all is well, some recognition that one's situation contains troubling difficulties and is somehow problematic. There must be self-correcting investigation that takes all considerations into account and constructs alternative hypotheses as ways in which the problem can be resolved. Above all, inquiry involves questioning, more narrowly a quest for truth, more broadly a quest for meaning. Here are some other features of communities of inquiry:

a. *Inclusiveness.* Communities may or may not be internally diversified – the participants may or may not be of one religion, or of one nationality, or of one age level – but within a community no one is excluded from internal activities without adequate justification.

b. *Participation.* Communities of inquiry encourage but do not require participants to participate verbally and as equals. There is a sense in which a community, like a book, is a cognitive *schema*. Schemata are Gestalt-like structures of relationships that draw participation out of participants the way an interesting book won't allow its reader to put it down. When the children's reader is an interesting novel the students become all the more anxious to read the next page and the next, to find out what will happen next.

c. *Shared cognition.* In a prolonged session of private reflection, an individual will engage in a series of mental acts aimed at penetrating and analyzing the matter at hand. Thus one will engage in wondering, questioning, inferring, defining, assuming, supposing, imagining, distinguishing, and so on. In shared cognition (also called "distributive thinking"), the same acts are engaged in, but by different members of the community. One person raises a question, another objects to an underlying assumption, still another offers a counterinstance. The intellectual distance traversed may be the same, but the second illustration demonstrates how there can be a thinking community.

d. *Face-to-face relationships.* These relationships may not be essential to communities of inquiry, but they can be very advantageous. Faces are repositories of complex textures of meaning that we constantly try to read and interpret. These meanings are produced by the highly animated features of the faces that are in close proximity to one another.

e. *The quest for meaning.* Children are avid for understanding, and as a result they try to squeeze the meaning out of every sentence, every object, every experience. Communities of inquiry

are therefore meaning seeking in somewhat the way that intensive care units in hospitals are life preserving.

f. *Feelings of social solidarity.* Young children are often found to
    bond together in intense but inarticulate friendships. Some
    teachers are inclined to find such classroom friendships a bit
    threatening to their authority, with the result that they adopt
    a divide-and-rule strategy. However, classroom communities
    and friendships should be defined and understood in such a
    way that no intensification of the one should be perceived as a
    threat to the other.

g. *Deliberation.* This involves a consideration of alternatives
    through examination of the reasons supporting each alterna-
    tive. Since the deliberation usually takes place in preparation
    for the making of a judgment, we speak of the process as a
    "weighing" of the reasons and the alternatives. Deliberation
    can be usefully contrasted with debate, inasmuch as delib-
    erators need not try to get others to accept the position they
    themselves may believe, while debaters need not believe in the
    position they are trying to get others to accept.

h. *Impartiality.* Impartial inquiry pursues an investigation of a
    matter of importance in an open, self-corrective, and contex-
    tualistic manner. It should result in a settlement that takes into
    account all the considerations and points of view, as well as the
    interests of everyone.

i. *Modeling.* In philosophical literature fictional children can be
    offered to the live children in the classroom as a model of
    philosophical inquiry. Contrast this with the traditional ele-
    mentary school pedagogy, which claims that the teacher serves
    as a model for the students. One can test this claim by con-
    sidering the important philosophical tactic of questioning. The
    students may be inclined to presume that the teacher who ques-
    tions wants answers, not further questions. It is likely, therefore,
    that many children prefer fictional children, as models, to live
    adults.

j. *Thinking for oneself.* The possibility that the community may
    become conformitarian, hostile to independent thinking, is not
    to be taken lightly. The powerful schemata that are at work in
    the community may demand both closure and agreement, as

they do in a jury, and the opinion of the individual may become a mere echo of the opinion of the majority. Nevertheless, it is possible to get students to take pride in the originality of their responses. The opinions of others need to be respected, but they do not have to be mimicked. In a healthy community of inquiry, students learn to build on each other's ideas, although not necessarily with identical architecture. They also learn that, in a community that urges the discovery of the other side of the question, there are many occasions on which one may well be proud to be on that other side.

k. *Challenging as a procedure.* When children argue among themselves, it is not uncommon for them to challenge one another, sometimes quite intensely. They demand to know the reason supporting this judgment, or the meaning of this expression. If they challenge heatedly, it is because they don't know any other way to challenge. The community of inquiry experience teaches them that challenging is good but it need not be heated. It is just one more cognitive procedure that the participants need to perform in the course of their inquiries. Children are usually relieved to find this out: Adults are not the only ones who aspire to be reasonable.

l. *Reasonableness.* To be reasonable indicates that one has the capacity to employ rational procedures in a judicious manner, in the sense that, say, a hospital physician dealing with a highly contagious patient must make reasonable judgments as to the employment of standard medical procedures. But to be reasonable can refer not just to how one acts, but to how one is acted upon: It signifies one's capacity to listen to or be open to reason. Both senses of the term are fundamental for the community of inquirers.

m. *The reading.* A class session involving a community of inquiry aims at inducing the members of the class to be reflective: to engage in reflective reading, reflective questioning, and reflective discussion. To the extent that we are successful with any of these, it is likely to promote reflection in the other two as well. This means that each session should begin with a procedure or incident that can be counted on to provoke the quest for meaning – something controversial perhaps, or something already rich in meanings that must be sought out and uncovered, and held up for consideration. In this sense, reading a philosophical text for the first time is analogous to viewing a painting for the first time or to listening to a piece of music for the first time. One must observe what is there to be observed, appreciate what is of value, understand what is stated, figure out what is assumed, infer what is implied, grasp what is suggested, and surmise what is being attempted. This is *deep reading*, as contrasted with superficial reading, and it is a goal for students to aim at.

We encourage having the children in the class one at a time read the text aloud. Having them read it singly is of some ethical value in demonstrating sequential sharing to them. Moreover, reading the text aloud – a practice not in great favor in reading departments – assists the children in appropriating the meanings of the text to themselves. Also, it is an opportunity to correct their tendency to read monotonously and inexpressively, a practice responsible for a considerable loss of meaning. A colorless reading fails to ignite in the reader those emotional responses that lend significance to the finer nuances and discriminations that the text aims to suggest. Finally, reading aloud lends support to the practice of careful, attentive listening, a prerequisite for accuracy and precision in thinking.

n. *The questioning.* With the completion of the reading the teacher invites those students who are puzzled or perplexed to formulate their puzzlement in the form of a question. These questions are then written on the chalkboard, each followed by the name of its contributor of something of assistance to the work of the community. It is a moment of which they are deservedly proud, one in which they can take responsibility for their ideas. Completed, the list of questions on the board represents the various interests and perspectives of the members of the community in the topic to be discussed. It also represents a possible agenda for that discussion.

This is a pivotal moment. If the teacher selects the questions to be discussed, the students are likely to interpret that act as a vestige of the old authoritarianism. Fortunately, a number of alternatives compatible with democracy are available. The order of questions to be discussed can be determined by lot or by asking someone who did not submit a question to make the necessary choice. In any event, this recognition of the elevated status of the question (and the reduced status of the answer) will help the students remember that questioning is the leading edge of inquiry: It opens the door to dialogue, to self-criticism, and to self-correction. Each question has a global potential of putting a portion of the world in question, and this helps pave the way to fallibilism, the practice of assuming one's incorrectness in order to discover errors one did not know one had made. To question is to institutionalize and legitimize doubt and to invite critical evaluation. It hints openly of new options and fresh alternatives, in contrast to the stale dichotomy of true/false answers. One must constantly be on the lookout for new ways of encouraging student questioning, not as a matter of habit, but because many practices and institutions, while poorly justified and of dubious merit, can be found out only by creative questioning.

An important type of questioning is follow-up questioning. The most noteworthy example of a follow-up question (once the lead question has been asked and answered) is "What do you mean by _____?" Skilled interviewers, such as experienced reporters, are able to ask follow-up questions one after another until the topic is exhausted. Teachers and students of philosophy are wise to seek the same expertise.

It is not usually a simple matter to surmise the purpose or intent of a questioner. Often a question serves as a lure to make students aware of an underlying problem. The problem is, in a sense, the iceberg, and the question is the visible tip of the iceberg. Earlier, however, it was suggested that questioning is the leading edge of inquiry. The equivocation is instructive, for both are correct. The question puts doubts in our minds and doubt is the beginning of inquiry.

o. *The discussion.* The discussion often begins by turning to the person who posed the question that the community decided should be discussed first. This student may be asked to say a few words about the sources of the question, the reasons for raising it, and why it seems important. With the student's reply, others join in so as to articulate their agreement or disagreement with what is being said.

In all probability, more than one line of reasoning will open up, as the reading and questioning have stimulated a variety of interests among the students, and they will want to follow up on these. The teacher may be able to juggle or orchestrate these different lines of inquiry, which usually seem to be more vexing to adults than to children, who are evidently capable of participating in several inquiries simultaneously. (This observation is supported by the fact that many students are able to remember what was said and with what they agreed with considerably more accuracy than adults.)

Nothing improves thinking skills like discussion. This is probably true in all disciplines, but it is particularly true for classes that aim to improve thinking. In a best-case scenario, the discussion involves one's colleagues in the same discipline who are discussing a controversial issue of some theoretical importance. This is when they employ their best reasoning, make use of their most relevant knowledge, and display their most reasonable judgment. The situation is not really different in a children's community of inquiry. The problems the children discuss may be trivial, but they may also involve concepts of considerable abstractness. And the students too try to employ their best reasoning, their most relevant knowledge, and their most reasonable judgments, because all of this is happening publicly, in front of their teacher and their peers. Seated in the circle of chairs, face-to-face with their classmates, they employ the same thinking skills and thinking tools (such as reasons and criteria) that they have seen others employ.

The discussion provides a setting for the negotiation of understandings, for deliberation about reasons and options, for the examination of interpretations.

TOWARD THE FORMATION OF CLASSROOM COMMUNITIES OF INQUIRY

To bring this chapter to a close, I want to suggest what might be brought out if we were to unpack the notion of the community of

inquiry by examining it stage by stage. In what follows, I have identified five relatively discrete stages, but I make no attempt to provide a
further analysis of the series of steps that might be taken within each
stage. My aim is, instead, to indicate what is going on, psychologically
as well as pedagogically, at each stage.

I have chosen to use as an illustration a *philosophical* community
of inquiry, not only because that is the kind I am most familiar with
but also because I think it provides a valuable prototype. It remains
to be seen whether communities of inquiry in other disciplines will
be successful only to the extent that this prototype is approximated.

I. *The offering of the text*
  1. The text as a model, in story form, of a community of inquiry
  2. The text as reflecting the values and achievements of past
     generations
  3. The text as mediator between the culture and the individual
  4. The text as a highly peculiar object of perception that carries
     mental reflection already within itself
  5. The text portraying human relationships as possibly analyz-
     able into logical relations
  6. Taking turns reading aloud
     a. The ethical implication of alternating reading and
        listening
     b. The oral reproduction of the written text
     c. Turn taking as a division of labor: the beginnings of class-
        room community
  7. Gradual internalization of the thinking behaviors of the fic-
     tional characters (e.g., to read how a fictional character asks
     a question may lead a real child to ask such a question in
     class)
  8. Discovery by the class that the text is meaningful and rele-
     vant; the appropriation by the members of the class of those
     meanings
II. *The construction of the agenda*
  1. The offering of questions: the initial response of the class to
     the text
  2. Recognition by the teacher of the names of the contributing
     individuals

     3. The construction of the agenda as a collaborative work of the community
     4. The agenda as a map of areas of student interest
     5. The agenda as an index of what students consider important in the text and as an expression of the group's cognitive needs
     6. Cooperation of teacher and students in deciding where to begin the discussion

III. *Solidifying the community*
     1. Group solidarity through dialogical inquiry
     2. The primacy of activity over reflection
     3. The articulation of disagreements and the quest for understanding
     4. Fostering cognitive skills (e.g., assumption finding, generalization, exemplification) through dialogical practice
     5. Learning to employ cognitive tools (e.g., reasons, criteria, concepts, algorithms, rules, principles)
     6. Joining together in cooperative reasoning (e.g., building on each other's ideas, offering counterexamples or alternative hypotheses, etc.)
     7. Internalization of the overt cognitive behavior of the community (e.g., introjecting the ways in which classmates correct one another until each becomes systematically self-corrective) – "intrapsychical reproduction of the interpsychical" (Vygotsky)
     8. Becoming increasingly sensitive to meaningful nuances of contextual differences
     9. Group collectively groping its way along, following the argument where it leads

IV. *Using exercises and discussion plans*
     1. Employing questions from the academic tradition: recourse to professional guidance
     2. Appropriation by the students of the methodology of the discipline
     3. Opening students to other philosophical alternatives
     4. Focusing on specific problems so as to compel the making of practical judgments

    5. Compelling the inquiry to examine overarching regulative ideas such as truth, community, personhood, beauty, justice, and goodness

  V. *Encouraging further responses*

    1. Eliciting further responses (in the form of the telling or writing of stories, poetry, painting, drawing, and other forms of cognitive expression)[20]

    2. Recognizing the synthesis of the critical and the creative with the individual and the communal

    3. Celebrating the deepened sense of meaning that comes with strengthened judgment

THE EPISTEMOLOGICAL STATUS OF DISCUSSION IN THE COMMUNITY OF INQUIRY

The community of inquiry wants to build a system of thought. It begins with a provisional scaffolding made up of the relevant beliefs that are already held, the aims of the project, and the values that are to be upheld. The procedure is dialectical: Specific judgments are molded to accepted generalizations, and generalizations are molded to specific judgments. Considerations of value are weighed against antecedent judgments of fact. The goal is a system of thought in reflective equilibrium. "A system of thought is in reflective equilibrium when its components are reasonable in light of one another, and the account they comprise is reasonable in light of our antecedent convictions about the subject at hand."[21] Now, how are the discoveries of any member or group of members passed along to other members?

---

[20] V. V. Davydov provides a helpful prescription for the employment of dialogue in art education, in "The Mental Development of Younger Schoolchildren in the Process of Learning Activity," *Soviet Education* 30:10 (1988), 3–16. This is a selection from his book *Problems of Developmental Teaching*, trans. Liv Tudge (Armonk, N.Y.: M. E. Sharpe, 1986). For more on the value of discussion in instruction, see Roland G. Tharp and Ronald Gallimore, *Rousing Minds to Life* (New York: Cambridge University Press, 1988); W. Wilen (ed.), *Teaching and Learning through Discussion* (Springfield, Ill.: Charles C. Thomas, 1990); and Luis C. Moll (ed.), *Vygotsky and Education* (Cambridge University Press, 1990).

[21] Elgin, *Considered Judgment*, p. ix; I have also paraphrased from various passages on pp. 102–6.

It would appear that there is a practice that takes place from one session to another, in which those who make the discoveries then use the ensuing intervals to acquaint the others in the community with what has been learned. Thus there is a "snowballing phenomenon," well documented by researchers, that takes place.

The use of argument stratagems snowballs. That is, once a useful stratagem has been used by a child during a discussion, it tends to spread to other children and occur with increasing frequency. After the first appearance of a stratagem, the probability that it will appear again usually rises and remains high. In general, there are fewer and fewer lines of discussion between successive appearances of a stratagem. The snowball phenomenon was more pronounced during discussions with open participation than during discussions with teacher-controlled participation.[22]

Another investigator, Barbara Rogoff, uses the concept of "participatory appropriation" to refer to "the process by which individuals transform their understanding of and responsibility for activities through their own participation."[23]

---

[22] Richard C. Anderson et al., "The Snowball Phenomenon: Spread of Ways of Talking and Ways of Thinking across Groups of Children," *Cognition and Instruction*, vol. 19, no. 1, (2001), p. 1.

[23] Barbara Rogoff, "Observing Sociocultural Activity on Three Planes: Participatory Appropriation, Guided Appropriation and Apprenticeship," in J. V. Wertsch et al. (eds.), *Sociocultural Studies of Mind* (Cambridge: Cambridge University Press, 1995), pp. 139–64.

5

The Community of Inquiry Approach to Violence Reduction

EDUCATION, NOT INDOCTRINATION

What I shall not do in this chapter is extol the virtues of peace and deplore the viciousness of violence. To do so would be to fall into the trap in which so many attempts to educate for peace and against violence have been swallowed up. To be sure, the face of peace is most attractive and that of violence is most unattractive. However, when it comes to education with regard to these values, it is not enough to cultivate immediate emotional responses or to reiterate how good peace is and how bad violence is. Instead, we have to help children *both understand and practice* what is involved in violence reduction and peace development. They have to learn to think for themselves about these matters, not just provide knee-jerk responses when we present the proper stimuli.

It follows, on the one hand, that students must become much more conversant than they presently are with the *meaning* of such concepts as peace, freedom, equity, reciprocity, democracy, personhood, rights, and justice, even though this may bring to the surface profound disagreements about such meanings. On the other hand, it follows that students must become much more practiced in the *procedures* of rational deliberation, of stereotype exposure, and of prejudice and conflict reduction.

These two requirements lead to the same culmination: the conversion of ordinary classrooms into *communities of inquiry*, in which students can generate and exchange ideas, clarify concepts, develop hypotheses, weigh possible consequences, and in general deliberate reasonably together while learning to enjoy their intellectual interdependence. Like juries, which they in many ways resemble, these classroom communities develop skills in inquiry, reasoning, and concept-formation, skills that enable them to isolate subsidiary problems for manageable discussion and resolution, even when the settlement of the larger issues is elusive.

If people are ever to learn to use improved methods of conflict resolution in their daily lives, it will have to be by first having learned to question together, to reason together, and to make judgments together. Valuable as debate and argument may be in some contexts, such as the courthouse, it must be admitted that students can benefit far more from acquiring foundational skills in thinking critically, creatively, and caringly, in engaging in exploratory dialogue, and in learning to take into account the other sides to each issue. Valuable, moreover, as research assignments can be, and helpful as books and libraries can be, it must be acknowledged that working together for peace is inherently a social, communal matter; it involves developing skills in analyzing evidence and reasons together, working out compromises, and reaching consensus about such matters as can be decided by consensus.

Students can acquire significant practice in mediating with one another and in arriving at settlements only if they are first confronted with problems that speak to them directly and are genuinely unsettling. It is here that the discipline of philosophy, suitably reconstructed so as to be accessible to even the youngest schoolchildren, can be of enormous service. Philosophy provides ideas for people to chew on – ideas that don't get used up because they are persistently contestable.

As good friends cherish friendship and as strong communities value community, peaceful societies recognize the value of understanding what peace means and what conditions must be in place if peace is to be maintained. Societies that make little effort to understand how peace is to be achieved and preserved are unlikely to have it or enjoy it.

Sermons and lectures denouncing violence and extolling peace are all too often exercises in stereotypical thinking. They frequently take it for granted that those who listen to them should be *for* peace and *against* violence without qualification – without consideration of the context or the circumstances, without wondering whether the violence in question was of a justifiable or an unjustifiable variety. What this leads to is a kind of one-dimensional moral thinking that feeds upon stereotypes. "She's passive; she must be good." "She's meek and mild; she must be virtuous." "He's dashing; he can't be a violator of other people's rights." In other words, we are taught to pay lip service to the stereotypes but in practice to indulge actions that represent clearly unjustifiable inferences or appraisals. Under such circumstances, it is hardly surprising that rape is often treated indulgently as a male prerogative. It is not simply that the protests of the victims are disallowed; they are not even heard. After a time, those who have been violated cease to protest because they see that it is hopeless to do so, and their failure to protest is taken as a sure sign of their having been permissive or of their having deserved the treatment they got.

Educating for violence reduction and educating for peacemaking are therefore two different sides of the same coin. It is the coin as a whole that has purchasing power, not just one side or the other. We are familiar with the fact that those who educate for violence reduction by first portraying violence and then condemning it utilize a strategy that seldom works, because their audiences revel in the depiction and ignore the condemnation. The same is often true of peace advocacy, which paints peace in such dull colors as to make people want to avoid it like the plague. After all, was this not what happened in the case of the tympana of Romanesque and Gothic cathedrals – with worshippers coming to enjoy the lively depictions of torture in Hell, rather than the bland serenity of Heaven?

Thanks to the obsessive curiosity that many people now have about violence, it is no problem for the mass media to play upon that weakness and exacerbate it still further. The books, movies, TV, and newspapers of the contemporary world play up every aspect of every violent incident because the people in the media know that it sells. Violence is associated with high-intensity experience, with thrills – which is similar to the reasoning of many who turn to drugs, because drugs yield experiential "highs." Violence is highly marketable. The passive television watcher finds satisfaction in the depiction of violence because it provides an experiential texture he can appreciate. Since it is a vicarious experience, it has none of the responsibilities of a real-life happening, while preserving much of its excitement.

What does this obsession with violence tell us? On the one hand, it suggests that this is the desperate recourse people have when their lives are indescribably dreary and when they long for a richly textured life experience, far more intense and enjoyable than the one they presently endure. On the other hand, it suggests that people who feel that their powers are alienated, their hopes betrayed, and their energies wasted are likely to be people who fantasize violence as a way of siphoning off their own repressed bitterness and resentment.

People struggle to find meaning in their lives, and when they cannot find it there, they struggle to make it. But their well-intentioned efforts frequently run aground, because they are incapable of distinguishing the meretricious thrills to be derived from surrounding oneself with images of violence from the excitement of living a life that is rich in meanings, intense in quality, and overflowing with constructive human relationships. So that is, all too often, how we are: incapable of distinguishing the fool's gold from the real gold. The education we must talk about has to help us avoid making egregious mistakes of this kind.

TO WHAT CRITERIA CAN WE APPEAL?

In educating for violence reduction and peace development, to what criteria can we appeal? This is a preliminary question of great importance.

- We can cite our own experience and endeavor to show that this makes us authorities on the matter.
- We can appeal to the child's experience.
- We can attempt to persuade the child through argument and rhetoric.
- We can make use of reason – both the child's and our own.
- All of the above.

We can cite our own experience

Agreed. As adults, we can claim that our experience has taught us that peace is commendable and violence is deplorable. Granted, children can learn from our experience. But can we simply assume that our experience is an adequate substitute for the child's? And is this, after all, the goal of education, that only *our* experience be utilized, in order that the children's views ultimately should coincide with ours? Isn't it important that children form their own independent judgments, rather than just make carbon copies of ours?

True, when we adults speak of "our experience," we do not mean only yours and mine. We mean the experience of humankind, as embodied in history. But is this what we are going to do, draw unequivocal lessons from history to the effect that, in the long run, violence achieves its goals less often than nonviolence? Does the history of the human past really provide clear moral standards for the human future? If we are inclined to think so, we could do worse than read Freud's *Thoughts for the Times on War and Death*, in which he notes how people perk up in wartime: Their lives have suddenly become more meaningful, and they can take pleasure in the sufferings of their enemies. No, the tangled skeins of history provide us with little that is unequivocal or unproblematic. Santayana was being glib when he said that those who had forgotten the past were condemned to repeat it, for he was as aware as anyone that, in some sense, what happens to us will always be like something that happened in the past and that, in another sense, our lives and experience are always unprecedented and fresh. The only way history can be of use to the child is if the child is capable of careful reasoning and sound judgment.

The same is true concerning the child's use of our adult experience. Unless the child is able to think for himself, we can fill his or her mind at will with our most outrageous notions. Not only must children be taught to think better, but they must be taught to think for themselves and to think self-critically.

We can appeal to the child's own experience

Obviously, for any particular child, experience is in short supply, although children probably do make up in quality what they lack in quantity. What is more, the experience the child has had may be more different from our own than we realize. And even if it is the same, the chances are that we have forgotten so much of our own childhood experience that we do not know what to appeal to in the child's.

A different picture appears when we take into account the children's experiences that are marshalled in a community of inquiry setting. Here children collaborate in citing experiences to back up each other's opinions, and they even combine their touchingly fragmentary observations into a massive whole. And so we definitely should not leave out the criterion of the *children's* own experience.

We can attempt to persuade the child

Of course we can attempt to persuade the child through argument and rhetoric. But should we? Argument is a reasonable thing to employ, insofar as the child is capable of constructing a counterargument. Besides, presenting the adult point of view in the form of an argument provides the child with a model of the kind of response that the parent would deem reasonable. Small children can construct small arguments – minimal arguments such as a conclusion supported by a reason. But if we attempt to employ *force majeure*, such as an enthymene or a chain of syllogisms, the child will see that he is outmatched and will withdraw into a resentful silence.

Likewise with our rhetorical stratagems. Recourse to irony or sarcasm is generally counterproductive, since children can rarely fight back using these same weapons. Besides, if our only goal is persuasion, and we are willing to employ any rhetorical means to attain that goal, we are no longer in the realm of education. We are approaching manipulation: getting children to do what we want them to do while making them think it is what they want to do. And manipulation – is it too not a form of violence against the mind of a child?

Conclusion: Using argument with children who can reply in kind is not unreasonable, but it is not the only reasonable alternative open to us.

We can make use of reason

An alternative form of reasonableness is to engage the child in discussion, in which conflicts of opinions regarding facts or values quickly come to the surface and can be deliberated upon and reflected upon. In other words, we can engage the child in dialogue, with neither party knowing quite how the inquiry will come out but willing to follow the investigation wherever it leads.

All of the above

In a community of inquiry, there is a pooling of experience in which each is as ready and willing to learn from each other's experience as from his or her own. There is also a commitment to reasonableness – that is, to rationality tempered by judgment. One can even condone efforts at persuasion in such a context, where it is evident that mutual trust prevails and that the effort to persuade is well-intentioned.

In a community of inquiry, students and teachers are co-inquirers engaged in deliberating together about the issues or problems at hand. Such dialogue is a form of reasoning together. It is not an attempt to substitute reasoning for science, but an effort to complement scientific inquiry. The information derived from science – its theories and data and procedures – are not in dispute. What reasoning helps do is (a) *extend* knowledge through logical inference; (b) *defend* knowledge through reasons and arguments; and (c) *coordinate* knowledge through critical analysis.

When we underscore the word "inquiry" in "community of inquiry" we emphasize the investigative role of such communities. This is the role that leads them to deliberate with regard to concepts, evidence, jurisdictions, reasons, definitions and other matters directly involved in or complementary to the experimental aspect of scientific inquiry. The dialogue in a community of inquiry is aimed at practical results, such as settlements, determinations, decisions, or conclusion. All of these are *judgments*.

VIOLENCE AND JUSTIFICATION

It is not my purpose to inquire whether or not there is such a thing as defensible violence, in the sense that Michael Walzer, in his book *Just Wars*, explores the possibility that, under certain circumstances, war can be justified. Nor am I concerned to examine the various aspects of violence and to show that some aspects are neither moral nor nonmoral, while other aspects (e.g., violations) are necessarily immoral. These are matters that are beyond the reach of this book, even if I cannot resist alluding to them from time to time.

What I am concerned about is that education for violence reduction and for peace is likely to go the way of countless other initiatives claiming to eliminate violence by reducing the dispositions that favor it. The problem is based on the fact that these educational efforts often aim to instill particular sets of values by taking for granted pedagogical techniques that even in the schools are being phased out as obsolete. I am speaking of the "lectures by authorities" approach. The public is expected to accept these values simply on the grounds that they have been recommended by experts. This approach works well with the gullible and poorly with the skeptical. The skeptics, aware that every interest group has its own experts, paid or unpaid, are inclined to distrust claims of any kind that are to be accepted simply on the basis of the authority of the claimant.

But there is another method of obtaining the public's consent, and that is by invoking value terms or value concepts that would seem to be established a priori. In this sense, there is really nothing to educate people about, since they already know, if they are at all familiar with the language, that certain words have approbation built into their very meaning, while other words or concepts carry with them, at all times, a built-in social disapprobation. Listen to David Hume:

It is indeed obvious that writers of all nations and all ages concur in applauding justice, humanity, magnanimity, prudence, veracity; and in blaming the opposite qualities...Some part of the seeming harmony in morals may be accounted for from the very nature of language. The word *virtue*, with its equivalent in every tongue, implies praise, as that of *vice* does blame; and no one, without the most obvious and grossest impropriety, could affix reproach to a term, which in general acceptation, is understood in a good sense; or bestow applause, where the idiom requires disapprobation.[1]

Thus, it might seem that moral education need merely alert students to the terminology of the vices and virtues, and the built-in

---

[1] "Of the Standard of Taste," p. 2, in David Hume, *Of the Standard of Taste and Other Essays*, ed. John W. Lenz (Indianapolis: Bobbs-Merrill, 1965), pp. 3–34. Note that Hume does not reduce all moral education to getting children to learn the built-in moral values of words. But his caution is helpful: Words lull us into a "seeming harmony" about moral matters, and children need to be made aware of just what it is they are taking for granted.

disapprobation or approbation will automatically teach the students the difference between right and wrong. One does not have to puzzle over these things: Generosity is always right and cruelty is always wrong. For any given culture, learning to speak and think in the indigenous language is sufficient to educate children and newcomers into the way the good and the right are viewed in that culture.

This conventional approach to ethics has the merit of conveying to students the importance of taking into account the hidden praise or blame with which the moral terms we use are infected. On the other hand, it is mischievously misleading, for it lulls us into thinking that ethical inquiry is superfluous. If cruelty is always wrong, then our only problems are empirical and logical. All cruelty being wrong, we need only ascertain if this particular act was indeed an act of cruelty, and we can deduce that it was wrong. The conventional approach claims to solve the problem of ethics by confining it to the formulation of minor premises.

One of the things ethical inquiry must do – and this applies to problems involving force and violence as to anything else – is examine precisely what is normally taken for granted in moral discourse. A community engaged in deliberative ethical inquiry might take up questions such as these:

Can a person be cruel and still be kind?
Are there circumstances under which it would not be right to be generous?
Can we love someone we don't like?
Can we be jealous of someone we don't love?
Is veracity sometimes inappropriate?
Are justice and freedom in principle incompatible?
Are all vices matters of self-deception?
Can there be violations where there are no rights?
Can there be rights where there are no remedies?
Can someone be both violent and benevolent?

Notice that questions such as these emphasize compatibility, coherency, and context. Thus, even if justice is always and everywhere good, there is the possibility that other goods, such as freedom, might delimit its practical applicability. Coherency is often the objective of conceptual analysis, as when we ask for the clarification of concepts, inferences, meanings, and so on. And, of course, even those concepts that we most frequently take for granted may turn out to be troublesome in special contexts, as in acts of omission, questions of avoidability of infliction of pain and suffering, and jurisdictional disputes.

It cannot be emphasized sufficiently that the reason value concepts are not fixed and stable is that our understanding of them and of the contexts in which they occur is not fixed and stable. We are a long way from knowing what freedom means, if indeed we will ever know such a thing completely, and the same is true for other moral notions.[2] Thus, we cannot be sure that what the twenty-first century will understand with regard to such notions as peace and violence will be the same as what the nineteenth or twentieth centuries understood them to mean. This much, however, is clear enough: The more we bend our efforts toward peacemaking and violence reduction, the better our understanding of these concepts will be.

What I am emphasizing is that values education ignominiously collapses when it is based solely on the notion that the values in question are somehow inherent or intrinsic, so that all the educator need do is *reveal* these intrinsic values to the student. Values are only as good as their justifications. We can agree that peace is fine and beautiful and that violence is nasty and ugly, but these characteristics are weak and unconvincing unless they are woven into the justificational fabric. The time is past when we could tell students that it is simply self-evident that, say, courage is good, without having them engage in the hard conceptual labor of distinguishing it from lookalikes such as rashness or foolhardiness, or of citing the reasons that would justify it in particular cases.

It may be objected that I am ignoring considerations of character and disposition, but I do not think that this is the case. First, I would maintain that the buildup of moral character is the result of the successive superimposition of layer upon layer of justified moral acts, performed under a variety of circumstances. A person who is characteristically disposed to be reasonable is one who early on recognizes the importance of connecting acts with the reasons that justify them,

---

[2] A good discussion of this point is to be found in Stuart Hampshire, "In Defense of Radicalism," *Dissent* (Spring 1956), 170–6. Hampshire argues that freedom must be defined in a way that allows for continual expansion.

and who expects such connectedness with one's own future conduct. Second, I would argue that we have seriously underestimated the role the intellectual virtues play in the makeup of moral character. Respect for other points of view, patience with other deliberators, dedication to rationality, intellectual creativity in the formulation of new hypotheses – all of these and many more form an indispensable portion of anyone's moral character.[3] And third, there are ways of building character and developing moral dispositions that do not rely on authority, persuasion, exhortation, or various other approaches of dubious validity. I am thinking of the character-building consequences of participating in communities of inquiry. But I will turn to this consideration shortly.

Here I would like simply to reiterate the point made in this section, that education for violence reduction and for peacemaking cannot do without linguistic, logical, and conceptual analyses, so as to get students to think carefully about the language, reasoning, and informational structuring that are typically involved in such educational initiatives. If one student in a classroom claims that another student has been violent, the opportunity is there for a reasonable dialogue, not about the violent act itself, but about the context in which it occurred and the reasons that might be adduced for and against it.

It may be said that we substitute thereby one set of self-evident values for another. In place of courage and cowardice, or patriotism and lack of patriotism, or benevolence and malevolence, we substitute moderation, temperance, and reasonableness, independently of *their* justification. But this is not so: Moderation, temperance, and reasonableness are no less susceptible to being made, at any moment, the subject matter of ethical inquiry, than are courage, generosity,

---

[3] It must be acknowledged that Hume is alert to the importance of the intellectual virtues, as when he writes,

> Should we lay hold of the distinction between *intellectual* and *moral* endowments, and affirm the last alone to be the real and genuine virtues because they alone lead to action, we should find that many of those qualities usually called intellectual virtues, such as prudence, penetration, discernment, discretion, had also a considerable influence on conduct ... Who did ever say, except by way of irony, that such a one was a man of great virtue, but an egregious blockhead? (From "Of Some Verbal Disputes," in Appendix IV, *Enquiry Concerning the Principles of Morals*)

and goodwill. What makes these and other virtues similar to them of special importance is that they happen also to be related to the *procedures* of ethical inquiry. The justification for the emphasis upon consistency, scrupulousness, reasonableness, considerateness, attentiveness, and so on, lies in the fact that inquiry relies on values such as these. Without them, inquiry cannot be effectively prosecuted.

Ethical inquiry, in turn, yields strengthened ethical judgment, and strengthened ethical judgment intervenes to bring about violence reduction, prejudice reduction, and the alleviation of other deplorable acts and attitudes. The problem, therefore, is to find a way of introducing ethical inquiry into the school, not so much to sit in judgment on previous acts of violence as to give *preventive* consideration to future acts of that character. The classroom devoted to ethical inquiry should not have the pressure-cooker atmosphere that prevails in the jury room: It should be freed to proceed at a more leisurely pace, without having to make decisions prematurely – indeed, without necessarily having to make them at all.

THE STRENGTHENING OF JUDGMENT THROUGH COGNITIVE WORK

It is a commonplace that one can strengthen one's judgment by frequently exercising it. But this really tells us very little, since so much depends upon the kinds of situations in which such exercises are performed. One makes judgments in doing crossword puzzles, answering riddles, and reviewing grocery receipts, but such challenges are relatively trivial and provide small satisfactions in return for mere cleverness.

Is it the case then that it takes no great wit to find the answer to a question, where that answer is already known to the person who asks the question? Of course not. Questions can be asked about matters of specialized knowledge, and one would have to be brilliant to come up with the answers to many of them, even though those answers are already known.

Nevertheless, there is a world of difference between asking a child a question the answer to which is known and asking a question the answer to which is unknown, or a matter of considerable controversy. If the questioner already knows the answer, what the child generally proceeds to do is to try to find out what the questioner knows, rather than embark on an independent investigation of the problem. The child knows better than to try to reinvent the wheel if he is merely asked what a vehicle is.

On the other hand, if the question is a meaningful one and the questioner does not know the answer, the classroom discussion that follows will likely demand that each participant think more and more judiciously. Consideration will be given to the circumstances under which violence is to be forbidden, under which it is to be tolerated or condoned, and under which it might be greeted with bouquets and accolades. Distinction making will be invited, so that seemingly similar behaviors can be differentiated from one another. (This is often necessary in the case of alleged sexual violence.) And careful attention will be paid to the bearings that existing legal statutes may have on the cases in question.

The strengthening of judgment that is a prerequisite for success in violence reduction or peacemaking is difficult to bring about unless students are seriously engaged in deliberative work. In physics, work is understood to be the overcoming of resistance. In reflective matters, its meaning – or one of its meanings, in any event – is quite the same. The resistances to be overcome are not things like friction and gravity, but things like prejudice, self-deception, conflicting emotions, illogicality, fallacies of reasoning, unwillingness to compromise where a matter is subject to mediation or arbitration, and lack of respect for the opinions of others. These are powerful resistances to be overcome; to do so requires patient, deliberative inquiry – in effect, cognitive work.

Ordinarily, however, the obstacles to the performance of deliberative work are latent rather than manifest. We are not aware, in practicing to become more reasonable, that in the process we are overcoming some of the prejudices or intellectual vices that have normally blocked our path. Breaking down these obstacles, or smoothing them out so that one can glide over them, can indeed be a long and arduous job – indeed, a never-ending job, since no one is able to get rid of such obstacles once and for all.

Nevertheless, just as we do not have to address ourselves directly to the notion of peace in order to engage in education for peacemaking, so we do not have to address ourselves directly to our prejudices or superstitions in order to develop in ourselves more reasonable ways of thinking. In the earlier stages of deliberative work, at any rate, one need not target the remaking of the self, even if it is going to have to come to that sooner or later. As Edwin Muir puts it:

> Will you, sometime, have sought so long and seek
> Still in the slowly darkening hunting ground,
> Catch sight some ordinary month or week
> Of that strange quarry you scarcely thought you sought –
> Yourself, the gatherer gathered, the finder found,
> The buyer, who would buy all, in bounty bought –
> And perch in pride on the princely hand, at home,
> And there, the long hunt over, rest and roam?[4]

In these earlier stages, the open-ended question can be sufficient to launch those powerful searchings that overcome resistances with hardly any awareness that they were there at all. For example, let a single student or a group of students be set the task of making a comparison between two things so similar that they might easily be taken for one another. The work that ensues is to spell out the differences – what Josiah Royce calls the process of interpretation.[5] Royce provides us with a simple, homely illustration. Take two strips of paper and paste the ends of one together to form a ring. Do the same to the other, but only after having first given the strip a half turn. This, of course, makes the second a Möebius strip. Now ask the students to identify the points of difference, and they will begin to articulate their observations, such as that the first strip has two sides while the second has only one, and that the first strip has two edges, the second only one. As we see, the elaboration of the distinction requires careful observation of specific points of difference, and these in turn provide criteria for further distinction making in other cases. Needless to say, the activity teaches children not only how differences are constituted but how some of them can be generated. After the children have performed cognitive work such as this, the distinction they make, after performing the comparison, will have become a knowing one, and their judgment, to that extent, will have been strengthened. And

---

4 Edwin Muir, "The Question," in *Collected Poems* (New York: Oxford University Press, 1965).
5 Josiah Royce, *The Problem of Christianity* (Chicago: University of Chicago Press, 1968).

not a few students will confess themselves perplexed by the mystery of the Möebius strip that they themselves brought into being.

EDUCATING FOR VALUES AND MEANINGS THROUGH THE COMMUNITY OF INQUIRY

Many of us have learned, often through bitter experiences, that peace is not merely desired but is actually *desirable*. It is something that we *may* approve of before reflection or inquiry but that we *do* approve of after reflection or inquiry. Furthermore, we would like students to share these convictions of ours, not just because they are ours, but because we are convinced that the students would benefit from accepting them as their own. And so we are strongly tempted to proselytize young people with these opinions of ours, barely managing to restrain ourselves by repeating to ourselves that preaching is not teaching.

For that matter, instruction is not very good education either, when it is a matter of educating for values. After all, in cases like these, where we feel sure we have already identified what is valuable, what we would like is for students to arrive at our conclusions through the use of *their* own reasonings.

There is a tendency to confuse the community of inquiry with cooperative learning, but the one should not be mistaken for the other. The chief point of difference is that cooperative learning stresses noncompetitive discussion while the community of inquiry stresses shared, collaborative inquiry. Inquiry, in turn, emphasizes moving forward to investigate a problem situation, and it also seeks to bring about a product. The product may be a settlement of disagreements, it may be a judgment, or it may be a judgment enacted in behavior, but in any case, it is more than a simple process.

In values education, the deliberative workload requires that consideration be given to

a. the value in question (in this case, violence or peace) as an *ideal-type*, requiring conceptual analysis;
b. the *phenomenology* of the value in question;
c. the concrete *conditions* or *powers* that seek to approximate or bring about the value as an ideal;

    d. the *relationships* between the ideal and the powers that seek to realize it;

    e. the *educational setting*, in which what takes place is not merely the study of the precede factors, but the bringing about of the desirable values that are under investigation.

These constitute five tasks for the community of inquiry. We can consider them briefly in a bit more detail.

(a) One way to begin a session of *education for peace* or *education for violence reduction* is to have the participants read a text in which a fictional community of inquiry is found attempting to define the key terms, "peace" and "violence." It will be discovered that the classroom community will allow itself to be influenced and guided by the fictional community, which it consciously or unconsciously attempts to emulate.

It should not be thought that the first task must be completed before beginning the second task, and so on. Work on all five tasks may be carried on concurrently.

Nevertheless, students find it useful to clarify what is to be understood by the terms "peace" and "violence." One task is therefore definitional in character and has to do with the elucidation of meanings.

(b) Second, in order to flesh out the meanings with which the community is attempting to come to grips, it may be necessary to engage in narrative or descriptive projects that can provide a phenomenology of the values or disvalues under investigation. Hobbes does some of this: He vividly describes the state of nature as a state of war in which human life is "nasty, brutish and short," denies there is an intermediate condition that we nowadays might call "cold war," and concludes, without further ado, that "all other time is peace." Peace itself is seldom described. And yet the implication in Hobbes is clear enough: Peace is a time of commerce and industry, a time of unimpeded communication, in which the arts and sciences flourish, in which people travel at will, and in which people live without fearing their neighbors.

(c) Third, the community must find out the *means* that are to be utilized in the attainment of the sought-after values or in the successful avoidance of the disvalues. Thus, democracy is often cited as a guarantor of peace, while political authoritarianism is held to be a guarantor of violence, just as protein-rich foods are thought to be in many cases conductive to health, while the lack of such foods brings about the lack of health.

(d) Then there are the means–end relationships to be considered. Clearly, the means–end relationship between protein-rich foods and health is what we call *nutrition*, and the means–end relationship between authoritarianism and violence may be thought of as *repression*. But obviously there are many things that can play the role of means and have a causal relationship with violence, other than authoritarianism. Child abuse, for example, is generally cited as a way of assuring antisocial attitudes in the children so affected, and of assuring their antisocial behavior in adolescence and adulthood. Abused children may turn into abusive adults. Adults who disturb others often turn out to have been disturbed by others when they were children. In short, the fourth task involves learning the causal relationships or etiologies that can account for the flourishing of positive values in certain cases and of negative values in other cases.

(e) Fifth and last, there is the educational setting or environment that is indispensable for the fostering of peacemaking behavior and for the inhibition of violence, either in disposition or in action.

There are two major sources of violence. One is the thoughtless impulsiveness of individuals. The other is the internal as well as external aggressiveness of institutions. These sources are often tapped at the very first sign of frustration. There is little patience with procedures that attempt to defuse the conflict so that the violence may be averted, even where such procedures are familiar to the parties involved. Yet it is only through the establishment of sound conflict-resolution procedures that the campaign for peace can be won.

REDUCING VIOLENCE IN A SCHOOL SETTING

What I shall conclude by discussing – the community of inquiry as a means of reducing violence and strengthening peace in a school setting – has already been alluded to. I have previously insisted that values like peace and the absence of violence cannot be effectively taught. They must be practiced, embodied, and lived. Yet we cannot just take it for granted that to achieve peace, we must simply learn to practice peace. For peace is an end, and what we must practice are the means to that end. Even to call such practice "peacemaking" is a distortion. To succeed, the process we are to employ must be one that students find satisfying for its own sake, while at the same time, one of its outcomes is the achievement of peaceful social relationships.

So there are really two aspects to the community of inquiry considered as a process. One is its *means–end* aspect, where peace is the long-range objective. The other is its *means–consequence* aspect, where the process is engaged in for its own immediate rewards but where peace emerges as a spin-off or consequence nevertheless. Unless this second aspect is present, the first is likely to be weak and ineffectual.

The community of inquiry is a wholesome social organization that provides a positive sense of belonging to its participants. In it, the participants are able to realize the reasonableness they are seldom able to practice amid the turmoil and turbulence of the rest of their lives. It is within the community of inquiry, then, that they can appreciate their own heightened powers, which, in turn, leads them to enhanced self-esteem.

In a community of inquiry, the contributions of all are welcomed, and not just the contribution of those who are quicker or more clever. As the participants learn to listen attentively to one another, they find their mutual respect being strengthened. And as they begin to recognize their dependency upon the community of inquiry procedures, they begin to care for and feel protective of those very procedures.

This is a community in which each participant can interpret any participant to any other participant, or can mediate between this one and that one. Each can offer hypotheses; each is free to build on or elaborate the hypotheses of others. Each can make claims; each can offer counterexamples or counterclaims. Each is free to question, to offer reasons or evidence, to express puzzlement, to portray ideals, to raise points of order.

Each community of inquiry in existence is likely to have been inspired by some ideal or fictional community of inquiry that it attempts to emulate. Furthermore, each participant is likely to be inspired by some other participant to do likewise. If I observe you questioning what all have hitherto taken for granted, I too am emboldened to question what is taken for granted. If I note the rigor you are able to introduce into your reasoning by your familiarity with elementary logical principles like the prohibition of self-contradiction, I will want to study the same things so as to have the same rigor.

The community of inquiry takes the problematic seriously. It recognizes that human institutions are imperfect, human experience is often only partial, and human knowledge is limited. It therefore recognizes the need for speculation as well as for analysis. It acknowledges that across-the-board solutions are seldom feasible and that often we must fall back on compromises that do not do violence to our principles. In short, it accepts the role of judgment – itself a coalition of the critical and the imaginative – in arriving at settlements where rules and precedents provide inadequate guidance.

The practice of deliberative dialogue in a community of inquiry setting introduces students to alternatives to violence. It enables them to see that a peaceful society cannot be a passive one, for such dialogue does not terminate with the achievement of peace. Rather, the continuation of dialogue is the best way of assuring that the tranquil conditions once achieved will be maintained.

So it is that education for peace can take place in every classroom, whether or not peace is the ostensible subject matter of study. The spirit of fallibilism that prevails in a community of inquiry is an invitation from all participants to have their errors pointed out to them, so that ways of correcting them might be sought. Such a spirit helps to defuse the contentiousness that absolutism and fanaticism inspire, and thereby it undercuts the violence to which such contentiousness often leads. The resolution to confront the problematic and deal with it in a spirit of reasonableness is a world apart from the inflexible insistence that education means the acquisition of knowledge that is authoritative and absolute. And if reasonableness prevails in the classroom today, then tomorrow, when today's students are adults and beginning to have children of their own, it will also prevail in the home. In time, other institutions may be transformed in a similar fashion, but it must all begin in the schools. It is in the schools that children learn to be self-critical – that is, critical of their own prejudices, biases, and destructiveness (which they do not recognize as destructiveness). It is there also that they can learn to be self-corrective – where they can learn how not to give offense by claiming more than

is their due. To be sure, they will also learn that the reduction of violence can hinge upon the reconstruction of unfair social, political,
and economic practices and institutions. But what cannot wait is the
understanding of how others understand us. Especially when they
think we have treated them offensively. Ultimately, violence will be
reduced by the reasonable adjudication of these claims. It is in the
classroom that these claims can first be articulated.

PART THREE

ORCHESTRATING THE COMPONENTS

6

The Emotions in Thinking and in Education

Among the noteworthy characteristics of reflective education is its willingness to reexamine the role of emotion. However, the objective of such a reexamination is called into question almost immediately. Are we talking about the emotions as a *subject matter* of education, or are we talking about the emotions as playing a role in education? (A third possibility would be to educate emotions themselves.)

Philosophers have long been fascinated by the "affects" *as subject matter* and have offered countless accounts and definitions of them. The propensities of human beings to experience this or that emotion under this or that set of circumstances fascinated the writers of the Early Renaissance, and their phenomenologies of the emotions were studied assiduously by students and scholars alike. The treatises on the emotions had formed a curriculum of sorts for centuries before Descartes and Spinoza, and have continued to do so for centuries afterward. We have only to think of Spinoza, carefully polishing his geometry of the emotions: joy, sorrow, astonishment, contempt, love, hatred, inclination, aversion, remorse, derision, hope, fear, and so on.

On the other hand, what about the *role* the emotions have played in education? To arrive at this point, we first have to consider the undesirable epistemological status often ascribed to the emotions. One's emotions are supposed to have a blurring, distorting effect upon one's thinking, and since clarity and distinctness have been taken for granted by the Cartesian tradition as the criteria of truth, the emotions have frequently been alleged to be the cause of error and falsehood.

More recently, however, writers have become more tolerant of the contribution of the emotions – I am thinking of the work of Ricoeur, Solomon, Scheffler, Elgin, Damasio, and a great many others. What had first to be done was to change the popular image of an emotion from a swirling, murky cloud that necessarily obscures and confuses our thinking to a set of conditions that may be able to clarify and organize it. Before considering the positive role that the emotions can play in thinking, I would like to mention Damasio's way of considering emotions as distinct from feelings. In brief, he sees emotions as expressing the ecological relationship between the organism and the world (as in the fear of heights or the anxiety about one's job), while feelings express the states of affairs within the organism itself (the pain in the knee, the twitch in the shoulder). We are to understand such emotions and feelings through a kind of imaging, similar to what goes on in the security center of any large modern building. For example, such a center in a bus terminal will have many television monitors, constantly sweeping all the corners in the building for anything amiss that might be of concern to the security forces in the building. Other television monitors are tuned in to happenings around the world. And so whether one feels peaceful or hostile, relaxed or wary, suspicious or naive, will depend largely on the sources of the imagery involved and on how that imagery is understood by the organism. Damasio even uses the phrase "the theatre of the body" in his account of feelings.[1]

I turn now to the role the emotions can play in thinking, and here I refer to the work of Catherine Z. Elgin.[2] (1) Emotions function cognitively, Elgin maintains, only when they *embed beliefs*. Thus an emotion cannot be genuine fear if one does not believe one is in danger. (2) An emotion provides a *frame of reference*. For example, parental love is a *framework* within which one organizes a set of feelings, attitudes, and

---

[1] Antonio Damasio, *The Feeling of What Happens* (New York: Harcourt, 1999), p. 7.
[2] Ibid., pp. 146–69.

actions. (3) Emotions help us *focus*. For instance, our interests determine what we notice. (4) In addition, emotions highlight; they make things stand out; they are sources of *salience*. This does not mean that they *necessarily* distort. They simply heighten our awareness, redirect our attention. They provide orientations, patterns of sensibility. (In this sense they function very much like beliefs. False beliefs can give us a false sense of security, and unjustified pessimism can give us an unwarranted sense of impending doom.)

For Elgin, an attitude is a sensitive stance that supplies an orientation as well as dispositions and expectations. If the attitude is oriented toward a proposition (whether true or false), we become disposed to accept or reject the proposition, utter it or reflect on it, deliberate upon it or insist upon it. These are usually described as "propositional attitudes," of which these are examples:

Josie knew that her son was ill.
Henry believed that there is a tooth fairy.
Conrad hopes his vote will count.

It is obvious that a propositional attitude has an important epistemic role, going beyond the mere assertion or denial of the proposition it contains. For the proposition is presented as encased in an emotional state that deftly manipulates the knowledge value of what is asserted. In the examples just presented, "knowing," "believing," and "hoping" can be taken as states of consciousness that entertain and qualify the statements they envelop. Propositional attitudes therefore have a more complex and significant role to play in communication than do mental-state verbs that do not have propositions as their objects. And by focusing attention, emotions bring about refinements in our sensory discriminations. For example, Elgin notes: "What we hear depends on what we listen for. Those who care about the child listen for more subtle features of his cries. When he discovers that his parents do this, he does it regarding his own cries."[3] This is a wonderful example of the view (based on Peirce and Mead) that what we generally come to think of ourselves is what we think other people think of us.

3 Ibid., p. 154.

IS THERE A PARADIGMATIC VERSION OF EMOTIVE THINKING?

Elgin's analysis of the contribution to thinking made by the emotions – contributions such as *focusing, framing, embedding,* and *emphasizing* – demonstrates conclusively that that contribution is *formal.* That is, we differentiate among different modes of thinking – inductive, deductive, conductive, distributive – not by differences in what they aim at or differences in what they accomplish, but by differences in their makeup, formal characteristics, structure, or composition. Emotive thinking is a form of thinking, and caring thinking is a form of emotive thinking – in a sense. It is in this sense that we can assert that all caring thinking is emotive thinking but not all emotive thinking is caring thinking.

But here the matter becomes still more complicated because there is another sense, one in which caring thinking is paradigmatic for all forms of emotive thinking. This sense is also synecdochic, in which a part is allowed to represent the whole. Nor is this just a figure of speech: We cannot think emotionally about something without caring about it, just as we cannot attend to something, be it good or bad, beautiful or ugly, without its having a sliver of meaning or importance for us. And so, in this second sense, I would have to say that caring thinking is emblematic of or paradigmatic of all forms of emotive thinking.

As musical composition is thinking in sounds, fiction writing is thinking in language, and painting is thinking in paints, so caring thinking is thinking in values. And just as the painter cannot think in paints unless she can appreciate color, so to think in values one must first be able to appreciate what is of value.

The emotional frames of reference in terms of which we think can affect not only the evaluational judgments we make but the classificatory judgments as well. Emotions focus attention, and how we classify is determined by the features we attend to. Just as a small dial controls the focus of a television image, ranging from distorted and blurry to clear and distinct, so the patterns of our emotional fields control the judgments we make about the world and how we justify those judgments. Even the kind of thinking we call "critical thinking" is attuned to the emotional requiredness one feels for exactitude, precision, consistency, and efficiency. We should therefore vigorously oppose the dualistic approach that considers the cognitive and the affective to be separate and autonomous functions that merely play off one another contrapuntally.

CAN WE EDUCATE WITH REGARD TO EMOTIONS?

The situation the emotions are generally in can be described as a "no-win" situation in that when something good happens as a result of our thinking, the emotions receive no credit, but when something troublesome happens, they quickly are given the blame. All too often, the emotions are treated as culprits, and we do not stop to wonder if they should be considered innocent until proven guilty.

Before we deliberate over whether or not the emotions *ought* to be educated, it might be well to consider if they *can* be educated. Part of the answer lies in how we treat them. If we want to assure that they will be irrational, we should treat them as irrational. If we want to assure that they are reasonable, it would help if we were to treat them as reasonable. And if we want to assure that they are educable, we should try treating them as educable.

Many people take a dim view of educating emotions. They think, "We don't choose our emotions: they just happen to us. We have no control over them. And besides, any scheme to educate the emotions would be more difficult than it would be worth." But this is a very harsh view of the matter. For example, a person may not allow himself to be happy; another person may not permit herself to be sorry. In these cases, it is not the emotions themselves that are being manipulated, but the gates – such as inhibitions – that pen them in. What still must be dealt with is the *appropriateness* of this or that emotion in the circumstances that prevail. In one sense, they may be considered inappropriate because they are not indicated, because they do not answer to the *requiredness* of the situation or to the needs of the context in which they make their appearance. In another sense, they may be considered inappropriate because they are unjustifiable: The *reasons* we offer in their support fail to do the job. Laughing at funerals can be inappropriate in both senses, while crying at weddings can be appropriate in both.

The moral education of the young child focuses frequently on the inappropriateness of this or that emotion. One is not to be amused at Aunt Minnie's way of walking because one hurts her when one does, and she has done nothing to deserve being hurt. By focusing on the reason for the emotion or on its contextual suitability rather than on the emotion itself, one can adjust and fine-tune the emotional dimension of the child's conduct.

Nonetheless, concern for Aunt Minnie's sensitivities is a highly specific mode of justification, and one may find it expedient to choose more general reasons. Of these latter, the one that most recommends itself is *reasonableness*. We can hardly be satisfied with a child whose conduct is inoffensive but whose flagrant exhibitions of emotion – such as dramatic displays of her hatred of minorities – succeed only in making everyone uncomfortable and some feel threatened. A classroom of ethical inquiry will want to examine such a situation, and to decide whether it is irrational, unreasonable, or strictly a personal matter. Needless to say, there are fashions in emotional displays, just as there are in the merchandising of clothing and automobiles.

The education of children's emotions begins with the earliest stages of their upbringing. During this period, an entire armory of rewards and punishments is employed to assure that the child has the kind of emotional life that the culture or the family deems proper. What one is taught to allow oneself in childhood frequently becomes fixated as one moves into adulthood, with the consequence that one finds oneself having emotions quite different from those conventionally called for by the adult-level situations in which one finds oneself.

Since human experience is so multilayered and complex, it is no easy task to dissect it and discover just what it is that the situation one finds oneself in can be said to need. There are layers and layers of intersecting motives and intentions, demands and obligations, habits and impulses. For many children, the easiest way out is to feel the emotions they are expected to feel, much as they already think as they believe they are expected to think. The emotional education of the child is part and parcel of the child's moral education.

EMOTIONS AND LANGUAGE

Many a job candidate has found himself passed over because his silence during an interview was taken to be evidence of ignorance or stupidity rather than lack of practice in articulating the terms and relationships representative of the domain under discussion. Some practice sessions beforehand, in which one prepares oneself for such a dialogue by discussing with a colleague the key concepts of the domain would be useful. This is so regardless of whether or not the concepts are directly relevant to the questions that may be asked. This can give the prospective job candidate a more warranted appearance of being knowledgeable about what matters in this situation.

One instance of this is the use of what psychologists call "two-level" terms, that is, ambiguous terms that are understood by one group of readers in one way and by another group in another way. This is the case of many "double entendres," which children may understand differently from adults. These should be distinguished, however, from terms that have the same meanings to some adults and some children but have a different meaning to other adults and other children. Here I have in mind terms like "rules," which some children in early childhood are able to consider as a concept, just as philosophers do, while other children and other philosophers may take it to be tantamount to a command, emanating from some unseen authority.

The upshot is that if we want to educate children with regard to emotions, we have to begin by teaching them the words by means of which these emotions can be identified. We must also teach them the relationships by means of which those emotions can be connected to other emotions, to ideas and concepts, to persons, to groups of persons, and so on. They can do this by discussing such questions as:

1. What is the difference between *bashfulness* and *meekness*?
2. What is the difference between *despair* and *desperation*?
3. What is the difference between *they loved each other* and *they were in love*?
4. What is the difference between *an angry crowd* and *a crowd of angry people*?

We are often able to make judgments about the appropriateness of the feelings of the various characters in the story, as well as about whether the characters were able or unable to allow those emotions to be acted out. We learn the procedure in literature; we practice it in life.

Children often seek to manage their lives carefully by managing their emotions carefully. One child learns that only crying will get him what he wants; as a result, even when grown, he whimpers whenever he wants to request something. No amount of crying will get another child what she wants; she is allowed to cry and cry, and no one will care for her. In time, she becomes apathetic – it's no use asking for anything. Still another child overreacts to approaching discomfort and expresses rage at the first faint signs of need. Thus, we have different levels of emotional tolerance, and we soon learn from our families how we are expected to respond to and control these powerful forces that attack us from within.

When children read world literature, they may discover that other children in other cultures experience discomforts and frustrations similar to theirs. Some of these children in other parts of the world may be found attempting to deal with their problems in much the same way we attempt to deal with ours. It is comforting to learn these evidences of emotional universality. We may be puzzled to discover, however, that other children understand the meaning of their emotions quite differently from how we understand them, either because their cultures have taught them these different interpretations or because the children themselves have arrived, through their own inquiries, at a quite different understanding.

We are so accustomed to seeing children who are virtually newborn laugh and cry that we infer that it comes equally natural to them to know on which occasions it is appropriate and reasonable for them to laugh, cry, or express other of their feelings. But this is surely not the case. They have to *learn* through experiences which situations call for which emotions. They have to *learn* under which circumstances fear or pride or joy are suitable and under which they are not. A well-constructed curriculum and pedagogy will seek to bring to better understanding and perhaps even to expression those emotions such as joy and friendship that are appropriate but are sometimes repressed, just as it will seek to inhibit those emotions that encourage self-destruction and other-destructive actions. The education of the emotions is not emotionally repressive; it is emotionally *redistributive*.

WORD CLUSTERS FOR BUILDING VERBAL FLUENCY
ABOUT EMOTIONS

In her book, *Teacher,* Sylvia Ashton Warner tells about her assumption that the five-year-old Maori children she taught needed to find some way of expressing their impulses that society would not interpret as antisocial behavior. She decided to try having them work with words that represented such conduct and in that fashion get them to sublimate their drives in ways that would not cause society to overreact. The writing and speaking of these words would alleviate the pressures the children experienced.

The experiment turned out badly, in that the educational authorities took a dim view of presenting children with opportunities to read and discuss these forbidden words. They could not bring themselves to condone it, even if the result of the experiment was that the behavior of the children markedly improved.

Until these children had experienced these words in an inquiry context rather than in a context of moral condemnation, they knew the forces and urges that were within them and among them only as blind pressures demanding outlet. The words served as counters for certain mental acts, and speaking them enabled the children to act out without doing harm.

Now, let us consider a somewhat connected aspect of education. We want to encourage students to improve their thinking. This means encouraging them to engage more often in creative thinking (as well as in thinking about creativity), critical thinking (as well as thinking about criticism), and caring thinking (as well as thinking about caring).

And to do so, they need relevant vocabulary. While children may have a wide range of emotions, they may not have much of an emotional vocabulary. However, they can't reflect upon and discuss their emotional life so long as they lack an adequate vocabulary and so long as they lack a suitable sounding board for their ideas, such as a community of inquiry can be. When introduced to the emotions, they may find themselves making use of the tiny vocabulary of the emotions that is available to them, and that is slowly growing larger. They may discover that the terms they are digging out of the text can be used for meta-level as well as for ordinary-level considerations.

Before long they may find that they are engaged in objective analyses of the emotions, thanks to the discussions that the community of inquiry has had involving these very terms.

In recent years, studies have been published that show that the use of philosophy and the community of inquiry pedagogy results in one-third to one-half of the student group's vocabulary being devoted to words or phrases associated with thinking. The following key word groups were outstanding:

1. Think, thinking, thought, thoughtful, wonder, wondering, idea, ideas, concept, analysis, explore
2. Argue, argument, explain, explanation, reason, justify, justification, because, reasoning, example, examples, true, false, correct, incorrect, right, wrong, relevance, relevant
3. Understand, understanding, understood, realize, know, knowledge
4. Perspective, view, standpoint, difference, different, distinction, big picture, big ideas, whole picture, alternative

The conclusions arrived at in the study cited here were that "the process of generating higher cognitive questions from the students at the beginning of the lesson, and encouraging question-asking of other students throughout the whole class lesson, appeared to transfer across into small-group behaviors." "The teacher's role fulfillment was highly effective and this expertise, coupled with high enthusiasm for Philosophy for Children, became infectious with the students who assumed the same kind of positive attitudes toward thinking."[4]

One of the important things this study (as well as associated ones by the same authors) appears to indicate is that there is a suggestive correlation between the character of teacher vocabularies and the character of classroom dialogue. If the teacher's vocabulary doesn't contain the kinds of terms that are typical of critical thinking discussions then presumably it will be more difficult to generate critical thinking about critical thinking.

[4] Kevin Barry, Leonard King, and Carmel Naloney, "Philosophy for Children and the Promotion of Student High Level Cognitive Talk in Small-Group Cooperative Learning," *Critical and Creative Thinking: The Australasian Journal of Philosophy for Children*, vol. 9, no. 1 (March 2001), pp. 31–45.

THREE CLUSTERS OF VALUE TERMS

precision
relevance   logical   ingenious
methodical   witty   consistency   self-controlled
clever   sensible   prudent   cunning
judicious   scrupulous   appreciative
thoughtful   alert   excogitating   considering
reckoning   pondering   cognising   concluding
infering   judging   reasoning   conceiving
subsuming   generalizing   inducing
apprehending   estimating   formulating
measuring   designing
predicting   **CRITICAL**   standardizing
substituting   expecting
understanding   doubting   knowing   assuming
associating   pretending   supposing
guessing   surmising   conceding   choosing
comparing   contrasting   grouping
classifying   defining   grading   ranking
seriating   exemplifying   questioning   relating
contradicting   sagacious
shrewdness   perspicacity
perceptive   acumen
insightful   keenness
competence   capability
intending   preparedness
efficieny

ingenious
witty   imaginative
clever   inventive   wise
appreciative   humorous
glowing   amusing   intuiting
designing   composing
constructing   wondering
believing   guessing   wishing
surmising   choosing   judging   deciding
exemplifying   questioning   generating
speculating   insightful   discerning   arranging
surprising   loveliness   ordering
organizing   elegant   graceful
attractive   beauteous
charming   delightful
bewitching   **CREATIVE**   exquisite
fine   fair   pretty
glorious   brilliant   dazzling   gleaming
splendid   scintillating   incandescent
radiant   spirited   quality
distinction   feature   sensitive
fascinating   winning
enchanting   delightful
entrancing   compelling   interesting
delicious   actualizing   consumate
animate   inspire   rousing
entertaining   beguiling   pleasing
recreating   making
whimsical   fabricated   contrived
choice   nice   exquisite

solicitous
vigilant
loving   generous
giving   respecting   forgiving   liberating
pardoning   releasing   clearing   adoring
enjoying   esteeming   approving   honoring   revering   venerating   agreeing   acquiescing
assenting   compliant   cooperating   concuring   consenting   harmonizing   uniting
pacifying   calming   appeasing   soothing   civilized   humane
refined   tender   benevolent   **CARING**   kind   unselfish   anxious
attentive   heeding   interesting   touching   solace   encouraging
comforting   sympathetic   moral   considerate   devoted   dedicated   dutiful
cheering   exciting   heartening   stimulating   tolerant   supportive   permissive
regard   ennobling   believing   faithful   civility   beneficial   magnanimous   open-handed
agreeable   serious   sociable   enjoyable   valuable   worth   deferential   charitable
gentle   merciful   tender   benign   patient   polite   responsible
careful

concerned   worried
proper   trusting   liking
apologetic   confessing
admiring   charming   obedient

FIGURE 6.1.

Caring thinking is a paradigmatic case of emotive thinking. More-over, a relevant vocabulary is needed to think, discuss, and learn about emotions. We can therefore conclude that if we want to educate children with regard to emotions, a vocabulary about what is of value and how we value it is needed.

The preceding clusters of value terms present words to which the teacher can alert the students. They are values either in the sense that persons who care think about them or in the sense that these are how we care about them.

It hardly needs to be said that these lists are representative of much larger lists or pools of terms that can be found in virtually any language. Students should be prepared to identify such words that are not listed here as well as those that are.

7

Mental Acts

Mental acts can be directly present within the student's own process of thinking. Because one of our purposes is to immerse students in thinking, the examination of mental acts can be advantageous. A mental act may play an important part in a dialogue by serving to move the inquiry along. It can be related to a speech act having a tactical role in discourse. The speech act is not something independent of the mental act yet somehow corresponding to it. Rather, it is that portion of the single discursive entity that has developed to the point of utterance. In this sense, speech acts have their roots in ongoing mental performances, while at the same time they interact with other speech acts that are parts of the communal dialogue, and they produce the phenomenon of *distributed thinking*, in which each participant contributes to the single thinking process. Without the activity of tiny molecules of thought – interacting mental acts – that process would be fairly unintelligible.

Insofar as our aim is to contribute to the understanding of teaching for thinking, it would be very useful to be able to refer to certain components that are understood to be mental performances – in short, mental acts. The intention here is to offer a phenomenological account, rather than an explanatory one, a depiction of how things appear to us to be, while making no claim to explanatory finality.

Since "thinking about thinking" is about as close as we have come so far to a characterization of reflective thinking, and since it seems to be what most proponents of these characterizations would agree to, then the concepts of mental acts and mental states are fairly indispensable. They are needed here, as they are needed in the philosophy of mind or in the ontology of mind, as units representative of the subject matter of the inquiry. Mental acts, such as deciding, selecting, gathering, are postulated as units of minding or mental functioning or thinking, much as an early scientist might postulate waves as units of light.

We need a theory of thinking because without it, our hard-won phrase "thinking about thinking" makes no sense. We need curricula that present mental phenomena in a *unified* and developmental manner, while letting students know that the actual connections are yet to be understood.

Language is in a sense a map of the mind, but it is difficult to determine how accurate a map it is. Philosophical and linguistic investigators such as J. L. Austin and Zeno Vendler have made some interesting forays into the field, particularly in the area of performatives, and in the distinguishing of mental acts from mental states. Mental acts are identified by them by means of "achievement" verbs, of which the prototype is *deciding*, while mental states are more a matter of mental mood, atmosphere, attitude, etc., the prototypes of which are *believing, knowing, doubting, trusting,* and so on.

Austin identifies one group of mental act verbs as performatives, meaning that utterance of the term is in effect performance of the act the term represents. For example, a couple comes to be married when a minister pronounces them "husband and wife." The utterance of the appropriate phrase is sufficient to enact the deed.

A mental act constitutes an achievement of sorts. We can contrast it therefore not just with steady-state expressions but with ascriptive expressions, which impute a particular property to something not already possessing that property. We attribute properties or qualities to one another all the time, often without bothering to verify or validate the attributions. Or we may defy the evidence, like the person who considers herself "fat" but whom most people would say is "skinny."

Nor should we omit mention of charismatic attributions. Indeed, one group of mental acts consists of *charismatic acts*, which are attributions of powers to an individual or institution despite the lack of accompanying evidence that the individual or institution thus targeted actually possesses such powers. For example, someone may skillfully praise a relatively nondescript group or population as having a special nature or destiny. The group in question responds that only a highly gifted individual or genius could have perceived the group's extraordinary character. In this fashion the group endows him with the virtues requisite for becoming their leader. The general formulation of such mental *activity* might be put in this way: If *x*, without relevant evidence, believes that *y* has extraordinary powers, then *y*'s charisma is the elicitation of that belief.

With some imprecision, we can distinguish between mental acts and *mental states*, by contrasting the verbs that we think correspond to them. Vendler has suggested some ways of understanding this distinction.[1] Mental acts, he says, are observable entities in contrast to mental states, which are not observable. Mental acts are exemplified by *decide* whereas the prototypical states are *believe* and *know*. Mental acts are achievement verbs: I don't have evidence that I have them. (No one would say, "How do you know you are in pain?") In contrast, mental states are expressed through verbs that do not indicate achievement. (*You* need evidence that I have them. I do not. I am immediately aware of them.)

Other examples of mental acts are *discover, learn, infer, deduce, gather,* and *realize*. Other examples of mental states are *think, suspect, surmise, imagine, suppose,* and *doubt*. Finally, it should be noted that some mental-state verbs, such as *remember, recall, anticipate,* and *expect,* have temporal connections.

BEING AWARE OF OUR MENTAL ACTS

To get children to learn something of the various species of creatures that are or have been alive on earth, we often resort to showing the students pictures and providing them with descriptions and to having

[1] This treatment of mental acts and states is based largely on Zeno Vendler's *Res Cogitans* (Ithaca, N.Y.: Cornell University Press, 1972), and J. L. Austin's *How to Do Things with Words* (Cambridge, Mass.: Harvard University Press, 1962). The pioneer in the study of mental acts was Franz Brentano. See his *Psychology from an Empirical Standpoint,* first published in 1874. Published in the United States in 1973 by Humanities Press, New York.

them connect these with terms for the genera and species involved. Similarly, we should be able to teach children the terms for various mental acts and mental states, together with ostensively identifying them. Unfortunately, the matter is not quite so simple. We can show children a picture of a cassowary and connect it with an illustration as well as a description, but we cannot so easily show children a deciding, a comparing, or a conceding. How then do we teach children about mental acts?

Suppose a student shows her teacher the following sentence in a novel: "Pamela surmised that Mr. Weatherbee was the spy they were looking for." The student wants to know the meaning of "surmised." You suggest that she use the dictionary. She does and announces, "It's a kind of guessing." "Okay," you reply, "Anything else?" "Yes," she says, "it could be a kind a accusation." "Does that fit?" you ask. "It could," the student says. "She thinks the man's a spy. Maybe he is one, maybe he isn't." "Did you get anything else from the dictionary?" you inquire. "It says 'an idea or opinion formed from evidence that is neither positive nor conclusive.' I'm not sure that helps me very much. It also says 'conjecture,' but I don't know what 'conjecture' means any more than I know what 'surmise' means." "I'm sorry I don't have a photograph of it," I say, as a kind of joke, but then I add, more seriously, "What do you think you can do to have a clearer idea of what it means to surmise?" "One thing I can do," she says, "is this: every time in my reading I come across the word 'conjecture' or the word 'guess,' I'll try substituting 'surmise.' In that way I can zero in on the meaning by finding a synonym for it. For example, 'guess' might serve as a synonym, but 'conjecture' might not. So that would be a little progress. But it wouldn't be sufficient." "Why not?" you ask. "Because I want to experience what actually goes on in my head and that I call a surmise." "You want to experience the mental act of *surmising*: You have the word for it; you know what it means, but what do you do when you do it, right?" "Right," she agrees. "It's like knowing what the word 'sneeze' means but never having heard or experienced a real sneeze. I need to know firsthand. Still, there have been times when I didn't know the right answer, but the evidence for one option being correct was just slightly better than the evidence for the other option. So I surmised that the first option was the correct one." "You sort of *gathered* it?" "That's it!" she exclaims with a laugh.

"I gathered the truth from the evidence just as our ancestors gathered nuts and fruit. A person who surmises is a mental gatherer!"

Enough of this fictitious dialogue has been presented to suggest that some students may be uneasy over the lack of a perceivable object corresponding to a term in their vocabulary, as occurs when the objects are mental (e.g., choosing, associating) or methodological (way, technique, problematic). This is the value of literature: It provides a surrogate context that helps us figure out what the term in question is doing in that context. We can't see a surmise or a gathering the way we can see a cassowary, but we can be conscious of performing the mental act of surmising or gathering. We can confront a cassowary in the zoo, but we can confront a surmise only by thinking about our own thinking, by being conscious of our own consciousness. Thus to think about our own thinking is to *objectify* a mental performance we have just engaged in, whereupon we can name it, describe it, correct it, substitute a synonym for it, and so on. To become aware of our own mental acts is to lift ourselves by our own bootstraps until we are functioning on a metacognitive level. To reflect is to be swept along by this metacognitive current of thought. Much of the success or failure of one's educational activity depends on one's ability to allow oneself to be carried along by this current.

MENTAL ACTS AS PERFORMANCES

A mental act is an achievement, a performance. One can feel oneself moving toward the making of a decision and then making it. In this sense it is like the making or fabrication of an object, like the making of a chair. The chair does not come out of nowhere: Some sort of design has preceded or accompanied it, and parts have been made that accord to the design, thanks to one's sawing, hammering, and chiseling. Other mental acts correspond to one's doings and to one's sayings. A mental act is therefore like a tiny work of art, a minuscule phrase or riff. In a sense it is to the mind what a computer chip is to a computer, except that the chip powers and prefigures a performance, while the mental act *is* a performance.

If we use the criterion of achievement, however, we come to realize that the borders of the domain of mental acts are very deep and that within those edges are many mental activities that are quite marginal and complex. Of particular interest are the combinations of mental acts and mental states. It is not that all mental states are deficient in achievement; it is just that the achievement factor in them is so slow moving that it appears to be standing still: This is what we mean by a "state." A person in a state of doubt is not paralyzed – mentally at any rate – in that condition. A person who knows may simultaneously be a person who learns, and what has been learned seeps slowly into one's pool of information until one deigns to know it or even to act on it. On the other hand, someone in a state of wonder or understanding or frenzy can be like a pot of applesauce on a stove, just bubbling away with all sorts of plans and initiatives.

If deciding is the most prototypical of mental acts, judgment is the unit of human behavior most representative of the person performing the judgment, and it is the most powerful in terms of the efficacy of its consequences. Buchler quite rightly asserts that each judgment is a microcosm of the person performing the judgment and is expressive of that person just as it is appraisive of that person's world.

Those who perform work or engage in sports that entail considerable physical activity are often so concerned with what they are doing that they do not think of their bodies as such, taking them for granted just as they may take their work or sports equipment for granted. It is only when something goes a bit wrong that they shift their focus from ends to means and institute repairs or therapy. In this way, they can get back to doing what they had previously been doing, with as little consciousness as before of the body itself or of the equipment itself. If this is the case with those who are engaged in physical activities, think of how much more it is likely to be true of those whose makings and doings are mental in nature. Whether or not one has suffered damage to the brain or the nervous system, one is hardly likely to image one's mental operations as they occur. More importantly, one is unlikely to be conscious of a mental sphere of operations, a mental dimension in which these activities are thought to take place. In no way should I be taken as suggesting that the mind is a real Cartesian substance or a theater in which the actors and actresses are all thoughts and feelings strutting about onstage for a brief time and then exiting to God knows where.

A classroom in which young children are being taught to read, write, and think better is somewhat like an intensive care unit in which patients are being treated for life-threatening damages. Such a classroom is not just an educational ambiance: It is an environment for thinking, and our job is to turn it into an environment for the support and the improvement of such thinking. To do so, the children must become aware of the cognitive ecology that can give them the support they need, as persons learning to fly must become conscious of the air around them that keeps them aloft. The student flyers' relationship with the planes they fly and the air that supports the planes is an ecological one. So is the relationship between student thinkers and the classroom environment – the community of inquiry, the books to be read and discussed, the teacher to facilitate the inquiry, the procedures and ideals to be considered and acquired, and so on.

Children are thrilled when they make their first paper airplane and can test the capacity of the air to support the plane as it sails across the room. Likewise they discover the power of thought to lend support to their decision-making process when they have to make a choice. The stream of thought becomes a fact they have to take into account, for it leads up to and down from the judgments they make, as these judgments are caught up in the currents of reasoning.

Compared with other mental acts, judgment is a massive and macroscopic accomplishment, a mental making/saying/doing of vast complexity. At the other end of the spectrum of mental acts are simpler, more microscopic ones, such as noting. If it is necessary to suggest a prototypical mental act it has been suggested that one offer *deciding*, because of the consciousness of a slight spasm of mental effort that accompanies the making of a decision. But deciding, like most mental acts, is far more complicated than it seems. We have little idea of what has to happen in order for us to remember, deduce, realize, and so on. It is evident that there are no atomic, indivisible mental acts, just as there are no atomic judgments. One cannot divide a mental act without creating new ones, just as we cannot repress a mental act without engendering a new awareness of it.

PROPOSITIONAL ATTITUDES

Human experience is comprised of more than its material infrastructure would lead us to believe, for it is also comprised of intentions, desires, emotions, convictions, attitudes, and countless other intangible, nonphysical qualities of personal presence. It is these qualities that give such experience its uniqueness and authenticity.

After all, it is not enough to say, here is this statement. What about the relationships between the statement and its maker? What attitude does the person take toward what is being asserted? You say he "believes" it. Well and good, he believes it. Let's say he believes that angels exist. Then "angels exist" is the proposition and "he believes" is the attitude he assumes toward that proposition. This promises to yield us a much more promising understanding of the person than if we sought to consider him and the proposition separately.

The attitude embeds the conviction, and as Elgin says, "the cognitive status of the emotion (is derived) from that of the belief it embeds."[2] An author can describe a group of people in a conference, sitting around a table. She can narrate what each of them says, and if she chooses, she can try to tell us what each of them thinks. With each new dimension, the narrative thickens, as if a rich layer of paint is being added to the surface of a painting. But more is possible. The author can tell us what each participant desires, hopes, regrets, despises, intends, perceives, feels. And she can tell us what each character's attitude is toward what he or she believes, understands, etc., these last being *propositional attitudes*. Of course, the *attitude of* a person may be quite out of synch with the content of his belief.

One of the things that beginning readers must master is the contextuality of *meaning*, and critical thinkers have been among the foremost in pointing this out. The child starting to read learns that *accent* can be tremendously important – the slight raising of the voice when an italicized word is being read, an inconspicuous lifting of an eyebrow, a gesture of diffidence – all of these affect the way in which we interpret an utterance. Likewise, the circumstances that prevailed at the time a statement was made may be quite unlike the circumstances that prevail today, so that the *truth* of the assertion may be dramatically different from what it was.

Some assertions carry a crucial bit of context along with them, as a snail carries its shell, with the result that we understand the assertion through the filter of this phrase that precedes the statement itself. In the so-called propositional attitudes, we are allowed a glimpse of a

---

[2] Ibid., p. 146.

person's attitude toward the proposition she is dealing with. Here are some examples:

George knew that John was ill.   *Harry supposed that* John was ill.
Mary thought that John was ill.   *Toni was thrilled that* John was ill.
Ed believed that John was ill.   *Melanie agreed that* John was ill.
Frank was certain that John was ill.   *Lillian regretted that* John was ill.
Polly doubted that John was ill.   *Max surmised that* John was ill.

These verbs all represent mental states that are attitudes toward the statement "John is ill" and together convey to the reader the psychological context in which the fact of John's illness is being understood. Obviously the fact of John's illness is surrounded by an animated circle of attitudes, feelings, judgments, mental states, and so on. It is through hints like these that people give away their intentions, their irritabilities, their confidences and promises. Austin's explanation of the various functions of verbs in discourse is very rich, and his classifications are intriguing: exercise of judgment verbs (like "grade," "assess," "rate," "acquit") are *verdictives*; exercising of power verbs (like "appoint," "dismiss," "command," "annul") are *exercitives*; verbs that commit one to a course of action (such as "promise," "undertake," "contract," "propose") are *commissives*; verbs that adopt an attitude (such as "apologize," "thank," "sympathize," "resent") are *behabitives*; and those verbs that clarify reasons, arguments, and communications (like "affirm," "deny," "mention," "report") are *expositives*.[3] This classification by Austin of many different functions of verbs in discourse is very helpful in understanding the mental acts and mental states that correspond to these terms. It enables us to name some of the most subtle of our feelings, our intentions, our doubts, and our desires. It helps us recognize the affective as well as the cognitive underpinnings of our mental life. It provides us with a vocabulary.

Austin says he prefers to call what he does "linguistic phenomenology" rather than "linguistic analysis." Neither term may do justice to what Austin is engaged in, and perhaps it would be best to see the two terms as involved in a *development*, such as "from linguistic phenomenology to linguistic analysis." If we do not see this process and

[3] J. L. Austin, op. cit., pp. 147–63.

development, we tend to look at mental activity as static rather than dynamic. Missing the developmental characteristic makes the overall mental setting resemble a set of transparencies for an overhead projector. We need to utilize narrative here, so as not to miss the elements of change and growth. The teaching of thinking needs to be set in an environment that is conducive to mental acts and states, and this is why propositional attitudes are so valuable, because they provide us twice our money's worth, each sentence concerning a statement and an attitude toward that statement. Citing a proposition but not citing the attitude with which that proposition is being received is like commenting on the observed surface of the moon but not revealing from where on the earth's surface the observation was made.

EPISTEMIC MOVEMENT: MENTAL ACTS AND STATES CAN DEVELOP INTO THINKING SKILLS

We are said to perform mental acts and to be engaged in mental states. What then is a *state*? a condition? a way of being? a set of circumstances? And what, in particular, is a *mental* state? a mood? an aspect of consciousness? a more or less fixed mental condition? As the term "mental state" is generally used, it would seem to be a homogeneously diffuse condition primarily psychological in nature but capable of making some cognitive contribution to the life of an individual. Mental states therefore may be depressed or enthusiastic, affirmative or denying, doubting or believing, recollecting or anticipating, as well as wondering, regretting, cherishing, loathing, and so on. Again conspicuous is the homogeneity of these states, as commonly described: their absence of detail, and yet the power they have to suffuse anything that falls within their scope with the deep dye of their condition. A person in a state of doubt is fully in that state; a person in a mental state of denial is permeated, as it were, with that denial.

But are mental states really so empty of any content of their own? Are they simply positive or negative attitudes? Do they contain some kind of psychic landscape that is being overlooked? One would expect that a person in a state of despondency would find himself environed by depressing sounds, sights, images, and the like. He might be struggling to hold on to certain "truths" that, while in reality nothing more than maxims or adages, he repeats to himself over and over. But this is all part of the mindscape.

Let's move on to considering other illustrations. In basketball there are moves to be made; there are the moves themselves, and there are the skills with which the moves are made. In dance also, there are moves to be made, moves that have their own names, like *sauté* and *pirouette* and *plié*, and then there are the skills with which the moves are made. In addition to the moves, in ballet, there are positions. Is there anything like this in thinking?

In thinking, there are (1) the moves themselves, of which we have concepts; (2) the making of the moves, that which philosophers call "mental acts"; and (3) the skills with which the moves can be skillfully performed. It is plausible that the counterparts in thinking of some *positions* in dance are "mental states."

Mental acts and mental states are components of the thinking process. Thinking comprises the more or less skillful orchestration of these acts and states. It also includes the awareness in memory of what has already been thought as it passes over into the past, and the imaginative anticipation (like peeking at the dancers in the wings, awaiting their turn on the stage) of the upcoming phases of the process.

I am not saying that *any* mental act can become a thinking skill, nor that a person with many such skills automatically would know how to orchestrate them – how to organize them coherently so that they might be applied appropriately when needed. Probably the best procedure for the development of thinking skills is the use of a classroom community of inquiry to *discuss* a provocative matter in which there is already considerable student interest. Students will not only strengthen their individual skills, but they will learn how to introduce them in subsequent discussions or inquiries at just the appropriate time and place.

For example, if *decision making* is to be taken as a thinking skill, then *deciding* is the mental act that is at its core. But deciding cannot do the job alone; in itself it is not a skill. It relies, among other mental acts, for example, on *distinguishing* so that it knows what it must decide between. Distinguishing in turn relies upon the *perception of difference*, and if the difference is hardly appreciable, then fine-tuned *discrimination* must be resorted to. These are some of the mental (and perceptual) acts that can lend their support to *deciding*, thereby suggesting that mental acts are not discrete. They are typically found in complexes resembling beehives of activity. If we can imagine a vast hive of such beehives, we might have a better idea of what someone means, who remarks that thinking is comprised of mental acts and mental states, to say nothing of *mental events*, which are somewhat of a favorite among contemporary philosophers of mind.[4]

THE DEVELOPMENT OF MENTAL MOVES INTO PHILOSOPHICAL DIALOGUE

As was noted in the last section, thinking consists in the development of mental acts into thinking skills, and their orchestration into further mental moves. In this sense, it is profitable to speak of the *moves* characteristic of philosophers, just as we speak of the distinctive moves made by a chess player, a gymnast, or a ballet dancer. When philosophers offer arguments, request definitions, correct invalidly drawn inferences, identify underlying assumptions, insist upon distinctions, they are making the moves that constitute the philosopher's repertoire, just as a dancer is doing so in performing a *glissade*, an *entrechat*, a *pirouette*, or a *plié*. Of course, these are merely techniques, and the body of techniques constitutes a craft rather than an art. For all that, excellent dancers perform *their* moves well, and excellent philosophers perform *their* moves well. In attempting to improve children's reasoning, therefore, one naturally turns to philosophers and studies their moves, so that these might be conveyed to and adopted by children in their own classroom dialogues.[5]

No move is simple: Each is a complex or composite. In the case of a dancer's moves, one would have to acknowledge them to be composed of countless smaller motions – the crook of a finger, a way of turning the chin, a certain lift to a heel, each of which has its own epistemic complexity but nevertheless must be accounted simple in comparison with the more complex moves familiar to the audience. Philosophical behavior likewise contains certain moves that are

[4] See Helen Steward, *The Ontology of Mind: Events, Processes and States* (Oxford: The Clarendon Press, 1997). See also, Donald Davidson, *Essays on Actions and Events* (Oxford: Oxford University Press, 1980).
[5] This passage is taken from "On Children's Philosophical Style," which was originally published in German in *Zeitschrift für Didaktik der Philosophie* (January, 1984), 3–11. Reprinted, in English, in *Metaphilosophy* 15, pp. 318–330 (1984).

EPISTEMIC MOVEMENT (I)

SOME MENTAL ACTS CAN DEVELOP INTO THINKING SKILLS

MENTAL ACTS	REASONING SKILLS
questioning	asking questions as part of problem-formulation and the initiation of discussions
generalizing tentatively	avoiding sweeping generalizations, such as occurs in stereotyping
challenging	asking that claims be supported by evidence
explaining	developing explanatory hypotheses
discriminating	recognizing differences of context
collaborating	building on the ideas of others
accepting	accepting reasonable criticisms
listening	welcoming hearing the "other side of the case"
respecting	acknowledging others and their rights
comparing	offering appropriate analogies
clarifying	seeking to clarify ill-defined concepts
differentiating	making relevant distinctions and connections
justifying	supporting opinions with convincing reasons
example-giving	providing examples and counter-examples
assumption-finding	seeking to uncover underlying assumptions
inferring	drawing suitable inferences; discovering implications
judging	making balanced evaluative judgments

FIGURE 7.1.

relatively elementary – moves that we realize as *mental acts*: supposing, intending, conceiving, recalling, associating, and so on – and that are characteristic of thinking itself. These comparatively atomic moves can in turn be developed and organized molecularly into thinking skills, examples of which might be deduction, categorization, contructing analogies, definition, generalization, and

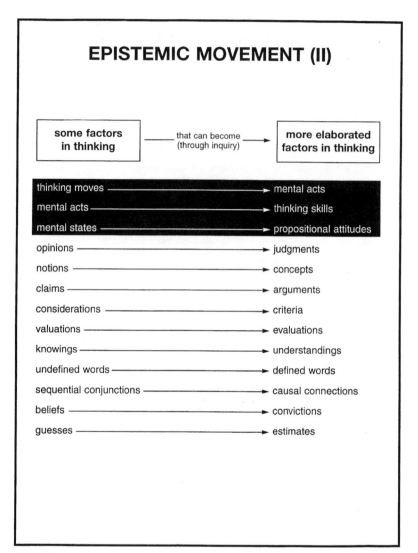

EPISTEMIC MOVEMENT (II)

some factors in thinking	that can become (through inquiry)	more elaborated factors in thinking
thinking moves	→	mental acts
mental acts	→	thinking skills
mental states	→	propositional attitudes
opinions	→	judgments
notions	→	concepts
claims	→	arguments
considerations	→	criteria
valuations	→	evaluations
knowings	→	understandings
undefined words	→	defined words
sequential conjunctions	→	causal connections
beliefs	→	convictions
guesses	→	estimates

FIGURE 7.2.

instantiation. Neither these individual skills nor their component acts are specifically philosophical; philosophy occurs when these skills are competently employed in the service of reflective inquiry. Thus the skills employed in the *craft* of philosophy can be taught, but whether the *art* of philosophy can be taught – in the elementary school or in the graduate school – is another matter. Perhaps the most that can be done, as with any art, is to put students into situations that invite their behaving philosophically.

Listening to a well-tuned philosophical discussion is like listening to an unfamiliar but excellent piece of chamber music. The moves are so complex, unforeseeable, and surprising yet at the same time so dissolved in the texture of what is taking place that they can be extricated only with considerable difficulty. Good philosophy is not reducible to technical virtuosity. This is why, in contrast with ordinary conversation, which is generally less than skillful, good philosophical conversation is generally more than skillful. Let's consider as an illustration an actual bit of children's dialogue:

(a) TEACHER: If it's true that all potholes are holes, is it true that all holes are potholes?

FIRST CHILD: It's not true that all potholes are holes. Holes go all the way through.

SECOND CHILD: And it's not true that all holes are potholes, because what about buttonholes?[6]

The occasion for this discussion was one in which the class had been studying that form of immediate inference known as *conversion*. There are several things worth noting about (a).

1. Throughout the entire conversation, concern is evinced for what is true and what is not true. The fact that conversion works only with true sentences compels the students to concern themselves philosophically with the notion of *truth*.

2. The teacher engages in *questioning* and confronts the students with a task in *immediate inference*.

3. The first student is invited to deal with the question of the truth of the consequent, but instead, declining the gambit, he proceeds to deal with the question of the truth of the antecedent, thereby exhibiting an interesting degree of intellectual independence.

4. The antecedent asserts that "all potholes are holes." The first student might have rejected this by recourse to *contradiction* (some potholes are not holes). Instead, he has recourse to the

---

[6] Dialogue from a sixth-grade philosophy class, reported in *Thinking*, vol. 3, no. 2, p. 44.

contrary, claiming in effect (by implication) that *no* potholes are holes. Once again, this is a daring maneuver.

5. Having made these moves, the first student proceeds to offer a *reason* for his position. This reason (holes go all the way through) also functions as a *criterion*. At this point, it is evident that the first student could, if he had to, offer a *definition*.

6. The second student's reply can be reconstructed in several ways. Here is one such way:

> If all holes were potholes, buttonholes wouldn't be holes.
> But we know that buttonholes *are* holes.
> Therefore it can't be true that all holes are potholes.

It may seem strange that students in elementary school should be prepared to employ hypothetical syllogisms or their equivalents. But the matter should not be all that mysterious. From the moment children begin to learn language, they begin to acquire, concomitantly, the grammar and the logic needed for the intelligible use of that language. Say to a little child, just learning to speak, "If it snows tonight, there'll be snowdrifts by the fence tomorrow." The next day the child looks out the window and murmurs, "No snowdrifts. So it didn't snow last night!" No one had to teach her specifically that the denial of the consequent requires denial of the antecedent. Everyone who learns the language acquires a minimal use of the reasoning skills, but not everyone employs those skills well. This is why teachers instinctively know that they must reinforce such reasoning patterns, such as by the use of enthymemes. A teacher will offer the minor premise "I don't see any hands," and the students supply the major premise ("If you know the answer, raise your hand") and the conclusion ("None of you knows the answer").

7. How could we, if we were to try, say what is said in (a) more economically? It is a masterpiece of compactness.

8. Both students seem content with a negative capability – they do not manifest an irritable reaching out for conclusions. They seem to prefer to be precise about what they are sure of and to be ready to leave the remainder of the problem open and contestable, a project for future inquiry.

9. In challenging the premise of the teacher's question, the first
   student reveals a preparedness to reappraise the given methodology of the inquiry.

One more illustration, this time involving some of the same logical
skills, plus analogical reasoning as well:

(b)   TEACHER: "Who can give me an example of an 'All' sentence that
      is false when reversed?"
      ELISE: "The sentence, 'All people are living things' is true. But
      when you turn it around, you get 'All living things are people'
      and that's false!"
      EUGENE: "What about *dead* people? All people are not living
      things, because some people are dead people! The first sen-
      tence isn't true!"
      SANDY: "If you're dead, you're not a person any more!"
      SEVERAL STUDENTS: "Yes, you are! Yes, you are!"
      STEVE: "A person has a heart, a soul and a body. His heart is a
      kind of bicycle pump. It's a bit like the air pump pumps air into
      a tire. Well, a heart pumps blood into a person. I mean, it's like
      the heart is pumping *life* into a person . . ."
      LISA: "I get it! Yeah, it's like that! When air goes out of a tire, it's
      still a tire, right? When the air goes out, it's not living any more,
      it's a dead tire." (The children laugh.) "So maybe if the life goes
      out of a person, he's still a person!"
      Several students protest that being dead and being a flat tire are
      very different.
      EUGENE: "But Steve, you can always blow a tire up again!"
      STEVE: "Yeah, but what if the tire had a hole in it?"[7]

There is an almost Doric simplicity and straightforwardness about
this interchange, but at the same time there is a breathtaking swift-
ness of movement. Also, there is confirmation here of the view that
when children participate together in a classroom community of
philosophic inquiry, they are able to make as much progress as a
smaller number of adults or as an adult working singly.

[7] Dialogue reported from a fifth-grade philosophy class, idem.

It is clear that the children in (b) are both *speaking* to one another and *listening* to one another. Shortly before they were *reading*, now they are *reasoning*. But what about *writing*? Surely if they are ever going to write, the time to challenge them to do so would be at this very moment, when they have become intrigued with an issue and have become excited by their own ideas on the matter. Their writing at this point will simply be a continuation of their thinking: highly compressed and compact, perhaps jumbled together a bit, rather breathless, and with no great concern for spelling and punctuation. It will probably be a long, long time before our procedures for teacher education are overhauled – thoroughly overhauled, as they must be – in order to accord philosophy its proper role in education. It will probably be an equally long time before we have curricula that are adequate to the task of challenging children's intelligence.

THROUGH THE MAGNIFYING GLASS: A CLOSER LOOK AT HOW PHILOSOPHY CAN IMPROVE THINKING

An example of an educational approach that seeks to facilitate the improvement of thinking in the schools is *Philosophy for Children* (P4C), whose curriculum is composed of novels for the students and manuals for the teachers. The novels are age-differentiated, and they aim to stimulate in children patterns of questioning and discussion that are first modeled by the fictional characters in the novels and subsequently continued, by internalization and appropriation, by the live children in the classroom, as they talk about what they have learned.

The first exemplar of this series of readers was *Harry Stottlemeier's Discovery*. One of the aims of *Harry* was to provide a user-friendly cognitive/affective environment that would nurture the earliest sparks of reflection in the hope that a full-scale discussion would soon begin to catch fire. A P4C reader is an inquiry-fostering environment because it is problematical, containing many ill-defined, essentially contested concepts, and because it displays the employment of many intellectual instruments, such as mental acts, reasoning skills, propositional attitudes, initial and follow-up questions, and judgments. Such a book facilitates thinking as a mountaineer's oxygen mask facilitates breathing. The process is then continued in the bracing dialogues of the community of inquiry, where the concepts and skills are tried out and appropriated.

We can employ an analogy between the ecological support provided by the environment for the growth of natural species and the support provided by texts and the community of inquiry for the development of thinking. In other words, thinking needs a habitat to facilitate its development.

As a way of illustrating the ecological service performed by the text, a list of concepts, cognitive skills, mental acts, and mental states, drawn from the four pages of Chapter One of *Harry*, is provided in Figure 7.3. In Figures 7.4 and 7.5, a mental activity matrix of just the first page of *Harry* is shown. Some of the mental states are merely reports of an affective or cognitive condition, such as "James was doubtful," or "Elinor was thrilled." But some are elements of propositional attitudes, such as "James was doubtful that he would win the race" or "Elinor was thrilled that her father was coming home." Propositional attitudes go beyond mere description and furnish us with an insight into the state of consciousness of the protagonists in the story, as well as their attitudes toward their own knowledge.

An analogous ecological service is performed by the community of inquiry, which provides models of reasoning and inquiry skills, as well as of concepts. (We speak of the concepts as being *appropriated* and the skills as being *internalized*.) As the intensity of the discussion in the classroom rises, the fact that the participants are engaged in shared inquiry becomes more evident. Instead of witnessing each individual thinking by himself or herself, observers can note the existence of distributed thinking, in which each participant utters what the situation calls for at the appropriate moment but from a differing point of view. Thus the community of inquiry provides a perspectival context for shared inquiry and an epistemic context for the formation of a reflective equilibrium.

It is not my contention that the provocation of reflective activity can take place *only* by providing a nurturing, animated environment in which it may flourish. That the flourishing of inquiry is much to be desired goes without saying, but this is an end that can be accomplished by a variety of means. Thus a human face

HARRY STOTTLEMEIER'S DISCOVERY   CHAPTER ONE

Concepts	Mental Acts and States	Thinking Skills	Underlying Reasoning Skills
• solar system = sun + revolving planets • all planets (as a class) revolve about the sun • comets are not planets • *all* planets revolve, but not *only* planets • sentences • nonreversible sentences • truth • truth and falsehood as mutually exclusive • discovery • understanding • being wonderful • kinds • distinction between classes of eagles and lions • working • rules • fault • failure • making a difference • conversation • mean (in sense of *imply*)	• daydreaming • listening • paying attention • humor • patience • puzzlement • trying to figure out • having an idea • being fascinated • being delighted • reflecting • being fond of • being thrilled • being embarrassed • being impatient • wondering • resenting • occurring to • feeling comforted • being serious • being grateful • wanting to thank • not wanting to interrupt	• judgment (assigning a predicate to a subject) • classification (all _____ members of the class of _____) • making distinctions • distinguishing *inclusion* from *exclusion* • recognizing nonconvertability of "all" sentences • "trying out" (exemplification) • "thinking up" (inventing? recalling?) • distinguishing one class from another ("No _____ are_____.") • converting "No" sentences (remain true when reversed) • "figuring out" (discovering? inventing? inquiring?) • offering evidence to substantiate a distinction ("My sentences weren't like yours because...") • exemplification of conversion of "No" sentences • broadening the rule to take the exception into account • listening • recognizing non-convertability of "all" sentences	• giving counterinstances (The comet is a counterinstance to the assertion that all things that revolve about the sun are planets.) • working with asymmetrical relationships (turning them around, or reversing them, to see if they stay true) • deductive inference (Lisa has discovered when it is *valid* to infer one sentence from another.) • working with symmetrical relationships • chapter prepares students to discover *identity statements*, which are the exception to Harry's rule

FIGURE 7.3.

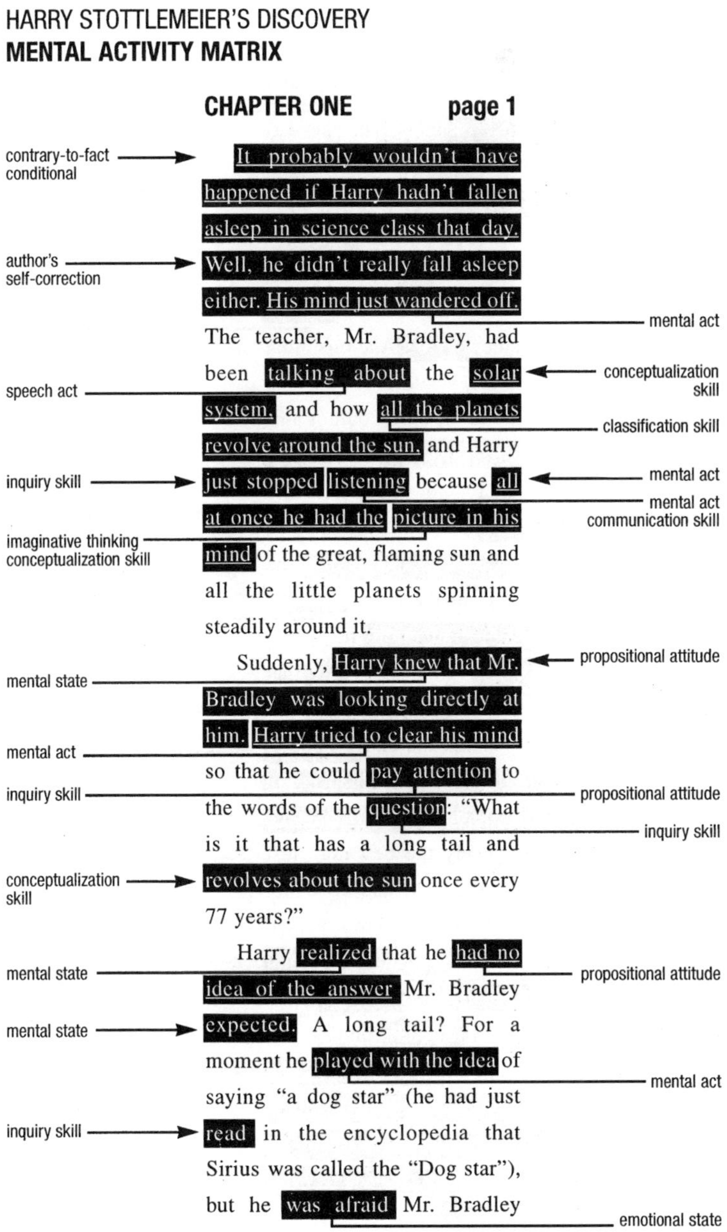

HARRY STOTTLEMEIER'S DISCOVERY
MENTAL ACTIVITY MATRIX

CHAPTER ONE   **page 1**

contrary-to-fact conditional → It probably wouldn't have happened if Harry hadn't fallen asleep in science class that day.

author's self-correction → Well, he didn't really fall asleep either. His mind just wandered off. ——— mental act

The teacher, Mr. Bradley, had

speech act ——— been talking about the solar ← conceptualization skill

system, and how all the planets ——— classification skill

revolve around the sun, and Harry

inquiry skill → just stopped listening because all ← mental act
——— mental act / communication skill

imaginative thinking / conceptualization skill — at once he had the picture in his

mind of the great, flaming sun and all the little planets spinning steadily around it.

mental state ——— Suddenly, Harry knew that Mr. ← propositional attitude

Bradley was looking directly at

mental act ——— him. Harry tried to clear his mind

so that he could pay attention to

inquiry skill ——— the words of the question: "What ——— propositional attitude
——— inquiry skill

is it that has a long tail and

conceptualization skill → revolves about the sun once every

77 years?"

Harry realized that he had no

mental state ——— idea of the answer Mr. Bradley ——— propositional attitude

mental state → expected. A long tail? For a

moment he played with the idea of ——— mental act

saying "a dog star" (he had just

inquiry skill → read in the encyclopedia that

Sirius was called the "Dog star"),

but he was afraid Mr. Bradley ——— emotional state

FIGURE 7.4.

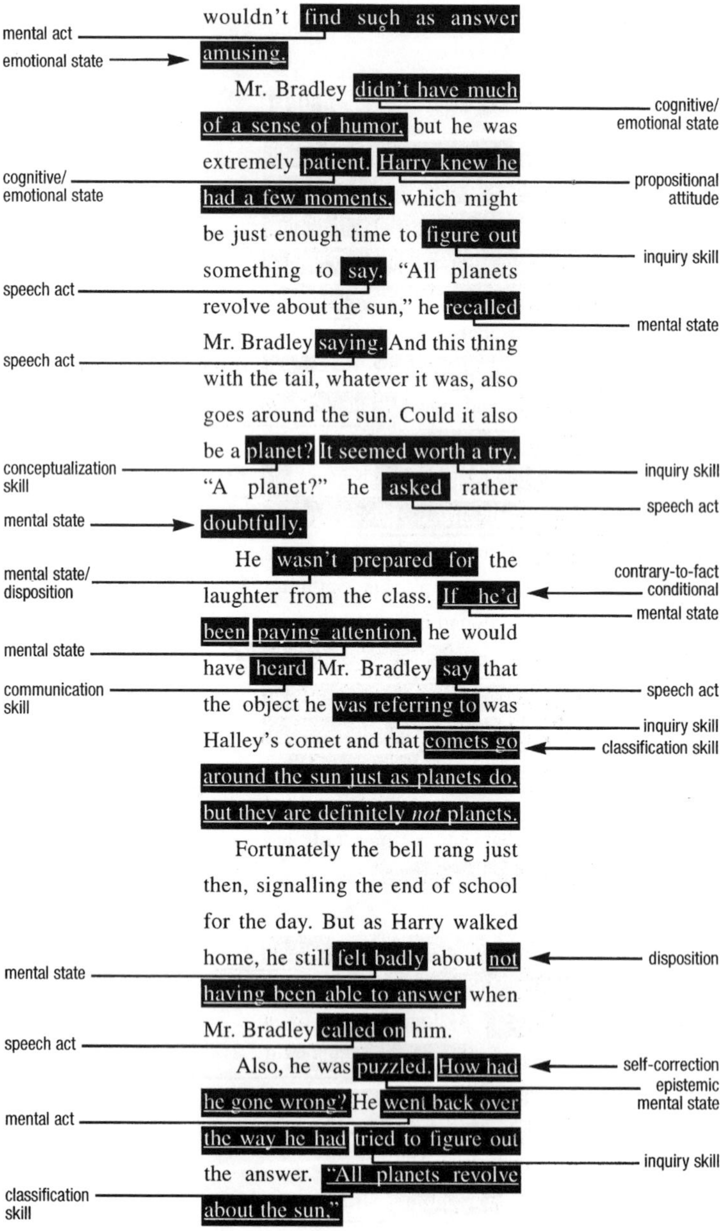

wouldn't find such as answer amusing.

Mr. Bradley didn't have much of a sense of humor, but he was extremely patient. Harry knew he had a few moments, which might be just enough time to figure out something to say. "All planets revolve about the sun," he recalled Mr. Bradley saying. And this thing with the tail, whatever it was, also goes around the sun. Could it also be a planet? It seemed worth a try. "A planet?" he asked rather doubtfully.

He wasn't prepared for the laughter from the class. If he'd been paying attention, he would have heard Mr. Bradley say that the object he was referring to was Halley's comet and that comets go around the sun just as planets do, but they are definitely *not* planets.

Fortunately the bell rang just then, signalling the end of school for the day. But as Harry walked home, he still felt badly about not having been able to answer when Mr. Bradley called on him.

Also, he was puzzled. How had he gone wrong? He went back over the way he had tried to figure out the answer. "All planets revolve about the sun."

Left margin annotations: mental act; emotional state; cognitive/emotional state; speech act; speech act; conceptualization skill; mental state; mental state/disposition; mental state; communication skill; mental state; speech act; mental act; classification skill.

Right margin annotations: cognitive/emotional state; propositional attitude; inquiry skill; mental state; inquiry skill; speech act; contrary-to-fact conditional; mental state; speech act; inquiry skill; classification skill; disposition; self-correction; epistemic mental state; inquiry skill.

FIGURE 7.5.

is a physical object, but it can convey, through animation or arrangements of its parts, an expression of extreme spirituality. Expression can be matched by evocation. A book contains language, language in which ideas are couched, and these ideas evoke the mental activity of the reader. These ideas can be the start of inquiry, which is accentuated by emotions and reinforced by deliberative discussions.

The epistemic matrix in Figures 7.4 and 7.5 represents the kind of analysis that teachers can be asked to make of a discussion transcript, so as to acquaint them with some of the more significant, if elusive, aspects of the logic of discourse.

8

Thinking Skills

"Thinking skills" is a catchall phrase.[1] It ranges from very specific to very general abilities, from proficiency in logical reasoning to the witty perception of remote resemblances, from the capacity to decompose a whole into parts to the capacity to assemble random words or things to make them well-fitting parts of a whole, the ability to explain how a situation may have come about to the ability to foretell how a process will likely eventuate, from a proficiency in discerning uniformities and similarities to a proficiency in noting dissimilarities and uniqueness, from a facility in justifying beliefs through persuasive reasons and valid arguments to a facility in generating ideas and developing concepts, from the power of discovering alternative possibilities to the power of inventing systematic but imaginary universes, from the capacity to solve problems to the capacity to circumvent problems or forestall their emergence, from the ability to evaluate to the ability to reenact – the list is endless, because it consists of nothing less than an inventory of the intellectual powers of humankind. Insofar as each intelligent human activity is different, it involves a different assemblage of thinking skills – differently sequenced, synchronized, and orchestrated.

[1] Adapted from M. Lipman, "Thinking Skills Fostered by Philosophy for Children," in Judith W. Segal, Susan F. Chipman and Robert Glaser, *Thinking and Learning Skills, vol. 1, Relating Instruction to Research* (Hillsdale, N.J.: Lawrence Erlbaum Associates, 1985), pp. 83–87, 97–99.

To dream of constructing a curriculum that would nurture and sharpen such an array of skills must certainly be considered quixotic: To have an impact on no more than a token selection of such skills is something we may aspire to without realistically hoping ever to achieve. Yet education has been at an impasse, and the improvement of thinking skills has been hailed for holding out the promise of lifting it to a new level of excellence.

Thus, we could do worse than to begin our attempts at instruction in thinking skills with the objective of converting the classroom into a community, if communality does indeed have a wholesome and positive effect upon cognitive proficiency. But what kind of community? Obviously it would involve shared experience, but beyond that, it would necessarily involve a common commitment to a method of inquiry. But what is that method? Surely it must be the collection of rational procedures through which individuals can identify where they may have gone wrong in their thinking; in short, it is the method of systematic self-correction. And such a classroom – one that had been converted into a community of inquiry – would find disrespect for persons repugnant. For the community would draw on the experience of each and make the resultant meanings available to all.

Now, it would be totally futile to expound such an objective to children themselves. Even if they could understand it in outline, they would hardly grasp its relevance to themselves. Somehow, they would have to be encouraged to hope that the ideal they had glimpsed might be feasible for those who, like themselves, were still young and inexperienced. This is where we must call upon their imaginative powers and have recourse to the magic of fiction. For instead of wearying them with an explanation of the merits of inquiry in the classroom, we can *show* them, in fictional form, a classroom community of inquiry, composed of children much like ordinary, live children, but thinking about matters of grave importance to children: matters like truth and friendship, personal identity and fairness, goodness and freedom. These fictional youngsters also spend a considerable portion of their time thinking about thinking, and about the criteria for distinguishing sound from unsound reasoning.

Again, let us take the educational approach P4C as an illustration. As the novels unfold, the characters in them are shown using the very thinking skills that one would hope the live children in the classroom,

DISCIPLINARY AND OTHER COMPONENTS FOR THE IMPROVEMENT
OF THINKING IN A COMMUNITY OF INQUIRY SETTING

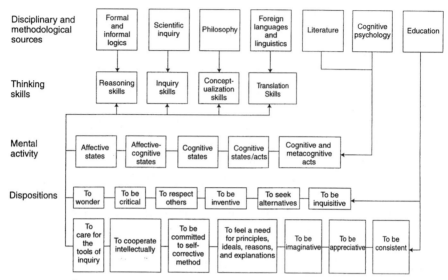

FIGURE 8.1.

through a process of identification, would likewise utilize. Perhaps "identification" does not suitably convey what occurs, for in fact, the students in the classroom tend to reenact the intellectual processes of their young heroes and heroines, much as, in reading romantic fiction, they reenact, live again, the emotional processes of their heroes and heroines. This occurs not merely in the private recollections of each reader but, more importantly, in the classroom discussions that follow the role playing or script reading of each episode in the novel. Children are quick to note that the fictional persons have their own styles of thinking, just as they have their own temperaments and moral characters. Some are quick to take intellectual risks; others are less venturesome. Some are analytical, others are experimental. Some are empirical, some are speculative. The variety of thinking styles is not provided merely for dramatic purposes. Children must be encouraged to express themselves with style, as well as efficiently, and they must also be encouraged to think with style, as well as efficiently. Indeed, we can hardly expect children's thinking to be well expressed, unless it is well reasoned, nor to be sensitively and gracefully expressed, unless it is sensitively and gracefully reasoned. There is not a precise way of separating the thinking that goes into writing – to take one form of expression – from the writing itself.

The sharpening of thinking skills does not take place exclusively in classroom discussions, but it is there that the exercise and strengthening of such skills is most evident. Some children like to read, some like to write, but many love to talk. The problem is to transform the energy of this impulse into cognitive skill, much as the transmission system of an automobile transforms the raw power of the engine into the disciplined and directed movement of the wheels. Mere talking must be converted into conversation, discussion, dialogue. This means learning to listen to others, as well as to respond effectively. It means learning to follow the various lines of reasoning taking place as the discussion proceeds: sizing up the assumptions that underlie each utterance, drawing inferences, testing for consistency and comprehensiveness, learning to think independently by freely choosing one's own premises. At any given moment in a conversation, each participant is engaging in countless mental acts, some in harmony with others, some quite independent of others, some convergent, others divergent. It is the task of the regimen of logic to discipline the dialogue. This is accomplished by enabling the participants to utilize the rules of logic as criteria of legitimate inference – in effect, as criteria for distinguishing between good and poor thinking.

But logic can do no more than impart a *formal* character to the dialogue. Unless children find something worthwhile to talk *about*, they will jabber about trivia, or lapse into silence and apathy. We need to show them how they can go beyond the mere exchanging of reports of their feelings and opinions to learning and discussing their ideas – ideas that many of them consider most precious because these are their most personal possessions, with which they most closely identify themselves.

That children should prefer primarily to discuss their own ideas – or what they take to be the ideas of children – should come as no surprise to us. We are all familiar with the experience of encountering in secondary sources ideas that in their original sources had seemed so thrilling and that now, in their restated version, appear so flat and stale. To be told about other people's thoughts is no substitute for having and thinking one's own. Moreover, we have the distinct impression that our thoughts regarding truth or friendship or justice are our own, whereas our thoughts of the Pyramids or of the Counter-Reformation are paler versions of a reality independent of us and remote from us in time and space. In short, we prefer our own, immediately presented thoughts to those that are re-presentational. This is a major reason for the warm response that children give to philosophy and poetry, for philosophical and poetic ideas are directly available to us in their original form and are not copies of things in a world beyond our immediate knowledge or experience.

No program of instruction in thinking skills can be thoroughly sound unless it strikes a balance between its encouragement of discovery and its encouragement of invention. Children are eager to discover both what lies within and what lies outside their powers. They are not distressed at finding that the rules of a game are coercive or that the laws of nature have a compulsory character that we flaunt only at our peril. But children also want to know what they are free to initiate and invent. They want to know the areas in which they can exercise creativity or, at the very least, discretion. "No fact in all the world is more wonderful than our understanding of that fact," one of Harry Stottlemeier's teachers tells him in the novel, and it gives Harry an insight into priorities that all children need to share.

The following list is not intended to exhaust the list of thinking skills. It is just a representative list, and for each skill, an example involving use of that skill is cited.

Skills and Dispositions Encouraged and Developed in the Community of Inquiry

Factor 1: *General Inquiry Skills*. Items 1–6 are characteristic of students engaged in deliberative inquiry.

Factor 2: *Open-mindedness*. Items 7–9 represent conduct that is considerate and cooperative with regard to others in the community.

Factor 3: *Reasoning Skills*. Items 10–17. These skills are more closely linked to logical reasoning than are the "General Inquiry Skills." (Both groups contain some items that represent "analysis" and others that represent "synthesis.)

Skills and Dispositions	*Examples*

1. *Formulates questions.*
   Students should be familiar with some of the defects with which questions are frequently contaminated. Formulating questions is fundamental in the inquiry process. Questions are formulated to enable students to understand the meaning of what is said or read. They also may point out underlying problems. However, not all questions are good ones.

1. Flawed questions are often:
   a. *vague.* "Where do animals come from?"
   b. *loaded.* "Have you stopped cheating on exams?"
   c. *self-contradictory.* "If the ship sank with all aboard, what happened to the survivors?"
   d. *nonsensical.* "What's the difference between a wrench and a grench?"
   e. *based on incorrect assumptions.* "Chicago is the busiest city in Texas, isn't it?"

2. *Avoids sweeping generalizations* (also known as stereotyping).
   Sweeping generalizations claim that what is true of one member of a class is true of the whole class.

2. "The guy who robbed the bank yesterday was almost seven feet tall. That just goes to prove that you can't trust tall people."

3. *Asks that claims be supported by evidence.*
   Those who make factual claims should be prepared to back them up with factual evidence, or should at least know how to find it.

3. "I assume that this medication is safe to take because it has been experimented with for ten years, its effects are still lasting, and it has shown no serious side effects. The research involved thousands of subjects under widely varying conditions."

4. *Develops explanatory hypotheses.*
   Often the evidence is available but a satisfactory

4. "This is a bad neighborhood. People lock their doors at night. If you never lock your doors, I

explanation of it is lacking. Or the evidence may be fragmentary or disconnected. The hypothesis gives it coherence and makes what happened appear to be a matter of course.

5. *Recognizes situational differences.*
Very slight contextual differences can invalidate an otherwise powerful inductive argument. Skilled inquirers are constantly on the lookout for subtle situational differences that would make their generalizations more hazardous.

6. *Builds on the ideas of others.*
Not building just on one's own ideas, but contributing to the strengthening and applicability of other people's ideas as well.

7. *Accepts reasonable criticisms.*
Those who are open-minded avoid becoming "defensive" about their own opinions. They will argue for their views, but at the same time they will

hypothesize that sooner or later there will be a robbery in your place. At least that's what you would normally expect."

5. "Under what circumstances could the following statements be *true*?
a. Water doesn't put out a fire.
b. A house floats away in the air."
"Under what circumstances could the following statements be *false*?
a. There is nothing living on the moon.
b. The capital of the U.S. is N.Y.C."

6. Teacher: "From where I stand, in the front of the room, I can see all your faces."
Johnny: "But on the other hand, from where we sit, at the back of the room, we can see only the backs of heads."

7. Marie: "My father's been reading that smoking causes cancer, so he's going to give up smoking."
Tom: "Why doesn't he just give up reading?"
Marie: "That won't do anything for the risk of cancer,

recognize the value of constructive criticism.

8. *Welcomes hearing "the other side of the case."*
Open-mindedness here is fair-mindedness: a willingness to take alternative perspectives into account.

9. *Respects others as persons.*
In a community of inquiry, one respects others as persons. One restricts one's negative criticisms to an argument rather than to the person who proposes the argument.

10. *Offers appropriate analogies.*
Analogies represent similarities not just of single traits, but of whole systems of traits. Once students have learned to identify relationships, they are prepared to recognize that analogies involve a relationship of similarity between two relationships.

11. *Seeks to clarify ill-defined concepts.*
Students assigned well-defined problems often find them unchallenging or uninteresting. They may prefer to start with ill-defined, problematic

although maybe it will reduce the risk of reading."

8. "Fran had no business pushing that boy like that." "He had no right obstructing the doorway to the classroom. You've got to see the matter from her point of view."

9. "Jeremy claims that although DDT kills mosquitoes, it can also be harmful to humans."
"You can't believe anything Jeremy says. Everyone knows he is scared of everything."

10. "Our toes function very much the way our fingers do."
"Can you be more explicit?"
"Sure. Fingers are to hands as toes are to feet."
"Maybe so, but you can't grasp with your feet the way you can grasp with your hands, and you can't walk on your hands the way you can walk on your feet."

11. "To call this painting 'unique' is simply to say that there isn't anything in the world like it. It's very rare."
"No, to call it 'unique' is to say that it's so individualized that it would still be

concepts in need of clarification and analysis.

12. *Makes relevant distinctions and connections.*

    In inquiry, if one makes a distinction, there should be a difference in the world that corresponds to that distinction; hence the saying, "No distinctions without differences." Analogously, one could say, "No connections without similarities"

13. *Supports opinions with convincing reasons.*

    In answering an opinion, one assumes responsibility for developing an argument that would justify that opinion. At the least this means finding a reason that is both strong and relevant.

14. *Provides examples and counterexamples.*

    To give an example is to cite a particular, specific instance of a general rule, a principle, or a concept. To give a counterexample is to cite an instance that refutes an argument advanced by someone else.

different even if there were a great many paintings more or less similar to it."

12. "I distinguish between 'doctors' and 'physicians' because physicians can do things that doctors can't do."
    "There's nothing a physician can do that a doctor can't do. The terms are completely synonymous."
    "But there's a connection between neurologists and psychiatrists?"
    "They're both professionals in the field of medicine."

13. "Percy's the best example I know of a solid citizen. He's so typical of everyone else when it comes to his opinions and his conduct."

14. "Parents always protect their children."
    "What about children who are abandoned by their parents?"

15. *Seeks to uncover underlying assumptions.*

The assertions we put forward are often based on assumptions that are concealed (from others and possibly from ourselves as well).

16. *Draws suitable inferences.*

Where possible, one should draw inferences that do not violate the rules of validity.

17. *Makes balanced evaluative judgments.*

Balanced evaluative judgments require an equilibrium between different kinds of criteria.

15. "Jeff's a plumber and a Conservative. He must come from Lancaster."

"You can draw that inference only if you first assume that all plumbers who are Conservative come from Lancaster."

16. "Is it true that only if today is Wednesday, will tomorrow be Thursday?"

"Yes."

"And is it true that tomorrow's Friday?"

"Yes."

"Then today can't be Wednesday."

17. "To determine which is greater, China or Japan, will you use quantitative criteria, like population, or qualitative criteria like cultural achievements?"

"Why couldn't I use both kinds?"

The *coordination* of thinking skills is of the very first order of importance. Thus, it is possible to induce improved student performance in some individual skill without such improvement being reflected in improved academic performance.

If the learning of individual thinking skills does not assure that such skills will be employed in a coordinated fashion, what needs to be done to obtain such assurance? The answer would seem to lie in the acquisition by children of certain cognitive dispositions. These dispositions are not themselves skills, but they represent a readiness to employ such skills – and to employ them in a coordinated and cumulatively reinforcing fashion. There are, of course, many dispositions that have long been considered desirable in students and that overlap with those under discussion. Examples would be trust, coop- erativeness, readiness to listen, attentiveness, and respect for others. These are certainly familiar features of a congenial and smoothly functioning classroom. But to the extent that the classroom is con- verted into a community of inquiry, new dispositions also emerge that are more cognitive in character. These include: trust that the method of inquiry will be self-correcting; care for the procedures of inquiry; a considerateness of others' points of view; and a readiness to apply the same critical spirit to oneself as one does to others, that is, to be self-appraising as well as appraisive of one's peers. When students acquire cognitive propensities such as these, all of which could perhaps be summed up in the term "commitment to inquiry," they are motivated to mobilize their skills effectively. Those students who can be counted on to use their intellectual resources in a uni- fied and consistent fashion are precisely those who have already developed habits of so doing. It is the job of a thinking skills pro- gram to develop these habits and dispositions, and not just the skills themselves.

If we want children to grow up to be reflective adults, we should encourage them to be reflective children. It is obvious that the con- tinuity between means and ends implies for us a rule of proce- dure: Tomorrow's results, whatever they may be, will bear the stamp and character of today's procedures and practices. Thus, if think- ing skills are to be taught, they should be taught in the context of ongoing communities of inquiry whose scrupulous attention to method can be internalized by each participant. And to the extent that this occurs, each participant becomes a reflective and reasonable individual.

SKILLS AND MEANINGS

The primary incentive for acquiring speech is probably the power speech affords to express meanings and acquire them.[2] It is not enough to be able to spit food out or pat the dog; the infant evidently

---

[2] This section is taken from my essay "The Seeds of Reason," originally published in Ronald T. Hyman (ed.), *Thinking Processes in the Classroom: Prospects and Programs* (Trenton: New Jersey Association for Supervision and Curriculum Development, 1985), pp. 1–15.

wants to be able to say, "Nasty food" or "Nice doggie." Likewise, it is not enough merely to observe the sky; the infant evidently wants to be able to say that it is blue. To be able to predicate nastiness of the food, niceness of the dog, and blueness of the sky – in short, to be able to make logical judgments – is a significant achievement. But at the same time the infant wants to know what other people mean by *their* verbal expressions, such as "The dog is dirty," the clue to which is usually given by the adult's facial expression. Our animal inquisitiveness is rapidly transformed into a lust for *meaning* – to acquire meaning and to express it through interpersonal communication. The acquisition of meaning gains added momentum through acquiring the ability to read, while the expression of meaning is enhanced by acquiring the ability to write.

It is not that the literary skills traditionally emphasized by language arts teachers are not "thinking skills." (The phrase is redundant; all skills involve thinking, and nothing can be a skill that does not involve thinking.) But these literary skills do not play the meaning-acquisitive role that reasoning and inquiry skills play in the reading process. Violations of the reasoning operations result directly in losses of meaning to the writer or reader, while violations of syntactical and spelling rules do not necessarily cause such losses.

To insist upon the primacy of meaning in motivation will be thoroughly unsurprising to those who have all along stressed comprehension as the chief incentive for children in getting them to read or to read better. What the primacy of meaning in motivation does spotlight, however, are those rudimentary activities that are more directly involved in meaning acquisition and those that are less so. By way of illustration of this point, let us consider some errors:

Error	*Comment*
1. "Thirty-five divided by seven equals four," said George.	1. George's error involves a violation of conventions and procedures within the system of arithmetic.
2. Ruth left a note saying, "Us going to the stor."	2. Ruth has violated English syntax and spelling

conventions, although she manages to convey the same meaning she would have conveyed had she written without errors.

3. Gary remarked, "Gems are defined as ordinary stones."

3. Gary's failure to define "gems" correctly rests on his failure to classify them correctly as precious rather than as nonprecious. As a result, the defining term ("ordinary stones") does not have the same meaning as the term to be defined ("gems"). Because Gary does not perceive the lack of synonymity, he fails to convey the meaning he attempts to convey.

4. Sally said, "All detectives are interested in crime and all criminals are interested in crime; therefore all detectives are criminals."

4. We may assume the premises of Sally's syllogism to be true, but then we discover that, owing to its formal invalidity, it fails to preserve the truth of its premises in its conclusion.

5. "The French word *chat*," said Tom, "means, in English, *an informal conversation*."

5. Tom's translation of the French word for *cat* into the English *chat* fails to preserve the French meaning by finding an equivalent English meaning.

6. The item in the reading comprehension test reads as follows: "The main idea of the statement 'One of the most alarming statistics in recent years has been the

6. This passage betrays a faulty understanding of the way the original statement is to be translated into a more colloquial (but still English) locution.

rapidly rising number of fires' is that false alarms are costly and dangerous, rather than that there are more fires now than there used to be."

The resulting lack of synonymity can also be described as a failure to preserve meaning.

These examples provide us with an opportunity to make two distinctions. The first is between errors that violate *meaning* and errors that do not. The second is between operations that preserve *truth* and operations that preserve meaning.

With regard to the second distinction, consider the cases of Gary, Sally, and Tom. Sally's syllogism failed to preserve the *truth* of its premises. Gary's definition failed to preserve the *meaning* of the term to be defined. And Tom's translation failed to preserve the *meaning* of a French word by failing to select an equivalent English word.

Now, in the light of these distinctions, let us reconsider the item in error number 6 on the reading comprehension test. The error is one that violates meaning but is independent of the question of truth, since we are expected to understand and correctly translate false statements just as we are expected to understand and correctly translate true ones. What lesson does this hold for us?

Strictly speaking, the truth-preserving process is *inference* and the meaning-preserving process is *translation*. Reading comprehension presupposes skill in translating not from one language to another but from one domain of a language to another domain of the same language, as when we read a passage in formal prose and then say what it means in colloquial language. But while the truth of the passage under translation is not at issue, the operations by means of which the translation is made may be inferential and hence truth-preservative.

There is, of course, a broader and narrower sense of reading comprehension. The broader sense involves a collaboration between author and reader that results in a common product that goes beyond what the author has stated or implied. I am deliberately putting aside this quite valid sense of meanings as generated by the act of reading and am restricting myself to the narrower sense employed by the constructor of tests of reading comprehension. These test-constructors apparently take into account only (1) whether or not the reader understands what the passage *states*, (2) whether or not the reader infers what the passage *implies*, and (3) whether or not the reader grasps the *underlying assumptions* on which the passage is based. All three of these considerations presuppose skills that are primarily logical in character. (1) Understanding what the passage states is held to be achieved when the reader can identify a second passage whose meaning is equivalent to the meaning of the first. In this sense, to understand is to recognize *identity* in the form of *synonymity*. (2) To infer correctly what a passage implies is obviously a logical procedure, whether it is formal and syllogistic or informal and linguistic (in the sense that "John beat Mary badly at cards" implies that "John beat Mary at cards"). (3) To grasp underlying assumptions is to ask what the premises might be if a given assertion were to be the conclusion of a valid argument; once again, logical procedures are involved.

The question, of course, is not whether we can show *identity* of meaning but whether we can show *similarity* of meaning. Take the case of the fourth-grade child who was asked, in a Philosophy for Children class, what it would be like to be the only person on earth and who replied, "It would be like being the only star in the sky." What the child noted was a telling likeness between the person alone in an empty world and the star alone in an empty sky. She evidently found the relationship between the person and the world much like the relationship between the star and the sky; in other words, she discovered a relationship of similarity between two part–whole relationships. And this is precisely what constitutes analogical reasoning: the finding of similar relationships among other relationships. The child's answer is impressive evidence that she has grasped the meaning of the question.

Reading comprehension can therefore be said to rest upon the formal skills of deductive inferential reasoning and upon such skills as analogical reasoning. It is likely that reading comprehension will be more effectively improved if these primary reasoning skills are strengthened than if attention is paid to syntactical lapses, vocabulary weaknesses, spelling deficiencies, and a lack of stylistic appreciation. This is because reasoning skills contribute directly to the reader's acquisition of meaning, and it is access to meaning that most effectively motivates the reader to continue pursuing the reading process. Teachers of reading and language arts insist that they teach thinking, and they do. But if we examine the skills they stress (the ones they grade for), it is clear that the emphasis is on the skills that are not meaning-bearing rather than on the semantic skills that are.

This is true not only of teachers of reading and language arts. In each elementary school discipline, education textbooks bend over backwards to cite thinking skills and to urge their fostering by the teacher because of the relevance of such skills to the mastery of the material, whether in science, math, or social studies. Consider a representative approach in education – for example, the eighth edition of *Social Studies for Children*, by John U. Michaelis.[3] Michaelis is a respected educator who has been concerned with the development of cognitive processing in educational contexts and who is the coauthor of *A Comprehensive Framework of Objectives*.[4] His advocacy of thinking skills in a social studies framework is clear and explicit. He presents four modes of thinking: critical thinking, creative thinking, decision making, and problem solving and inquiry. These four approaches intersect with a knowledge base derived from other thinking skills: remembering, interpreting, comparing, gathering data, and classifying.

Michaelis says that concepts must be developed to supplement the knowledge base. Examples he gives of concepts are conjunctive, disjunctive, and relational. The strategies of concept-formation include defining, distinguishing examples from nonexamples, listing–grouping–labeling, and "problem solving or inquiry." He lists, as skills to be emphasized, generalizing, inferring, predicting, hypothesizing, analyzing and synthesizing information, and evaluating. For each skill, a few hints are given as to the kinds of questions the teacher should ask in order to foster the skill, and then the text turns to other important matters. Judging from this text, it is as if only a quick brush-up or tune-up is needed to get these skills operating and plugged into the discipline.

The fact is that elementary school teachers, like teachers at every other level, are in no position to read the now-obligatory chapter on thinking skills that virtually all new textbooks such as this one by Michaelis contain and to operationalize the taxonomies of skills set

3 Englewood Cliffs, N.J.: Prentice-Hall, 1985, pp. 233–63.
4 John U. Michaelis and Larry B. Hannah, *A Comprehensive Framework of Objectives* (Reading, Mass.: Addison-Wesley, 1977).

forth. Indeed, many teachers become rebellious and vow not to be distracted from their lesson plans by futile efforts to strengthen skills that students should have brought with them on school opening day. It may be somewhat useful to teachers to have a neat new definition of inference if they are to be answered correctly, but teachers must be extraordinarily naive to believe that such hints even remotely prepare them to strengthen the inferential proficiencies of those students who perform uncertainly when inference is called for. And the educators who prepare such teachers in schools of education must be extraordinarily naive to believe that an educational process that fails to provoke students to think can be successful at making them think better.

FOUR MAJOR VARIETIES OF THINKING SKILLS

For educational purposes, the most relevant skill areas are those relating to inquiry processes, reasoning processes, information organizing, and translation. It is likely that very small children possess all of these skills in a rudimentary way. Education is therefore a matter not of cognitive skill acquisition but of skill strengthening and improvement. In other words, children are naturally disposed to acquire cognitive skills, just as they naturally acquire language, and education is needed to strengthen the process.

Inquiry skills

By "inquiry," I mean self-correcting practice. I do not call a behavior inquiry if it is merely customary, conventional, or traditional – that is, simply practice. But if the supervening practice of self-correction is added to that practice, the result is inquiry. I do not think this definition of inquiry is too broad just because it spans the behavior of the exploring infant and that of the exploring scientist. The fumbling, groping infant, trying to guess where the ball went – perhaps under the sofa – is engaged in considering alternatives, constructing hypotheses, testing, and other forms of behavior that will gradually become recognizable as "intelligent."

Inquiry skills, like the other varieties of cognitive skills, are continuous across age levels. The differences, from childhood to old age, are much more of degree than of kind. It is primarily through inquiry skills that children learn to connect their present experiences with what has already happened in their lives and with what they can expect to happen. They learn to explain and to predict and to identify causes and effects, means and ends, and means and consequences, as well as to distinguish these things from one another. They learn to formulate problems and to estimate, measure, and develop the countless proficiencies that make up the practice associated with the process of inquiry.

Reasoning skills

Knowledge originates in experience. One way of extending knowledge, however, without recourse to additional experience, is through reasoning. *Given what we know, reasoning permits us to discover additional things that are the case.* In a soundly formulated argument, where we begin with true premises, we discover an equally true conclusion that "follows from" those premises. Our knowledge is based upon our experience of the world; it is by means of reasoning that we extend that knowledge and defend it.

One of the merits of logic is almost purely educational. To students eager to vaunt their newfound relativism, it provides a superb reminder that what may be true for one may not be true for all, that not everything follows from everything else, and that relativism does not necessarily exclude objectivity. What logic does beautifully is demonstrate to incredulous students that rationality is possible, that there is such a thing as logical correctness or validity, and that some arguments are better than others.

In Plato's day, inference had something living and fresh and surprising about it, and we have attempted to explain this away by saying that it must have been because, to Socrates and Plato, logic was so *new*. But this was only part of the matter. The vitality of reasoning then was much more closely connected to the nature of *dialogue*. When we think by ourselves, rather than in conversation with others, our deductions are derived from premises we already know. As a result, the conclusion we infer is totally unsurprising. But when no person knows all the premises, as is often the case in dialogue, the reasoning process has much more vitality, and the conclusion can come with considerably more surprise.

Information-organizing skills

For purposes of cognitive efficiency, we have to be able to organize the information we receive into meaningful clusters or units. These conceptual clusters are networks of relationships, and since each relationship is a unit of meaning, each of the alternative networks or clusters is a web of meanings. Three basic types of informational clustering are the sentence, the concept, and the schema. There are, however, also organizational *processes* that are not merely parts or elements of a larger whole but are global ways of formulating and expressing what we know. I am thinking here of narration and description, very comprehensive skills that can take into account the whole of an experience and break it down into its constituents, whether viewed sequentially or simultaneously.

Sentences. Sentences, rather than individual words, are *basic contexts of meaning*. They are larger units than, say, the relationship between any two words in a sentence, but they are elementary as contrasted with such larger units as paragraphs and arguments. It is true that individual words have reference to things in the world, but they make sense only when organized with other words and when understood in the context of the language as a whole.[5]

When we deal with reasoning, we are primarily preoccupied with relationships among sentences. We tend to forget, therefore, how great an achievement an individual sentence can be for the language learner. What goes on in a sentence is no less exciting than what goes on among sentences. Some writers, for example, say something different in each sentence they construct, so that we comprehend

---

[5] I take it that the most elementary unit of meaning is a relationship. In this sense, since words have semantic or referential relationships to things in the world, words participate in and partake of the meanings of those relationships. (Obviously, I hesitate to say that the relationship, and hence the meaning, is in cases of this sort in the connection between the word and the thing referred to. Rather, the relationship spans the word and the thing it refers to in an overarching way so as to include and comprise them in the meaning. In other words, I see connections as interactional and words as transactional. Cf. John Dewey and Arthur F. Bentley, "A Trial Group of Names," in *Knowing and the Known* [Boston: Beacon, 1949], pp. 287–312.) But I see no conflict between this and the assumption that the sentence (because it includes a complex nesting of linguistic and not just referential relationships) is in a better position to be taken as the basic unit of meaning. Cf., for example, Michael Dummett, "Meaning and Understanding," in *The Interpretation of Frege's Philosophy* (Cambridge, Mass.: Harvard University Press, 1981), pp. 74–82.

the whole of what they say only by understanding each of the sentences in the order in which they are presented. Other writers write epigrammatically or aphoristically, so that each of their sentences intimates something of the sense of their work taken as a totality. Nietzsche's sentences are something like this. And there are still other writers whose individual sentences are fairly atomistic in content, so that their larger compositions are like mosaics with each of the tiny units united with every other by means of a consistent texture or style. We readily recognize Hemingway in the repetitions and adjectival choices of a sentence such as "The cows were big, gray, striped-flanked antelope with ridiculously small heads, big ears, and a soft, fast-rushing gait that moved them in a big-bellied panic through the trees."[6]

Sentences are the basic building blocks of reading and writing, and they may be of many kinds: questions, exclamations, commands, assertions. From the point of view of traditional logic, assertions or statements are of the greatest interest; each statement is said to represent a judgment. An example of an elementary logical judgment is "All mice are rodents."[7]

Concepts. When we cluster things in terms of their similarities, we are said to have a concept of them. As Rom Harré says, concepts are the vehicles of thought, entities by means of which thought is carried on.[8] Analysis of concepts involves clarifying and removing ambiguities, as in Figure 8.2, an example by Katz and Fodor. In another example (Figure 8.3), students are presented with a targetlike map; two concentric areas, identified by a pair of antonyms, are separated by a "fuzzy area." The students are given a list of words that they are to distribute as appropriately as possible among the three areas. The synonyms in the inner zone are to contribute to the massed meaning in that zone, while the unique meaning of each term is to be found by contrasting it with its synonyms. This method was suggested by J. L. Austin.[9]

---

[6] *The Green Hills of Africa* (New York: Scribner, 1935), p. 138.

[7] John Dewey argues, in contrast, that "all particular propositions are relational," and propositions about the relationships among kinds are also relational – logically, if not verbally. See *Logic: The Theory of Inquiry* (New York: Holt, 1938), pp. 307–9.

[8] "The Formal Analysis of Concepts," in H. J. Klausmeier and C. W. Harris (eds.), *Analysis of Concept Learning* (New York: Academic Press, 1966), p. 3.

[9] *Philosophical Papers*, 3d ed. (New York: Oxford University Press, 1979), pp. 94–5.

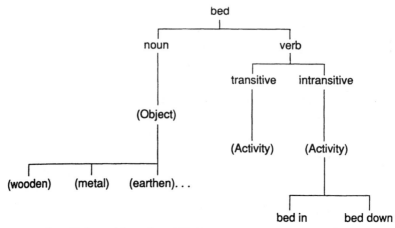

FIGURE 8.2. (Adapted from Jerrold J. Katz and Jerry A. Fodor, "The Structure of a Semantic Theory," in Katz and Fodor [eds.], *The Structure of Language* [Englewood Cliffs, N.J.: Prentice-Hall, 1964], p. 485.)

Schemata. There can be no doubt that working with concepts is more efficient than trying to deal with each and every entity in the work independently. But concept-formation and concept-analysis may be very hard work. Many students, confronting an assigned number of pages in a text, find themselves drained of energy as they attempt to grasp and understand the concepts that the author uses with such facility.

On the other hand, there are organizing systems that impart energy rather than soak it up. An example is the schema; an example of a schema is a narrative, such as a story. Narrative organization, in contrast to expository organization, tends to unfold as it is explored. As it unfolds, it gathers momentum and energy and transmits this to the reader. It is not simply the sequencing of information that makes this possible. It is made possible by the organic relationship that the parts have to one another and to the whole. This is in contrast to the jigsaw part–whole relationship found in a technical text. Additionally, the narrative form readily encompasses affective strands as well as cognitive ones, and this further intensifies the reader's interest and attentiveness.

Schemata are dynamic rather than static. They represent an active requiredness that urgently demands completion or equilibrium. A work of art in the process of being created exhibits this demand

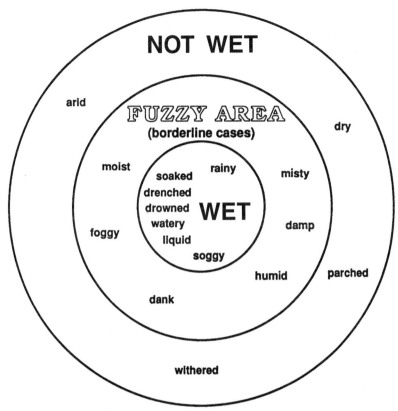

FIGURE 8.3. (From Matthew Lipman and Ann Margaret Sharp, *Wondering at the World* [Lanham, Md.: University Press of America, 1986], pp. 74–5.)

character; so does an organism when it resists or rejects what it finds alien to it and accepts what it can tolerate or find congenial. But whatever a schema (such as a story) incorporates is bound to affect and modify the whole of that schema.[10]

When we employ schemata in perceptions we tend to impose structure on what we observe. An example is the three-dimensional structure of space that we impose on the blur of perceptions with which we begin our postnatal experience of the world. This is what makes the three-dimensional renderings of space by artists intelligible to us. However, there are times when we impose schemata upon the world

[10] For an understanding of the organic nature of schemata, see Paul Schilder, *Image and Appearance of the Human Body* (London: Routledge and Kegan Paul, 1935).

Characterizations

Inquiry is a self-corrective practice in which a subject matter is investigated with the aim of discovering or inventing ways of dealing with what is problematic. The products of inquiry are judgments.

Reasoning is the process of ordering and coordinating what has been found out through the inquiry. It involves finding valid ways of extending and organizing what has been discovered or invented while retaining its truth.

Concept-formation involves organizing information into relational clusters and then analyzing and clarifying them so as to expedite their employment in understanding and judging. Conceptual thinking involves the relating of concepts to one another so as to form principles, criteria, arguments, explanations, and so on.

Translation involves carrying meanings over from one language or symbolic scheme or sense modality to another and yet retaining them intact. Interpretation becomes necessary when the translated meanings fail to make adequate sense in the new context in which they have been placed. *Thus, reasoning is truth-preservative, and translation is meaning-preservative.*

---

gratuitously, as when we impute to whole social groups characteristics common to only a few of their members. In cases of prejudice, which is what I am describing, it is difficult to correct the matter simply by direct communication or instruction, for the power of the schema to resist radical reconstruction is very great.[11]

Description and narration. Description and narration are not simply ways of organizing information; they are ways of organizing and expressing experiences. But at the same time they are capable of

---

[11] For more on the role of schemata in contributing to ethnic stereotypes, see M. Rothbart, M. Evens, and S. Fulero, "Recall for Confirming Events: Memory Processes and the Maintenance of Social Stereotypes," *Journal of Experimental Social Psychology* 15 (1979), 343–55.

organizing the informational content of such experiences, they are also modes of transmission.

Authors think in flights and perchings. There are details on which our thought rests long enough to permit a description. These details are perchings. Then there are flights of thought as we move from observation to observation or from idea to idea or from premises to conclusions. As we read what the author has written, our thought tends to recapitulate the flights and perchings of the author's thought. If the author's thought pauses to examine and describe something, we become absorbed in that description. If then the author's thought takes wing, ours may do the same, as when we breathlessly follow a narrative so closely that our thinking keeps pace precisely with the unfolding of the story.

Translation skills

We usually think of translation as a process in which what is said in one language is then said, without loss of meaning, in another. By "language" here is meant natural languages like Spanish and Chinese. But translation is not limited to transmission of meaning from one natural language to another. It can occur among different modes of expression, as when a composer attempts, by means of a tone poem, to tender literary meanings in musical form, or a painter tries to give a title to her work that will be true to the painterly content. No doubt all translation involves an element of interpretation; preservation of meaning is not always assigned the highest order of priority by those doing the translating. But the fact remains that translating skills enable us to shuttle back and forth *among* languages, and this may be no less important than discovering or constructing meanings *within* a given language.

One of the values of learning formal logic is that it requires the learning of rules for the standardization of everyday language so that the complexities of ordinary discourse can be reduced to the simplicities of logical language. This does considerable damage to meaning, but it demonstrates to students that natural language has an underlying musculature that makes possible such pushings and pullings as are involved in inference, causal expressions, and the like, and that natural language can be translated into this rudimentary but powerful logical language. Thus the rules of logical standardization form a paradigm of translation as well as a model that encourages students to carry their thinking proficiencies over from one discipline to the next.

In a pluralistic world composed of diverse communities, some of which overlap others or are nested within others, and each of which has commitments, some of which are local and particularized and others universal, it becomes more and more important to articulate and specify what precisely is being translated into what, what is being converted into what. It is impossible to have an ethics or politics of distribution unless we are clear about the values or meanings involved in the transactions with which we are concerned.

Economic terms like "exchange" and "distribution" have to be employed here, because thinking is a form of productivity, and this entails problems that extend far beyond questions of patents, copyrights, and permissions. For if thinking is a form of productivity, then communal deliberations can be seen as resulting in communal judgments, and a fresh appraisal is needed to determine our entitlements to public or private, shared or unshared values. All the more reason, then, to cultivate thinking skills in the schools.

When thinking is understood as a kind of productivity, then translation can be understood as a form of exchange. When we translate from poetry into music, as a composer does in writing a tone poem, or from body language into ordinary language, we are exchanging and preserving meanings. Indeed, just as reasoning is that form of thinking that preserves *truth* through change, so translation is that form that preserves *meaning* through change.

IS TEACHING REASONING WORTHWHILE?

Just a few years ago, the mammoth testing organizations were assuring us that reasoning could not be taught. This was a self-serving move. Significant portions of their tests involved reasoning, and if they could convince the schools that reasoning was unteachable, there would be no need to worry about the schools preparing students to do better on the tests by teaching them reasoning.

SKILLS AND THEIR ORCHESTRATION

Generations of laborers go by before a specific task or set of tasks is identified. Workers show their skill in the way they perform their

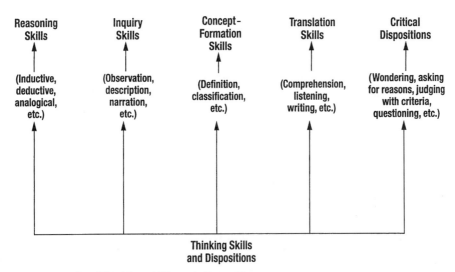

Reasoning Skills	Inquiry Skills	Concept- Formation Skills	Translation Skills	Critical Dispositions
↑	↑	↑	↑	↑
(Inductive, deductive, analogical, etc.)	(Observation, description, narration, etc.)	(Definition, classification, etc.)	(Comprehension, listening, writing, etc.)	(Wondering, asking for reasons, judging with criteria, questioning, etc.)
↑	↑	↑	↑	↑

Thinking Skills and Dispositions

FIGURE 8.4. Thinking skills and dispositions.

tasks. First the tasks are specified, and then the workers turn in their skillful or nonskillful performances. Choreographers design *moves* to be performed by dancers, who perform the moves more or less skillfully. Likewise, athletes are expected to engage in certain actions in accordance with the rules of the game or sport. In baseball, the swing of the bat by the batter is specified by the handbook, and it is then carried out by the batter. The most skillful batters hit the ball where no one can catch it; the least skillful players miss it completely.

So it would seem to be with thinkers. There are various moves that a thinker *could* make, and there are various corresponding moves that a thinker *does* make. The politician who has just lost a race already knows what it is to concede well before she decides to concede, and she decides to concede well before she concedes in her own mind, which generally happens a bit sooner than she utters a concession. Even if Lucy, much to her own surprise, asks Henry if he will marry her, the form of a marriage proposal precedes the asking of Henry of the actual question. It is by means of such moves that the game is played.

The same situation evidently prevails in the case of thinking skills. They are antecedently designed moves skillfully performed. The skill is a matter of the degree of excellence of the performance. Take the mental act of *affirming*, in contrast to *realizing*. To affirm is a simple, zero-sum deed: It would be difficult to do by degrees. Either one does it or one does not. But realizing may be a very slow affair that can occur under very dramatic circumstances. For if by "intuitive" we mean "able to come to a true conclusion with a minimum of evidence," then we can say that some people are intuitive in the sense that they realize amazingly soon what the implications of the scanty evidence actually are.

From what I have been saying, it is apparent that there is a wide range of thinking skills, and for each skill a wide range of performances with regard to their degree of excellence. The skills of the athlete are only roughly comparable to the skills of an investigator involved in an inquiry. Nevertheless, with regard to the *acquisition* of skills, including thinking skills, certain common characteristics may stand out. For example, the skilled person usually acquires the skill as one acquires a habit, in the sense that both skills and habits involve dispositions to act in certain ways. The first way has to do with a peculiar excellence of performance. The second has to do with a certain sameness of performance. But some habits are not acquired deliberately, while skills often are. To learn a skill is to teach oneself a proficiency through persistent *self-correction*. This is what a Sunday golfer must do and it is what a Tiger Woods does do. Thus self-correction, already identified as one of the most characteristic of the defining features of critical thinkers, also plays a key role in skill acquisition.

I have said earlier that thinking skills *develop* out of mental acts. This suggests that if a sizable layer or seedbed of mental acts is lacking, it will be all the more difficult for the skills to grow and flourish. Thus, to *conceptualize* is to perform an important mental act, and *conceptualization* is a major cognitive skill. Thinking skills form more readily when they grow out of childhood experience that is shot through with ideas.

Not that one need be able self-consciously to identify the thinking skills one is employing at the very same moment one is using them. They should be perfected by use or by practice, to the point where they form a "second nature" and can be called into play, like the muscles in the hands of a concert pianist, without one's having to be conscious of them, for they would then form a distraction.

Merely to acquire a set of skills, such as inquiry skills or reasoning skills, will not take one very far: It is necessary to know how and when and where to use them. If an automobile mechanic purchases a kit of tools, we can assume that he already knows how to use them. But the ordinary person lacks the skills of appropriate orchestration that the mechanic, the surgeon, and the orchestra conductor all possess. Consequently, she does not know the *timing* that would be best for her intervention. Presumably this is what very young children learn, along with some values and a vocabulary, from their parents and siblings: a sense of timing and a sense of context. When a skillful writer racks her brains for *le mot juste*, it is probably indicative of a concern for fidelity to the entire context that has already been established, rather than a concern for a word that will make just a particular sentence true.

Thinking skillfully, then, entails a keen appreciation not just of the context in which one is thinking but also of the *quality* of that context. Thus an interior decorator, concerned to add a chair to a room, must take into account not just the furniture that is already there but the quality of the existing arrangement of what is there.

But now we have begun to reach out beyond the paradigm of thinking that is merely *critical*, and we have begun to involve thinking that must be accounted *creative*, as well as thinking that can be called *caring*. Much will have to be said before a case can be made for this tripartite division of modes of thinking, but for the moment we probably see the problem sufficiently clearly if we recognize the usual dependence of creative and caring thinking upon qualitative rather than nonqualitative considerations.

It should be added that although, in one sense, every educational level is the equal of every other, in another sense, education has to be seen as an ascent from the earliest stirrings of consciousness to the most refined states of judgment.

FROM BASIC SKILLS TO ELEMENTARY SCHOOL SUBJECTS

The ultimate basic skills – reading, writing, speaking, and listening – exercise a kind of academic sovereignty over the subject areas that are taught in the elementary school. They are distribution channels or clearinghouses of information and of the means of understanding that information. They are central to cognition.

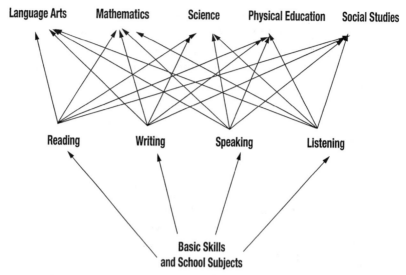

Language Arts   Mathematics   Science   Physical Education   Social Studies

Reading   Writing   Speaking   Listening

Basic Skills
and School Subjects

FIGURE 8.5.

But reading, writing, speaking, and listening, as well as computation, are incredibly sophisticated megaskills. They are orchestrations of vast numbers of highly diversified skills and mental acts that have been developed previously. Reasoning is not another of these megaskills; it is not a fourth R. It is instead, with reference to the basic skills, foundational. It is fundamental to their development.

To the extent that we can make the students' reading, writing, speaking, and listening more critical, we can be sure that they will pass the new advantage along and apply it to the subject areas they are expected to study. Failure to do so could have serious consequences, as if it were some kind of academic embolism.

It should be noted that all four of the basic skills just referred to are also known as "inquiry" skills, and "inquiry" is a term that is used promiscuously, but what is it, and how is it relevant? As one scholar has defined it, inquiry is "the single process of students asking relevant questions about issues to which they do not possess predetermined answers.... Student discovery is key to effective inquiry.... The role of discussion is almost always incorrectly associated by educators with the didactic end of the (inquiry/discovery) continuum, but discussion is a natural outgrowth of inquiry/discovery processes."[12] This use of the term "inquiry" would not be acceptable in some contexts, but in education it can be of major value. It has the merit of connecting discussion and discovery with cognition and education. We need more such definitions, that connect the content of education with the process of education in ways that show their interdependence, just as we need to confront the skills that enable inquiry to take place and not pretend they do not exist. Inquiry without deliberation or discussion, without reasoning or concept-formation or communication skills, would be like putting on a performance of *Hamlet*, but without the cast.

THE BOUNDARIES OF SKILL

Philosophers have always been suspicious of talk of skills and have insisted that intelligent making, saying, and doing are not reducible to a repertoire of skills. Once we know what is to be done, we may do it either skillfully or unskillfully, but how do we know what is to be done? This is not a matter of skill, Aristotle tells us, but a matter of understanding. Understanding is "about things which may become subjects of questioning and deliberation,"[13] and it is the understanding that enables us to make judgments; that is, to decide what is appropriate in a given situation. To have judgment is "the right discrimination of the equitable," and the equitable is "a correction of law where it is defective owing to its universality."[14] So according to Aristotle, it is not skill that governs the adaptation of rule and case to one another or means to ends, but judgment.

For Kant, Aristotle did not go nearly far enough in distinguishing between that which governs and that which obeys. When reason acts in a self-serving fashion, it makes use of skills in accordance with "hypothetical imperatives," so that if a certain end is desired, then the appropriate means for obtaining that end can be specified and skills can be learned to facilitate the desired result. But this is all contingent, Kant argues. Nothing requires me to recognize that some

---

[12] Frank X Sutman, "We Need a Better Understanding of Inquiry in Instruction" *Harvard Education Letter* (September-October, 2000), p. 8.

[13] Aristotle, *Nicomachean Ethics*, 1143a, in Richard McKeon (ed.), *The Basic Works of Aristotle* (New York: Random House, 1941), p. 1032.

[14] Ibid., 1137b (p. 1020).

ends are more important than others, and I am left free to indulge myself however I choose. It is only when we bring our "good will" or moral character into play that we invoke the *categorical* imperative and choose to do what we would like everyone to have to do in our situation. There is only one moral criterion, according to Kant: Only actions done solely for the sake of the moral law are good.[15] When we follow a *hypothetical* imperative, Kant says, even if we are acting *as* duty requires, we are not acting *because* duty requires, and our actions lack moral worth. Skilled performances are precisely of this kind; they lack moral worth to the extent that they are contingent and self-serving.

A contemporary version of the disparagement of talk of skills, if not of skills themselves, is to be found in W. A. Hart's "Against Skills."[16] Hart is nauseated by educational jargon according to which everything becomes a matter of skill: language skills, social skills, moral skills, skills of relevance, skills of loving and caring, skills of leadership, religious skills, imagining skills, and perhaps even skills for coping with innovation and skills of humility. Take reading, Hart says. It is not just a matter of mechanically mastering the left-to-right convention or of decoding the look and sound of the words. Reading involves skills, he argues, but it is not itself a skill. Comprehending and appreciating significance cannot be skills because "it is open to argument whether one has 'read' a certain passage correctly." In order to be able to read well, says Hart, "you have to be able to bring something to your reading. But what you have to bring isn't skills; it's yourself."

An analogous situation prevails with regard to learning to speak, Hart says, and he invokes Wittgenstein. Learning to speak is not mastering a technique or acquiring a skill; it is coming to have something to say. At least this is Rush Rhees's interpretation of Wittgenstein.[17] But Hart is not satisfied with our merely participating in the conversation; we have to bring a perspective of our own. We have to bring

---

[15] Immanuel Kant, *Groundwork of the Metaphysics of Morals* (New York: Harper and Row, 1964).

[16] Hart's article appeared originally in *Oxford Review of Education* 4:2 (1978), 205–16. It was reprinted in *Thinking: The Journal of Philosophy for Children* 5:1 (n.d.), 35–44.

[17] Rush Rhees, *Discussions of Wittgenstein* (London: Routledge and Kegan Paul, 1970), pp. 81–3, 89.

ourselves, and to do this we must *be* someone. Learning to speak is not a matter of what we can skillfully do, but of who we are. If we keep this in mind, we see that skills are peripheral; they are at one remove from the person exercising them. But thinking, reading, and loving are not to be put at one remove from our humanity; according to Hart, they *are* our humanity. The narrating of great writers like D. H. Lawrence is not external and manipulative; great writers concentrate on exploring what they have to say and let the language take care of itself. (I wonder if, by this criterion, Hart would consider Flaubert a great writer.)

There is a definitely Kantian ring to Hart's argument. I have some problem with the dualism whereby he exiles skills to a peripheral realm outside the human, just as I have difficulty swallowing Kant's separation of the technological and the moral; it gives rise to the myth of "value-free" science and technology. It seems to me that to vest morality wholly in persons and to divest it wholly from method-ologies, procedures, and institutions is the way to go if we want to compound our problems rather than resolve them.

But Hart's critique is not to be shrugged off. He is right to insist on a difference between the mastery of the mechanics of reading and what goes on in comprehension, appreciation, interpretation, and evaluation. The first involves technical skills, the criteria for which we know in advance. But in the second instance we are not sure what the criteria are, and this is why Hart says that what a passage says is "open to argument."

Hart's comments on Wittgenstein also bear out, I think, what was expressed at the end of the preceding section with regard to the order of priorities that schooling should establish. There must first be es-tablishment of the human setting – a community of inquiry; second, there must be demonstration that the function of the community is to deliberate and arrive at (or suspend) judgments; and third, schooling should establish the environment in which to cultivate skills and ac-quaint students with procedures. Children learn their first language readily because they are born into a family, which is a form of life that calls forth the learning of language. Children will more readily learn what the schools have to teach *if* the schools too begin by immersing them in a form of life – the community of inquiry – that will stimulate them to respond as persons. From the very first, then, young readers should be taught to evaluate what they read and to argue for their interpretations rather than be confronted with years of mechanical reading before they can be entrusted with the formation of critical judgments.

It should be added that Hart's invocation of Wittgenstein cuts in two ways. There is the Wittgenstein for whom it is the form of life – and not the criteria – that seems relevant, that dictates the form our judgments are to take. But there is also the Wittgenstein (in *On Certainty*) who ponders the question of the relative worth of skills versus rule-gained behavior and comes down on the side of skills. How can we help seeing, in this crucial disjunction, how Kant contrasts acting *as* duty requires and acting *because* duty requires? To Kant, we are virtuous only if we consciously obey the moral law; we are not virtuous if our action happens merely to coincide with rule-governed behavior. But Kant's disjunction I think is too severe: Skill represents a third choice, in which the rule is completely internalized by the practitioner and dissolved in the skill itself. In a sense, skills transcend Kant's distinction, because they represent conduct in which we act both ways, *as* the rule requires and *because* the rule requires.

This leads me in turn to reject Hart's rigid dichotomy between the technical and the human. Skill does not have to fall on either side of the fence. The violinist who plays a sonata skillfully is not therefore doing something that has no relevance to what is human. The very existence of the score presupposes a human product and a human performance. We can no more separate the humanity of the *product* from the person than we can separate the humanity of the creative *process* from the person.

PART FOUR

EDUCATION FOR THE IMPROVEMENT
OF THINKING

9

The Transactive Dimensions of Thinking

A MULTIDIMENSIONAL THINKING APPROACH

For the improvement of thinking in the schools, the most important dimensions of thinking to be cultivated are the critical, the creative, and the caring. A prototype of the critical thinker is the professional, the expert, the model of good judgment. A prototype of the creative thinker is the artist. Some prototypes of the caring thinker are the solicitous parent, the considerate environmental planner, the thoughtful and concerned teacher.

In each of the three cases, it will be assumed that the pedagogy will involve the community of inquiry, while the epistemology of that community will be that of the reflective equilibrium. This equilibrium should be understood in the fallibilistic sense that, in the classroom of the community of inquiry, the aim is not to find an absolute foundation of knowledge, like a bedrock. Instead, there is a constant remaking, improving, revising of all its failing parts in order to maintain the equilibrium. It is not based on a notion of absolute truth. That is why self-correction has to be always part of the inquiry process. Insofar as the inquiry process includes a caring dimension, it is concerned to protect and maintain the equilibrium. And insofar as it includes a creative dimension, it is concerned to look for new solutions and ways to maintain this equilibrium.

There are, of course, differences among the communities. A community of reflective, deliberative inquiry, the kind most likely to foster critical thinking, generally emphasizes such values as *precision* and *consistency.* A community of creative inquiry, as best illustrated by an artist's atelier, tends to stress both technical prowess and adventurous imagination. And a community of caring inquiry, one that cultivates the appreciation of values, is likely to study how such cultivation can best be accomplished and how to live so that the values of what is worthwhile will be disclosed for all to perceive.

When we work, our hands enter into dialogue with one another. Each does what it has to do: One holds while the other shapes or cuts. These behavioral differences are readily observable and describable but not so readily explainable. Similarly with instances of multidimensional thinking: We can distinguish "analytic" from "intuitive" thinking (another pair of terms might do as well), but it would be much more difficult to explain how each functions, and for our present purposes it might not even be particularly profitable to attempt to do so. It may be enough to note for the present that some thinking is criterion-governed and some is governed by values that flood the entire context in which the thinking takes place. Some thinking moves smoothly and routinely, like a train on its tracks; some ranges at will, like a bird in flight, with the result that we see one kind of thinking as linear and explicative and the other as inventive and expansive. Some thinking seems to be purely computational; some seems conjectural, hypothetical, and imaginative. Some thinking is a mere collecting of thoughts that are pressed together mechanically, like a package of figs. In other cases, the thoughts are related to one another organically, each assuming a distinctive role but cooperating with the others in the overall division of labor to give us a more complete picture. Some thinking is quantitative; some is expository, some narrative. The list goes on and on, but it will be enough if we recognize that thinking entails an interpenetration and interbreeding of different forms of mental behavior, which we are free to conceptualize as reasonableness, creativity, and care. Each form of these behaviors is a form of inquiry; put together, the result is not merely additive but multiplicative.

As long as education was considered to be merely a matter of transmitting information about the world from teachers to learners, the way in which that information was processed in transmission – in other words, the way it was *thought about* – seemed of no great consequence. But once the cognitive processing began to take precedence as the forward edge of the educational transaction, it was clear that the old priorities had been worn out and needed to be replaced by a set that was wholly new. For example, while the acquisition of knowledge might still be a worthwhile aim, it was not nearly as worthwhile as the careful honing of the *judgment* with which such knowledge was to be used. And while the use of knowledge could still be construed as what was centrally involved in theoretical understanding, it had become clear that successful education required even more the *practical application* of such knowledge to problematical settings.

We are so transfixed by the implications of the rise of the computer and its impact upon contemporary society that we are distracted from recognizing that this technological shift can be only a symptom of a more general revolution that has been quietly taking place in society. The changes we wish to introduce into human behavior should be the result of laws and policies that govern that behavior. Even more they should be the result of changes in the criteria by means of which we judge that behavior. We can talk all we want to about how the human brain is the consequence of the dexterity of the hand, and subsequently of the tools and the machinery that succeeded the hand. We can describe how the brain is now being affected by the extension of its powers the computer makes possible. The fact remains that thinking is coming to be recognized as the operations center of human activity. Consequently, for better or for worse, the revolution consists in our addressing to people's thinking what we previously had addressed to the people themselves.

The temptation will be great indeed to draw from this last statement the inference that people are to be treated as Cartesian machines: robots piloted by their intellects. This might be true if what I meant by "thinking" was what Descartes meant by it. But this is not the case. To Descartes, the notion of thinking that counts is mathematical and logical thinking. The exclusion of the mind from the body and its attributes – its perceiving, its ways of feeling, its valuing, its creating, its imagining, its acting, and so on – was total and absolute. In contrast, significantly improved thinking – *multidimensional thinking* as I understand it – aims at a balance between the cognitive and the affective, between the perceptual and the conceptual, between

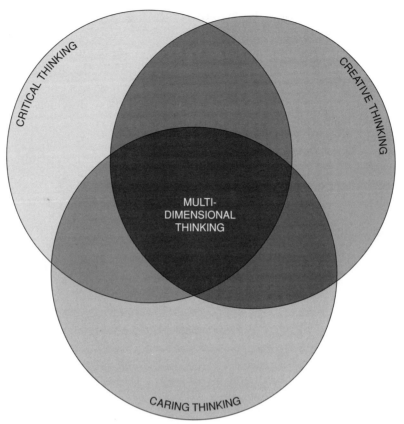

FIGURE 9.1.

the physical and the mental, the rule-governed and the non–rule-governed.

In times past, these distinctions would have been tripartite, and the mind would have been contrasted with the appetites and the senses, or with one's perceptions and one's passions, but always giving the intellect the upper hand, so to speak. The mind was the monarch, and the others merely its ministers, commoners whose overweening aspirations were destined to be repressed by the sovereignty of reason. Time was when any proposal making a case for a more pluralistic or democratic approach was immediately castigated as a brief for anarchy. It was of such notions that ancient Stocism was constructed and the valuational presuppositions of Renaissance writers such as Shakespeare were formed.

In contrast, the trinity of criteria now proposed as prerequisites for multidimensional thinking are or should be thoroughly equalitarian. Unless an instance of thinking satisfies all three of these criteria, it cannot be considered excellent. The three aspects of thinking to which these criteria apply are the critical, the creative, and the caring aspect. The challenge faced in this book has to do first with the lack of accord one encounters in describing these three features as dimensions of thinking – that is, as critical thinking, creative thinking, and caring thinking. In the case of critical thinking, the opposition one meets is relatively negligible. With respect to creative thinking, the opposition may allow itself to be sufficiently won over as to grant the term a grudging acceptance. By far the foremost objections have to do with the notion of caring thinking, for caring, in the diverse senses in which it is used here, is ordinarily thought of as falling in the affective rather than in the cognitive camp.

The second challenge has to do with the proposal to treat these three aspects of thinking as of equal significance. This is in sharp contrast to the hierarchical approach that ranks the purely theoretical over that which is practical and applied and that ranks the general and the abstract over anything that manifests itself only in its particularity.

At this point, one would be entitled to ask what the educational significance might be of granting the contentions that I have just been describing. So what if critical, creative, and caring thinking are to be counted as equal instances of multidimensional thinking to be encouraged at all levels of education? What difference would it make? How can this difference be taught?

In teaching for multidimensional thinking, one must be on one's guard not to give the impression to students that critical thinking is equal to the whole of thinking. Likewise, one should not give the impression that the three different modalities of thinking are independent rather than in continual transaction with each other. For this reason, it is helpful for the teacher to inquire of the class what instances of creative thinking in the chapter under discussion they can point out, or what sorts of caring do the characters in this episode manifest. The teacher will recognize that this takes deep reading on the part of the students. They have to be able to infer that A's persistent demanding of explanations expresses her caring for understanding; B's frequent yielding expresses his need for acceptance; C's insistence upon precision and consistency reveals her concern for the instruments of inquiry; and D's habit of interrupting others may indicate a lack of respect for others in the community. The teacher must encourage students to look beneath the more superficial levels of discourse to discover what these levels conceal. Thus a doctor's prescription, brief and abstract though it may be, may hide a passionate commitment on that doctor's part to heal the afflicted. A poem about a cloud may contain only meager information about the cloud but may betray nevertheless an intense love of language. Our behaviors, our utterances, our inventions – whatever we make, say, or do – disclose how much we value, how much we appreciate, how we enjoy, how we love, but give only the faintest hint that these are all species of caring. (There are a thousand verbs that are indicative of *saying*, but we do not use them. We prefer to use the overworked phrases "he said" and "she said." But, though there may be a thousand terms that indicate species of caring, we prefer to employ them rather than the generic term.) Teaching of creative and caring thinking requires an enormous vigilance on the teacher's part *not* to overlook the floodplain of emotion in which the writing in question stands or the flow of care that is an essential part of our experience.

For the schools to be committed to eliciting from each student an equilibrium among the critical, creative, and caring aspects of thinking would result, it seems to me, in a dramatic change in the nature of education. The present pedagogical techniques that seek the critical at the expense of the creative and caring would themselves have to be excluded. A classroom would *have* to be a community of inquiry that facilitates creative and caring thinking. It could not be a factory for the production of solely intellectual operations, wholly indifferent to or actually hostile to the consideration, respect, and appreciation that the members of the class might have for each other or for the subject to be studied. Granted, we need to know a great deal more than we know right now about how to move away from the regimentation of thinking that is today characteristic of education and toward that liberation and restructuring of feelings and values and meanings that ought to be characteristic of education. Nevertheless, one has a sense of forward movement these days, an impression that we are ratcheting our way beyond the trade school mentality that can conceive of education only as preparation for tiers upon tiers of pigeonholes in a multitiered society. What is said in this book represents an effort to make a contribution to that forward movement, by specifying some of the concepts and criteria that are indispensable to the devising of an education that can do justice to the spirit of humanity's greatest discoveries and inventions.

THE RIGHT TO THINKING CAPABILITY

It is well-established throughout the world that children have the right to physical education, a right that will guide and develop their physical growth. They also are thought to have a right to literacy, for it is through reading and writing that we can become connected with our society, our culture, and our civilization, as well as the society, culture, and civilization of other peoples.

It is less clear that children have a right to the development of their thinking capabilities, other than what occurs to them as they move from one educational level to the next. It is not clear, judging by the words and deeds of some of us, that children are to be seen as having thinking rights, that is, rights not just to acceptable reading and writing skills, but rights to standards that go beyond mere acceptability: to reasonableness, judiciousness, imaginativeness, and appreciativeness. Instead, we settle for a small number of minimal literacy standards, such as relevance and consistency, and fail to press for the much higher standards of children's thinking capabilities. And yet children do have a right to perform up to these higher standards, so that they can bring their potentials into closer connection with the requirements of modern communal life.

If the human musculature is neglected, the individual becomes progressively weakened and cannot engage in the self-care that a member of society is expected to engage in. Just as we have a right to physical strengthening, we have a right to moral strengthening, so that we can engage in moral self-criticism, self-correction, and self-control. Likewise we have a right to creative and emotional strengthening, so that we can think reliably and resourcefully, and so that we can meet the trials of life with stamina and resiliency.

In educating for the improvement of thinking in an inquiry-driven society, critical thinking, creative thinking, and caring thinking enable us to identify the primary aspect of its educational process. In such a

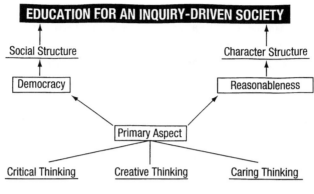

FIGURE 9.2.

society, two most important regulative ideas have to be considered: democracy and reasonableness. These are the essential components of the educational process. By "primary aspect" is meant not the whole of the educational process – in the sense of the sum of its parts – but the network of policies, principles, and procedures to which we appeal when we organize the structure of that process.[1] In this sense, we can consider *democracy* as a regulative idea for the development of the social structure, while *reasonableness* is a regulative idea for the development of the character structure, either of the individual citizen or of a particular procedure of a society.

---

[1] For a brief explanation of the concept of *primary aspect*, see pp. 243–4 in this book.

10

Education for Critical Thinking

CRITICAL THINKING: WHAT IT CAN BE

Outstanding among the intellectual virtues treasured in the ancient world were knowledge and wisdom. Knowledge was needed for cases in which the required decisions could be made by rational means, such as the relationship between cause and effect or between means and end. But wisdom was necessary for cases that were rationally undecidable and where what had to be relied on instead were Solomonic judgments.

In highly stable, tradition-bound societies, knowledge was often conceived of as a stockpile of truths transmitted from the older to the younger generations. It was thought of as a body of eternal verities, perennially applicable to an unchanging world. In times of change, however, traditional knowledge was likely to become inapplicable or obsolete. What was emphasized instead were intellectual flexibility and resourcefulness. Wisdom was cultivated, by the Stoics and others, in preparation for whatever might happen, whether for good or for ill.

We no longer divide things up the way the ancients did. With modern experimental science, the mountains of knowledge accumulated in the past are no longer looked upon with awe. And the notion of wisdom seems more remote than ever.

On the other hand, we are ready to acknowledge that past experience is not always a reliable guide to the future, with the result that judgments of probability must be made. Yet it is precisely in cases like these that we are most prone to jump to conclusions and to make sweeping generalizations that reveal our biases and prejudices. Nor is our logical understanding infallible, since logic fits only imperfectly our everyday language and the world that surrounds us. We are constantly called upon to make reasonable judgments that neither our reason nor our experience prepares us to make.

As I have already said, in recent years we have become more conscious of the profound abyss separating the thinking that the schools have prepared us to engage in and the decisions that we are called upon to make in everyday life. And we have become aware of how dangerous it is to hold uncritically such knowledge as we do possess. Consequently, there has been a turn in recent education toward critical thinking.

What is known as "critical thinking" is not altogether new, just as experimental science did not originate in just the past four centuries. Efforts to improve the quality and quantity of thinking, like those aimed at improving the quality and quantity of knowledge, are probably coextensive with human history itself.

Despite the ongoing nature of this struggle, there are periods in our past that are characterized by remarkable advances in both fields of inquiry. It is well-known that the seventeenth century witnessed an almost explosive development of theoretical and experimental science. What is less well-known is that during the same period there was also a determined effort to strengthen the quality and quantity of thinking. Indeed, the arch exponents of the new science were as often as not to be found with one foot in each camp. Galileo's *Dialogue Concerning the Two Great World-Systems* is a commentary on the method of thinking as well as on the method of science, as are the *Rules for the Direction of the Mind* of Descartes and Spinoza's *On the Improvement of the Understanding*, not to mention the important work of Bacon. One is led to suspect that the major thinkers of the period were hedging their bets, for they were not altogether confident that the future lay with the improvement of scientific inquiry and not with the improvement of reasoning, concept-formation, and judgment.

Nor can it be denied that there were many, such as Erasmus, who misread the promise of science and instead sought to eliminate the flaws in our thinking due to prejudices, stereotypes, fallacies, ambiguities, appeals to emotion, and so on. What was needed, according to these thinkers, was not the experimental method of the new science, but some mental regimen or hygiene that people could impose upon themselves so as to immunize themselves against the vicissitudes of bad thinking.[1]

Now the advocates of scientific inquiry could not escape the fact that there was a schism in their own ranks. It was not a quarrel but a difference of emphasis. There were those who thought of the knowledge they sought and acquired as pure; there were others who unrepentantly acknowledged that their quest was only for knowledge that could be applied. Those who considered themselves to be representatives of pure science disdained dirtying their hands with practical applications of what they knew. But those in the professions – doctors, architects, engineers, jurists, and the like – recognized that their standings in the professions were based not on the thoroughness of their knowledge but on their judgment: the facility with which they could put their knowledge to appropriate use.

If scholars stressed the justifiability of their convictions, professionals stressed the justifiability of their *actions*. Certainly, each appealed to accepted criteria, evidence, and modes of inductive and deductive reasoning to provide the warrant for what they asserted or did. However, professionals could also point to a by-product of the application of their knowledge, which afforded their approach a particular attractiveness. The point can be grasped simply by recalling Charles Peirce's 1878 definition of the pragmatic principle: that the meaning of an idea was to be found in the practical consequences to which it led.[2] An illustration Peirce offers is the concept of hardness. The meaning of the concept, he says, is to be found in the "scratch test." Diamonds are harder than glass if diamonds scratch glass but glass cannot scratch diamonds. And so with any idea: To prevent

[1] See Antoine Arnauld's *The Art of Thinking*, also known as the "Port Royal Logic," originally published in 1662. There is good reason to believe that a fair number of philosophers, over the following three centuries, received their education in logic from his work.

[2] See Charles S. Peirce, "How to Make Our Ideas Clear," in Charles S. Peirce, *Selected Writings*, ed. Philip P. Wiener (New York: Dover Publications, 1958), pp. 113–36.

the idea from becoming a meaningless abstraction, consider how to demonstrate its practical bearings.

Educators sympathetic to students' claims that classroom materials were meaningless and irrelevant perked up when they realized that the pragmatic principle could have a special significance in their schools. Students would think better if they could be provided with conditions that would encourage the application of their thinking to the world in which they lived. The attraction that would spur them on would be their discovery of the meanings of the ideas they were attempting to master.

Still another major consideration of critical thinking needs to be addressed. It has to do with the fact that generalizations, universals, principles, and the like can be ever so reliable, and yet they may seem unduly rigid and schematic when one confronts a particular, concrete situation with its own individual composition and its own unique quality. Aristotle pointed this out when discussing the difference between justice and equity in the *Nichomachean Ethics*. Some situations are universal, and principles apply to them with certainty. Other contexts are special, and our knowledge applies to them only approximately and only probably. (Aristotle even goes so far as to say that equity is actually superior to some forms of justice.[3]) Advocates of better thinking have usually pointed out that such thinking would generally involve an intense sensitivity to contextual individuality. The Aristotelian emphasis on the need to balance justice and equity can be generalized by the contention that rationality needs to be tempered by judgment – the sense of the appropriate, whether in the proportionate adjustment of parts to wholes, of means to ends, or of any other relationship.

I have been attempting to show that what is today called critical thinking is only the latest version of long-standing concerns that have accompanied the spread of civilization, to which have been added more recent concerns about the adequacy of our thinking to the increasingly difficult tasks at hand. Thus, the spread of democracy has made us aware of how important it is that democratic citizens think

---

[3] Aristotle, *Nichomachean Ethics*, 1137b1–1138a1. Aristotle says that the equitable is "not better than absolute justice but better than the error that arises from the absoluteness of the statement."

flexibly but responsibly. If they do not, they are ready prey for authoritarian and conformitarian propaganda. Critical thinking can provide
a degree of protection against the less subtle forms of brainwashing.
Also, the emergence of universally mandated education has made us
realize that traditional education often fostered an uncritical acceptance on the student's part. Not to teach a discipline with attention to
critical thinking, many people now believe, has become equivalent
to not teaching it at all.

If we want to foster and strengthen critical thinking in the schools
and colleges, we would do well to keep in mind the persistent concerns to which it has been addressed. We also need a clear conception of what critical thinking can be. Therefore, it will be very useful
to know its defining features, its characteristic outcomes, and the
underlying conditions that make it possible. Let us begin with the
outcomes.

The outcomes of critical thinking are judgments

If we consult current definitions of critical thinking, we cannot help
being struck by the fact that the authors often stress the *outcomes* of
such thinking but generally fail to note its essential characteristics.
What is more, the outcomes that are specified tend to be limited to
solutions and *decisions*. Thus, one writer defines critical thinking as
"the mental processes, strategies and representations people use to
solve problems, make decisions and learn new concepts."[4] Another
conceives of critical thinking as "reasonable reflective thinking that
is focused on deciding what to believe and do."[5]

These definitions provide us with insufficient enlightenment; the
outcomes (solutions, decisions, acquisitions of concepts) are too
narrow, and the defining characteristics (reasonable, reflective) they
suggest are too vague. For example, if critical thinking is whatever
thinking it is that results in decisions, then deciding what doctor to

---

[4] Robert Sternberg, "Critical Thinking: Its Nature, Measurement, and Improvement,"
in Frances R. Link (ed.), *Essays on the Intellect* (Alexandria, Va.: ASCD, 1985),
p. 46.
[5] Robert H. Ennis, "A Taxonomy of Critical Thinking Dispositions and Abilities," in
Joan Boykoff Baron and Robert J. Sternberg (eds.), *Teaching Thinking Skills: Theory
and Practice* (New York: Freeman, 1987), p. 10.

go to by picking a name at random out of a phone book would have to count as critical thinking. *We must broaden the outcomes, identify the defining characteristics, and show the connection between them.*

It was suggested earlier that the present concern for critical thinking is reminiscent of the ancient concern for wisdom. It would be worthwhile to return briefly to that point. What is wisdom conceived to be? Phrases commonly taken to be synonymous are "intelligent judgment," "good judgment," and "judgment tempered by experience." We can hardly fail to notice how the term *judgment* keeps cropping up.[6]

But what is judgment? Here again, recourse to equivalent expressions suggests that it is the forming of opinions, estimates, or conclusions. It therefore includes such things as solving problems, making decisions, and learning new concepts, but it is more inclusive and more general. Every outcome of inquiry is a judgment.

As for wisdom, it is generally explained that those who are wise exercise *good judgment*. What is the difference between mere judgment and good judgment? This distinction is not an unfamiliar one; we commonly distinguish between mere singing and singing well, between mere living and living well. Nor is it unusual to distinguish between mere thinking and thinking well.

The line of inquiry I have been following is one that shows good judgment to be the modern descendant of the ancient notion of wisdom and to be, at the same time, the chief characteristic of critical thinking. Perhaps the point we have come to, where we want to know how ordinary judgment and good judgment are different, is a good place to pause and consider some illustrations.

Wherever knowledge and experience are not merely possessed but *applied to practice*, we are likely to see clear instances of judgment. Architects, lawyers, and doctors are professionals whose work constantly involves the making of judgments. The same is true of composers, painters, and poets. It is true of teachers and farmers and theoretical physicists as well; all of them have to make judgments as part of the practice of their occupations and their lives. It is

---

[6] For a penetrating discussion of judgment, see Justus Buchler, *Toward a General Theory of Human Judgment* (New York: Columbia University Press, 1951).

again true of any of us when we are in moral situations: We have to make moral judgments. There are practical, productive, and theoretical judgments, as Aristotle would have put it. Insofar as we consistently make such judgments well, we can be said to behave wisely.

Good professionals make good judgments about their own practice as well as about the subject matter of their practice. A good doctor not only makes good diagnoses of patients and prescribes well for them but also makes good judgments about medicine and his or her ability to practice it. Good judgment takes everything relevant into account, including itself.

A judgment, then, is a determination – of thinking, of speech, of action, or of creation. A gesture, such as the wave of a hand, can be a judgment; a metaphor like "John is a worm" is a judgment; an equation like $e = mc^2$ is a judgment. They are likely to be *good* judgments if they are the products of *skillfully performed* acts guided or facilitated by appropriate instruments and procedures.

Critical thinking is applied thinking. Therefore, it is not just process – it seeks to develop a product. This involves more than attaining understanding: It means producing something, said, made, or done. It involves using knowledge to bring about reasonable change. Minimally, the product is a judgment; maximally, it is putting that judgment into practice.

There is another sense in which critical thinking develops a product. Critical thinking is involved in all responsible interpretation (the production of meaning) and in all responsible translation (the preservation of meaning). Just as book, film, and music reviews are products about products, judgments about judgments, all instances of critical thinking are thinking about thinking, rather than thinking about some mute subject matter. A critical paleontologist thinks about life forms of the past and about *how* people have thought about life forms of the past. A critical geologist considers, in addition to rocks, the assumptions people have made in their thinking about rocks. In this fashion, the critical thinking that accompanies every discipline helps refine the end products – the meanings – that that discipline produces. If we now look at the process of critical thinking and identify its essential characteristics, we will be in a better position to understand its relationship to judgment. I will argue that critical thinking is *thinking that* (1) *facilitates judgment because it* (2) *relies on criteria,*[7] (3) *is self-correcting, and* (4) *is sensitive to context.*

Critical thinking relies on criteria

We suspect an association between the terms "critical" and "criteria" because they resemble each other and have a common ancestry. Also, we are all familiar with book, music, and film critics, and it is not uncommon to assume that those among them whose criticism is considered excellent are those who employ reliable criteria.

We are also aware of a relationship between criteria and judgments, for a *criterion* is often defined as "a rule or principle utilized in the making of judgments." It seems reasonable to conclude, therefore, that there is some sort of logical connection between critical thinking and criteria and judgment. The connection, of course, is to be found in the fact that critical thinking is reliable thinking, and skills themselves cannot be defined without criteria by means of which allegedly skillful performances can be evaluated. So critical thinking is reliable thinking that both employs criteria and can be assessed by appeal to criteria.

Furthermore, it might be profitable to consider what uncritical thinking might be. Surely uncritical thinking suggests thinking that is flabby, amorphous, arbitrary, specious, haphazard, and unstructured. The fact that critical thinking can rely upon criteria suggests that it is well-founded, structured, and reliable thinking. It seems to be defensible and convincing. How does this happen?

Whenever we make a claim or utter an opinion, we are vulnerable unless we can somehow back it up. We should therefore ask ourselves questions such as these: "When our opinions come under fire, to what do we appeal?" "When our claims are contested, what do we invoke?" "When our assertions are not convincing, what do we cite to strengthen them?" In attempting to answer questions like these, we are led to see that claims and opinions must be supported by reasons. What is the connection between reasons and criteria?

---

7 Useful discussions of the nature of criteria are to be found in Michael Anthony Slote, "The Theory of Important Criteria," *Journal of Philosophy* 63:8 (April 1966), 221–4, and Michael Scriven, "The Logic of Criteria," *Journal of Philosophy* 56 (October 1959), 857–68.

Criteria *are* reasons; they are one kind of reason, a particularly *reliable* kind. When we have to sort things out descriptively or evaluationally – and these are two very important tasks – we have to use the most reliable reasons we can find, and these are classificatory and evaluational criteria. Criteria may or may not have a high level of public acceptance, but they have a high level of acceptance and respect in the community of expert inquirers. The competent use of such respected reasons is a way of establishing the objectivity of our prescriptive, descriptive, and evaluative judgments. Thus, architects will judge a building by employing such criteria as *utility, safety,* and *beauty*; magistrates make judgments with the aid of such criteria as *legality* and *illegality*; and critical thinkers rely upon such time-tested criteria as *validity, evidential warrant,* and *consistency*. Any area of practice – like the examples just given of architectural practice, judicial practice, and cognitive practice – should be able to cite the criteria by which that practice is guided.

The intellectual domiciles we inhabit are often of flimsy construction; we can strengthen them by learning to reason more logically. But this will help little if the grounds or foundations upon which they rest are spongy. We need to rest our claims and opinions, as well as the rest of our thinking, upon a footing as firm as possible.

Here, then is a brief list of the sorts of things we invoke or appeal to and that therefore represent specific kinds of criteria:

- Standards
- Laws, bylaws, rules, regulations, charters, canons, ordinances, guidelines, directions
- Precepts, requirements, specifications, gauges, stipulations, boundaries, limits, conditions, parameters
- Conventions, norms, regularities, uniformities, covering generalizations
- Principles, assumptions, presuppositions, definitions
- Ideals, purposes, goals, aims, objectives, intuitions, insights
- Tests, credentials, factual evidence, experimental findings, observations
- Methods, procedures, policies, measures

All of these are instruments that can be employed in the making of judgments. They are part of the apparatus of rationality. Isolated in categories in a taxonomy, as they are here, they appear inert and sterile. But when they are at work in the process of inquiry, they can function dynamically – and critically.

It has already been noted that by means of logic we can validly *extend* our thinking; by means of reasons such as criteria, we can justify and *defend* it. The improvement of student thinking depends heavily on students' ability to identify and cite good reasons for the opinions they utter. Students can be brought to realize that for a reason to be called good it must be *relevant* to the opinion in question and *stronger* (in the sense of being more readily accepted or assumed to be true) than the opinion in question.

Since the school or college is a locus of inquiry, procedures employed therein must be defensible, just as job applicants are provided with specifications for hiring or promotion. When assigning grades to students, teachers must be prepared to justify such grades by citing the reasons – that is, the criteria – that were employed in arriving at the judgments at issue. It will hardly do for the teacher to claim that a judgment was arrived at intuitively or to say that criteria were unnecessary and irrelevant. Critical thinking is *cognitive accountability*.[8] When teachers openly state the criteria they employ, they encourage students to do likewise. By providing models of *intellectual responsibility*, teachers invite students to assume responsibility for their own thinking and, in a larger sense, for their own education.

This does not mean that all aspects of our lives are always and necessarily occasions for inquiry. There are things we prize that we may not care to appraise; there are people we esteem whom we may not want to estimate. Where the harm done to intimacy and privacy

---

[8] I see no inconsistency between urging "cognitive accountability" (i.e., feeling an obligation to supply reasons for stated opinions) and urging the development of intellectual autonomy among students. If providing students with cognitive skills is a form of empowerment, such increased powers entail increased responsibilities, especially to and for oneself. There are times when we cannot let other people do our thinking for us, and we must think for ourselves. And we must learn to think for ourselves by thinking for ourselves; other people cannot instruct us in how to do it, although they can put us in a community of inquiry where it becomes a relatively easy thing to do. The point is that students must be encouraged to become reasonable for their own good (i.e., as a step toward their own autonomy) and not just for our good (i.e., because the growing rationalization of the society requires it).

outweighs the benefits to be derived from such evaluations, the call for criteria and standards may well be ignored. In any event, if there are matters about which we do not care to reflect publicly, the drawing of such boundary lines should be as far as possible of our own choosing.

Metacriteria and megacriteria

When we have to select among criteria, we must of course rely on other criteria to do so. Some criteria serve this purpose better than others and can therefore be said to operate as *metacriteria*. For example, when it was earlier pointed out that criteria are especially reliable reasons and that good reasons are those that reveal strength and relevance, this is another way of saying that *reliability, strength,* and *relevance* are important metacriteria. Others that might be cited are *coherence, precision,* and *consistency*.

Some criteria are of a very high level of generality and are often presupposed, either explicitly or implicitly, whenever critical thinking takes place. Thus, the notion of knowledge presupposes the criterion of *truth*, and so wherever something is said to be knowledge, the claim also being made is that it is in some sense true. In this sense, philosophical domains such as epistemology, ethics, and aesthetics do not dictate the criteria relevant to them; it is rather the other way around: The criteria define the domains. Epistemology consists of judgments to which truth and falsity are relevant; ethics comprises judgments to which right and wrong are relevant; and aesthetics contains judgments to which beautiful and not-beautiful are relevant. *Truth, right, wrong, just, good, beautiful* – all of these are regulative ideas of such vast scope that we should probably consider them *megacriteria*. And they in turn are instances of the great galactic criterion of *meaning*.

Criteria as bases of comparison

One of the primary functions of criteria is to provide a basis for comparisons. When an isolated, context-free comparison is made and no basis or criterion is given (as in the case of, say, "Tokyo is better than New York"), confusion results. Or if several competing criteria might be applicable (as when someone says, "Tokyo is larger than New York," and we don't know whether the speaker means larger in area or larger in population), the situation can be equally confusing. Just as opinions should generally be backed up by reasons, comparisons should generally be accompanied by criteria or expressed in contexts that can be as illuminating as criteria.

Sometimes criteria are introduced informally and extemporaneously, as when someone remarks that Tuesday's weather was good compared with Monday's, while Wednesday's weather was bad compared with Monday's. In this instance, Monday's weather is being used as an informal criterion. The same is the case if someone says, "Compared with a dog, an elephant is large, but compared with a dog, a mouse is small"; this case also involves the informal, impromptu use of criteria. Even figurative language can be understood as involving the use of informal criteria. Thus, such open and closed similes as "The school was like an army camp" and "The school was as regimented as an army camp" use the army camp as an informal criterion against which to measure the orderliness of the school.

On the other hand, when criteria are considered by an authority or by general consent to be a basis of comparison, we may speak of them as "formal" criteria. When we compare the quantities of liquid in two tanks in terms of gallons, we are employing the unit of the gallon on the say-so of the Bureau of Standards. The gallon measure at the bureau is the institutionalized paradigm to which our gallon measure is comparable.

So things can be compared by means of more or less formal criteria. But there is also the distinction between comparing things with one another and comparing them with an ideal standard, a distinction Plato addresses in *The Statesman*.[9] For example, in grading test papers, we may compare a student's performance with the performances of other students in the class (using "the curve" as a criterion), or we may compare it with the standard of an error-free performance. In

---

[9] The Stranger remarks to Young Socrates, "We must posit two types and two standards of greatness and smallness. . . . The standard of relative comparison will remain, but we must acknowledge a second standard, which is a standard of comparison with the due measure" ("Statesman" 283e, in Edith Hamilton and Huntington Cairns [eds.], *Plato: The Collected Dialogues* [Princeton: N.J.: Princeton University Press, 1961], p. 1051).

baseball, we may compare pitchers' averages with one another, or we may compare their performances with what is entailed in pitching a perfect game – a no-hit, no-walk performance.[10] Standards represent the degree to which a given criterion must be satisfied. Thus, passing arithmetic is a criterion for graduation, while getting 70 or more in the final examination is an example of a standard for the satisfaction of that criterion.

The indispensability of standards

"Standards" and "criteria" are often used interchangeably in ordinary discourse. It would appear, however, that standards represent a vast special kind of criteria. It is vast because the concept *standard* can be understood in many different ways. There is the interpretation cited in the preceding paragraph, where we were talking about an ideal standard or a standard of perfection. There are, in contrast, standards as minimal levels of performance, as in the oft-heard cry, "We must not lower our standards!" There is a sense in which standards are conventions of conduct: "When in Rome, do as the Romans do" provides a conventional standard for our guidance. There is also the sense in which standards are the units of measurement defined authoritatively by a Bureau of Standards.

There is, of course, a certain arbitrariness about even the most reliable standards, such as units of measurement, in that we are free to define them as we like. We could, if we liked, define a yard as containing fewer inches than it now does. But the fact is that we prefer such units, once defined, to be unchanging; they are so much more reliable that way. When concepts are vague, arbitrariness may be unavoidable. Thus the concept of maturity is vague; it lacks clear cut-off points. But once the voting age is set at, say eighteen, a precise decision procedure is available for deciding who is and who is not eligible to vote.

Criteria – and particularly standards among them – are among the most valuable instruments of rational procedure. Teaching students

---

[10] For a contemporary interchange regarding comparison of things with one another versus comparison of things with an ideal, see Gilbert Ryle, "Perceiving," in *Dilemmas* (New York: Cambridge University Press, 1966), pp. 93–102, and D. W. Hamlyn, *The Theory of Knowlege* (London: Doubleday and Macmillan, 1970), pp. 16–21.

to recognize and use them is an essential aspect of the teaching of critical thinking.

The quest for critical thinking is likely to mean a search for reasons of greater and greater leverage – and this in turn may make criteria a glamorous elite among logical operators. That seems to be the inference to be drawn when teachers urge students to emulate professionals and found their thinking upon firm criteria.[11]

Critical thinking is self-corrective

Much of our thinking moves along uncritically. Our thought unrolls impressionistically, from association to association, with little concern for either truth or validity and with even less concern for the possibility that it might be erroneous.

Among the many things we may reflect upon is our own thinking. We can think about our own thinking, but we can do so in a way that is still quite uncritical. And so, granted that "metacognition" is thinking about thinking, it need not be equivalent to critical thinking.

The most characteristic feature of inquiry, according to C. S. Peirce, is that it aims to discover its own weaknesses and rectify what is at fault in its own procedures. Inquiry, then, is *self-correcting*.[12]

---

[11] Ludwig Wittgenstein, *Philosophical Investigations* (Oxford: Blackwell Publisher, 1953). See in particular I, para. 242. Needless to say, virtually all of Wittgenstein's writings allude in one way or another to the problem of criteria. A remark like this, in *On Certainty*, is characteristic: "some propositions are exempt from doubt, are as it were like hinges on which those turn" (para. 341). What better description of the mode of operation of criteria could there be than that they are the hinges on which our judgments turn? A sustained backward glance on criteria would start with Plato, who is persistently intrigued with the topic, while a focus on the near distance would take into account such works as Urmson's "On Grading" (*Mind* 59 [1950], 145–69) and Crawshay-Williams's *Methods and Criteria of Reasoning* (London: Routledge and Kegan Paul, 1957), particularly pp. 26–40 and 235–62. The Urmson article has been persistently seminal, as is shown by two of its impressive progeny: Such as Bruce Vermazen's "Comparing Evaluations of Works of Art," in W. E. Kennick (ed.), *Art and Philosophy*, 2d ed. (New York: St. Martin's, 1979), pp. 707–18.

[12] C. S. Peirce, in "Ideals of Conduct," *Collected Papers of Charles Sanders Peirce*, ed. Charles Hartshorne and Paul Weiss (Cambridge, Mass.: Harvard University Press, 1931–5), vol. 1, discusses the connection between self-correcting inquiry, self-criticism, and self-control.

One of the most important advantages of converting the classroom into a community of inquiry (in addition to the undoubted improvement of moral climate it brings about) is that the members of the community begin looking for and correcting each other's methods and procedures. Consequently, insofar as each participant is able to internalize the methodology of the community as a whole, each is able to become self-correcting in his or her own thinking.

Critical thinking displays sensitivity to context

An astute copyeditor going over an essay prior to publication will make innumerable corrections that can be justified by appeals to recognized canons of grammar and spelling. Idiosyncratic spellings are rejected in favor of uniformity, as are grammatical irregularities. But stylistic idiosyncrasies on the author's part may be treated with considerably greater tolerance and sensitivity. This is because the editor knows that the style is not a matter of writing mechanics; it has to do with the context of what is being written as well as with the person of the author. At the same time, thinking that is sensitive to context involves recognition of:

1. *Exceptional or irregular circumstances.* For example, we normally examine statements for truth or falsity independent of the character of the speaker. But in a court trial, the character of a witness may become a relevant consideration.
2. *Special limitations, contingencies, or constraints wherein normally acceptable reasoning might find itself prohibited.* An example is the rejection of certain Euclidean theorems, such as that parallel lines never meet, in non-Euclidean geometries.
3. *Overall configurations.* A remark taken out of context may seem to be flagrantly in error, but in the light of the discourse taken as a whole it can appear valid and proper, or vice versa. Critical thinking in this sense is a descendent of Aristotle's awareness that individual situations need to be examined on their own terms and not forced into some Procrustean bed of general rules and regulations: "For when the thing is indefinite

the rule also is indefinite, like the lead rule used in making the Lesbian moulding; the rule adapts itself to the shape of the stone and is not rigid, and so too the decree is adapted to the facts."[13]

Critical thinking is thinking that is sensitive to particularities and uniqueness. It is the very opposite of that kind of casuistry that forces general rules upon individual cases, whether such rules are appropriate or not. It follows that critical thinking is hostile to all stereotyping; and since such stereotyping is the mechanism through which biased thinking operates, to all prejudice. There is a close alliance between critical thinking and informal logic, inasmuch as the latter deals with inferential reasoning that does not have certain conclusions but merely probable ones and does not claim the universality that is claimed by, say, deduction. The informal logician strives to identify the many fallacies to which thinking is prone, and to identify as well those individual cases that are not fallacious. The informal logician will examine the many varieties of inductive and analogical reasoning but will also give thought to the logical basis of figurative language, as for instance in simile and metaphor.

4. *The possibility that evidence is atypical.* An example is a case of overgeneralizing about national voter preferences based on a tiny regional sample of ethnically and occupationally homogeneous individuals.

5. *The possibility that some meanings do not translate from one context or domain to another.* There are terms and expressions for which there are no precise equivalents in other languages and whose meanings are therefore wholly context-specific.

With regard to *thinking with criteria* and *sensitivity to context*, a suitable illustration might be an exercise or assignment that involves the application of a particular criterion to a set of fictional situations. Suppose the criterion in question is *fairness*, which is itself a way of construing the still broader criterion of justice. One form that fairness assumes is *taking turns*. Look at an exercise taken from *Wondering at*

---

[13] *Nichomachean Ethics*, 1138 3 1.

Taking Turns: Exercise from "Wondering at the World"

There are times when people engage in sharing. For example, they go to a movie and share the pleasure of looking at the movie together. Or they can share a piece of cake by each taking half.

In other cases, however, simultaneous sharing is not so easily accomplished. If two people ride a horse, someone has to ride in front. They can take turns riding in front, but they can't ride in front at the same time. Children understand this very well. They recognize that certain procedures must be followed in certain ways.

For example, ask your students to discuss the number of ways they "take turns" in the classroom during the ordinary day. They take turns washing the blackboard, going to the bathroom, going to the cloakroom, and passing out the papers. On the playground, they take turns at bat, they take turns lining up for basketball, and they take turns at the high bar.

Ask your students what they think the connection is between "taking turns" and "being fair." The resulting discussion should throw light on the fact that sometimes being fair involves the way children are to be treated simultaneously, while at other times it involves the way they are to be treated sequentially. For example, if it is one child's birthday and there is going to be a party with cupcakes, there should be at least one cupcake for every child. This is being fair simultaneously. Later, if you want to play "Pin the Tail on the Donkey," children should sequentially take turns in order to be fair. (The prospect of everyone *simultaneously* being blindfolded and searching about with a pin boggles the mind.)

---

the World,[14] the instructional manual to accompany *Kio and Gus*,[15] a Philosophy for Children program for children nine to ten years old.

[14] Matthew Lipman and Ann Margaret Sharp, *Wondering at the World* (Upper Montclair, N.J.: IAPC, 1986), pp. 226–99.
[15] Matthew Lipman, *Kio and Gus* (Upper Montclair, N.J.: IAPC, 1982).

Exercise: The appropriate or inappropriate interpretation of "taking turns."

		Appropriate	Not Appropriate	?
1.	Pam: "Louise, let's take turns riding your bike. I'll ride it Mondays, Wednesdays, and Fridays, and you ride it Tuesdays, Thursdays, and Saturdays."	☐	☐	☐
2.	Gary: "Burt, let's take turns taking Louise to the movies. I'll take her the first and third Saturday of every month, and you take her the second and fourth Saturday."	☐	☐	☐
3.	Jack: "Louise, let's take turns doing the dishes. You wash and I'll dry."	☐	☐	☐
4.	Chris: "Okay, Louise, let's take turns with the TV. You choose a half-hour program, then I'll choose one."	☐	☐	☐
5.	Melissa: "Louise, what do you say we take turns doing our homework? Tonight I'll do yours and mine, and tomorrow you can do mine and yours."	☐	☐	☐

6. Hank: "Louise, I hate to
   see you struggle to school
   each day, carrying those
   heavy books! Let me carry
   yours and mine today, and
   you can carry yours and
   mine tomorrow."   ☐   ☐   ☐

The students performing this exercise are applying the criterion of *turn taking* (that is, *reciprocity* or *fair play* or *justice*) to half a dozen specific situations requiring sensitivity to context. Classroom discussion should be able to distinguish between those situations in which the procedure of turn taking is appropriate and those in which it is dubious. When exercises like these are employed in a community of inquiry setting, the stage is set for critical thinking in the classroom. It is not the only way to accomplish this, needless to say. But it is one way.

PRACTICAL REASONING BEHAVIORS THAT SIGNIFY CLOSURE

The question most frequently asked by teachers expected to teach for critical thinking is "How can I tell when I am teaching for critical thinking and when I am not?" Revealingly, the question is itself a demand for criteria.

The definition I have offered is a kind of bridge over four supporting piers: self-correction, sensitivity to context, criteria, and judgment. What a teacher would like to know is what classroom behaviors are associated with each of these categories.[16] And even if the teacher does observe these behaviors separately, does it follow that he or she is applying the definition?

[16] A number of instruments are available to evaluate the thinking of elementary school children. Although there appear to be none that effectively evaluate children's judgment, there are some that concentrate more or less successfully on children's reasoning. I would cite here the *New Jersey Test of Reasoning Skills* (Upper Montclair, N.J.: IAPC, 1983). For an instrument to evaluate possible changes in teacher attitudes toward students' cognitive potentials, there seems to be very little available other than the *Cognitive Behavior Checklist* (Upper Montclair, N.J.: IAPC, 1990).

We can take up the supporting concepts one by one:

Self-correction
Examples of associated behaviors

    a. Students point out errors in each other's thinking
    b. Students acknowledge errors in their own thinking
    c. Students disentangle ambiguous expressions in texts
    d. Students clarify vague expressions in texts
    e. Students demand reasons and criteria where none have been provided
    f. Students contend that it is wrong to take some matters for granted
    g. Students identify inconsistencies in discussions
    h. Students point out fallacious assumptions or invalid inferences in texts
    i. Students identify the commission of fallacies in formal or informal reasoning
    j. Students question whether inquiry procedures have been correctly applied

Acquiring sensitivity to context
Examples of associated behaviors

    a. Students differentiate among nuances of meaning stemming from cultural differences
    b. Students differentiate among nuances of meaning stemming from differences in personal perspectives or points of view
    c. Students recognize differences due to language differences, disciplinary differences, and differences of frames of reference
    d. Students contend to establish authenticity and integrity of interpretations of texts
    e. Students contest accuracy of translations
    f. Students point out how definitional meanings are modified by contextual circumstances
    g. Students note changes in meaning due to alterations of emphasis
    h. Students recognize changes in meaning resulting from shifts in speakers' intentions or purposes

i. Students note discrepancies between present situation and seemingly similar past situations

j. Students search for differences between seemingly similar situations whose consequences are different

Being guided (and goaded) by criteria
Examples displayed by students, who invoke

a. Shared values, such as ideals, purposes, goals, aims, and objectives

b. Conventions, such as norms, regularities, uniformities, and precedents or traditions.

c. Common bases of comparison, such as shared respects, properties, or characteristics

d. Requirements, such as precepts, specifications, stipulations, and limitations

e. Perspectives, including areas of concern, frames of reference, and points of view

f. Principles, including assumptions, presuppositions, and theoretical or conceptual relationships

g. Rules, including laws, bylaws, regulations, charters, canons, ordinances, and directions

h. Standards: criteria for determining the degree of satisfaction needed to satisfy a criterion

i. Definitions: assemblages of criteria that together have the same meaning as the word to be defined

j. Facts: what there is, as expressed in warranted assertions

k. Tests: probes or interventions for the purpose of eliciting empirical findings

Judgment
Examples displayed by students, who seek

a. Settlements of deliberations

b. Verdicts of trials or inquests

c. Decisions, as by administrators, executives, parents, teachers, etc.

d. Determinations: conclusive findings of investigative proceedings

e. Solutions to actual or theoretical problems

    f. Classifications or categorizations

    g. Evaluations of performances, services, objects, products, etc.; assessments

    h. Distinctions, in the form of negative predications

    i. Connections, in the form of affirmative predications

    j. Deliberate, intentional makings, sayings, or doings

PROFESSIONAL EDUCATION AND THE CULTIVATION OF JUDGMENT

It should be evident now why law and medicine were cited earlier as likely places to look for exemplary instances of critical thinking. Medicine and law both involve the flexible application of principles (criteria) to practice (judgment), extreme sensitivity to the uniqueness of particular cases (context sensitivity), refusal to allow either principles or facts to become Procrustean beds to which the other is to be fitted, and a commitment to tentative, hypothetical, self-correcting procedures as befits a species of inquiry (self-correction). Both judges and doctors recognize the importance of being judicious: of making good judgments in the carrying out of their practice. Law and medicine at their best illustrate what critical thinking can be and ought to be. It remains for educators to design appropriate courses in critical thinking and to help teachers and professors recognize the critical thinking elements in their present practice that need to be strengthened.

What, then, is the relevance of critical thinking to the enhancement of elementary school, secondary school, and college education? Why are so many educators convinced that critical thinking is the key to educational reform? A good part of the answer lies in the fact that we want students who can do more than merely think; it is equally important that students exercise good judgment. It is good judgment that characterizes the sound interpretation of a written text, the well-balanced and coherent composition, the lucid comprehension of what we listen to, and the persuasive argument. It is good judgment that enables us to weigh and grasp what a statement or passage states, assumes, implies, or suggests. And this good judgment cannot be operative unless it rests upon proficient reasoning skills that can assure competency in inference as well as upon proficient inquiry, concept-formation, and communication and translation skills. If critical thinking can produce an improvement in education, it will be because it increases the quantity and quality of meaning that students derive from what they read and perceive and that they express in what they write and say.

The infusion of critical thinking into the curriculum carries with it the promise of the academic empowerment of the student. Once this is recognized, it will be necessary to come to grips with the question of the best way to bring about such infusion. In the meantime, it will be well to keep in mind that students who are not taught to use criteria in a way that is both sensitive to context and self-corrective are not being taught to think critically.

Last, a word about the employment of criteria in critical thinking to facilitate good judgment. Critical thinking, as we have seen, is skillful thinking, and skills are proficient performances that satisfy relevant criteria. Without these skills, we would be unable to draw meaning from a written text or from a conversation, nor could we impart meaning to a conversation or to what we write. But just as in an orchestra there are such families as the woodwinds, the brasses, and the strings, so there are these different families of thinking skills. And just as within an orchestral family there are individual instruments – oboes and clarinets and bassoons, each with its own standard of proficient performance – so there are families of thinking skills, like induction, questioning, and analogical reasoning, that represent particular kinds of proficient performances in accordance with relevant criteria. We are all familiar with the fact that an otherwise splendid musical performance can be ruined if so much as a single instrumentalist performs below acceptable standards. Likewise, the mobilization and perfection of the thinking skills that go to make up critical thinking cannot neglect any of these skills without jeopardizing the process as a whole.

This is why we cannot be content to give students practice in a handful of cognitive skills while neglecting all the others that are needed for the competency in inquiry, in language, and in thought that is the hallmark of proficient critical thinkers. Instead of selecting and polishing a few skills that we think will do the trick, we must begin with the raw subject matter of communication and inquiry – with reading, listening, speaking, writing, and reasoning – and we must cultivate whatever skills the mastery of each process entails. When we do this, we come to realize that only philosophy can provide the logical and epistemological criteria that are now lacking in the curriculum.[17] This is far from saying that these are the only skills and criteria that are lacking, but they do represent a significant proportion of what is needed to make student thinking more responsible.

At the same time, it should be evident that, just as individual skills are not enough, the orchestration of skills is not enough either. Critical thinking is a normative enterprise in that it insists upon standards and criteria by means of which critical thinking can be distinguished from uncritical thinking. Shoddy work may be due less to a lack of skill than to the worker's having low standards, an insufficient commitment to quality, or a lack of judgment.[18]

Of course, psychologically oriented studies of critical thinking are often considered normative in the sense that the behavior of the "most successful" thinkers is described and recommended as a model for the way one ought to think. But this is a narrow and precarious base on which to set criteria and standards. Consider how much more broadly based in human experience are the logical criteria that guide our reasonings. Or consider the standards that prevail in the arts, crafts, and professions in contrast to the questionable implications of successful problem solving in this or that experiment. If critical thinking is to be insisted upon in education, it will have to develop conventions and traditions of cognitive work and accountability that teachers will readily recommend to their students. It is not enough to initiate students into heuristic and algorithmic procedures; they must also be initiated into the logic of good reasons, the logic of inference, and the logic of judgment.

[17] An earlier version of the preceding portion of this chapter appeared in *Educational Leadership* 16:1 (September 1988), 38–43, under the title "Critical Thinking – What Can It Be?"

[18] This point has been well made by Mark Selman in "Another Way of Talking about Critical Thinking," *Proceeding of the Forty-third Annual Meeting of the Philosophy of Education Society,* 1987 (Normal, Il, 1988), pp. 169–78.

Even if the claims I have been making on behalf of critical thinking up to this point are conceded to be true, much has been omitted, just as a witness may manage to tell the truth but not the whole truth. What I have in mind in particular is that critical thinking alone should not be considered the only dimension of thinking to be cultivated in order to improve thinking in the schools. Although it represents a component that contributes a great deal to such cognitive improvement, critical thinking skills are complemented by creative and caring thinking.

Any empirical instance of thinking is likely to involve aspects of all three modes, for no thinking is purely critical or purely creative or purely caring, and certainly excellent thinking will be strongly represented in all three categories. Determining the generic traits of creative and caring thinking may be more difficult than defining the specification of such traits in critical thinking. But there can be little doubt that, to improve thinking, the creative and the caring complement the critical. An education that nurtures uninventive thinking is no better than one that nourishes uncritical thinking. And how can we meaningfully address issues that involve, say, children, embryos, animals, or the environment if at the same time we care nothing for these things? What sort of architect would it be who cared nothing about the houses she designed and the people who were to inhabit them?

Finally, there is the question of the role of critical thinking in education. I have already suggested that all courses, whether in primary, secondary, or tertiary education, need to be taught in such a way as to encourage critical thinking in those subjects. Indeed, this opinion is so common in such areas as the social sciences as to be fairly uncontroversial. What I would add, however, is that critical thinking should be added to the curriculum as an independent course. Without an independent course that teaches the generic aspects of critical thinking, it will be difficult for the teachers in the particular disciplines to convey to their students why critical thinking is important.

It cannot be sufficiently emphasized, however, that there is nothing in the practice of critical thinking that does not already exist in some form or other in the practice of philosophy, even if there is an enormous amount in philosophy that is not in critical thinking. Educators would do well to try to understand the relationship between the two. My own opinion is that there is no better way of involving students in an independent course in critical thinking than by making it a course in philosophy. Not the traditional, academic philosophy of the university tradition, but the narrative philosophy that emphasizes dialogue, deliberation, and the strengthening of judgment and community. Such redesigned philosophy has existed now for a quarter of a century and has repeatedly demonstrated its viability. It would be a pity if it were overlooked in favor of glib commercial approaches that have only a glimmer of academic merit.

CRITICAL THINKING AND INFORMAL FALLACIES

The fallacies as a rogues' gallery of reasoning defects

Thinking can be manipulated and misused: It is highly exploitable. It is not surprising therefore that, since ancient times, people have sought to expose those who used their thinking harmfully, and to look for additional ways of defending themselves against these tricksters, as well as against those whose misuse of their powers of thought was unwitting or was simply due to ignorance.

The fallacies, on the other hand, switch the focus from the person or subject to the practice. The fallacies are a kind of rogues' gallery of reasoning, and their main value is to alert the naive reader or listener to the booby-traps that lie just below the surface of language.

These are not fallacies of formal logic, although obviously there are such things. They are informal fallacies. They do not violate strict rules of inference, the way the formal fallacies do. The conclusions of formal reasoning are considered certain and universal, while those of informal reasoning generally fall short of certainty as well as of universality. Formal logic seeks an ideal, symbolic language; informal logic prefers to deal with ordinary reasonings in natural languages. Informal fallacies disclose improprieties of reasoning. But that does not mean they are violations of truth or certainty. It should be remembered that most of them were formulated at a time when there was no discipline of informal logic. They were part of the long tradition of critical thinking as a popular exercise, a tradition that took on new life with the rise of democracy.

The significance of the value-principles

One of the first things children who are beginning school are encouraged to do, and quite rightly, is to make comparisons. Comparisons are a fundamental category of relationships, and without understanding relationships, students will have a hard time understanding arithmetical relationships, historical relationships, family relationships, and so on. But of course one has to have a *basis* of comparison. We cannot tell which is larger, Romania or Bulgaria, unless we can compare them in some specific respect, such as area or population. These bases of comparison, these specific respects, are *criteria*, which I shall also call "value-principles."

Criteria, as we have seen in earlier parts of this chapter, enable us to make more or less reasonable and reliable judgments. They lend a helpful consistency to the comparisons we make in the course of our conversations or inquiries. They are useful when it comes to specifying exactly what differences, similarities, and identities are.

Of course, there is no question that there are such things as similarities and differences. We refer to differences by formulating distinctions, and in an instance in which there is no difference, it is unnecessary to make a distinction. Differences are in the world; distinction making is a skill, a matter of practice.

Sometimes a distinction is made that is blatantly obvious, such as a distinction between elephants and mice, or between remembering and forgetting. At other times a distinction may be extremely subtle and may require magnification (like the differences between fingerprints) or clarification.

Some differences rest on a comparison of primary characteristics, but this may not always be feasible, so they are made by comparison of secondary or other characteristics, as when, in certain cultures, the distinctions between male and female are expressed through differences of dress.

An example of making an analogous distinction is to be found in the practice of chicken sexing. Those who operate chicken hatcheries usually cull out most of the male baby chicks during the first twenty-four hours after the chicks have broken out of their shells. The sexers ignore the primary sexual characteristics, which are much too difficult to perceive, and observe instead the coloration of the chicks' wing tips, where the readily visible differences in coloration correspond perfectly to the birds' barely visible differences of sex.

Therefore instead of trying to tell the differences among the various styles and manners of thinking by means of primary (but obscure) features, perhaps we can find more obvious characteristics that would normally be considered insufficient, when taken by themselves, but that may be strongly correlated with the differences we are looking for. Like the wing tip colorations among the baby chicks, these differences are not so much criteria as they are features functioning as criteria.

Thus it may be possible to identify the type of thinking called "critical" by means of a small number of characteristic values, and as I said earlier, I shall call such features *value-principles*. If this were the whole of the matter, we would not have to formulate a complex definition of "critical thinking" that would work in a large variety of contexts. We could rely more on characteristic values that were better related to critical thinking and were reliably correlated with it. We could put greater trust in the highlights.

This is not contrary to established inquiry procedure. When Thomas Kuhn, for example, writes about the outstanding characteristics of scientific concepts, he specifies them in terms of five features that apply equally well to scientific thinking: *accuracy, consistency, scope, simplicity,* and *fruitfulness*.[19] When Wölfflin contrasts the painting styles of Renaissance and Baroque painters, he is in effect specifying the outstanding differences in values between the two styles of inventive thinking (in paints).[20] We are talking now of the procedures of experts: Kuhn, an expert in scientific thinking, and Wölfflin, an expert in the history of European painting. Some experts are able to specify the characteristic values they look for, as is the case with experts judging dancers, divers, gymnasts, and so on. Others find such verbalization difficult although not impossible. I am thinking of wine tasters, perfume smellers, and the like.

The traditional informal fallacies can be taken to represent the violations of fundamental principles of informal logic and therefore

[19] Thomas S. Kuhn, "Objectivity, Value Judgment, and Theory Choice," *The Essential Tension* (1979), Chicago: University of Chicago Press, pp. 320–2.
[20] Heinrich Wölfflin, *Principles of Art History* (New York: Dover, 1950).

of critical thinking. Evidently these principles also formulate some of the more characteristic values of critical thinking. This is why they are here called "value-principles." (Of course, they may not represent our most important findings so much as they represent our most important expectations of what we think critical thinking is all about.)

Examination of a sizeable number of the traditional fallacies suggests that inept reasoning violates only a relatively small number (five) of value-principles: *precision, consistency, relevance, acceptability,* and *sufficiency*. Inclusion of the last two can be considered questionable on the ground that they are chiefly applicable to the *premises* of arguments, rather than to cases of reasoning per se. For this reason, attention is here concentrated on the first three value-principles. *Precision* has been retained because of its indispensability in correcting for ambiguity and vagueness. *Consistency* has been retained because of the powerful backup it receives from the "Laws of Thought." Finally, *relevance* has been retained on the ground that it assures the rejection of irrelevancy – another unacceptable characteristic.

A quick review is in order:

Precision. There are two general kinds of precision: quantitative and qualitative. Quantitative precision is perhaps best exemplified by measurement. Qualitative precision is best exemplified by specificity. Both are instances of the demand for exactitude.

Consistency. A person is said to be inconsistent if he asserts or believes two propositions that cannot both be true at the same time. (This is the Principle of Non-Contradiction: A statement cannot be both true and untrue – one or the other but not both.) Moreover, consistency requires that if a statement is true, it must be true. This is the Principle of Identity: Each thing is exactly what it is and not some other thing.

Relevance. To support the conclusion of an argument, the premises must be related to it. The more forms the relatedness takes, the more relevant the truth of one statement is to the truth of another. As one logician puts it, "A statement is positively relevant to another statement if its truth counts in favor of the other statement. That is, if it is true, that gives us some reason to think the other statement is true. A statement is negatively relevant to another statement if its truth counts against the truth of the other statement."[21]

Acceptability. Here is Govier again: "If you could accept – that is, *believe* – the premises of an argument without violating any standard of evidence or certainty, then you find its premises *acceptable*. . . . The premises of an argument are *unacceptable* if any one of the following conditions applies:

1. One premise or more is known to be false.
2. Several premises together produce a contradiction.
3. At least one premise depends upon an assumption that is either false or highly controversial.
4. At least one premise is unbelievable to a person who doesn't already believe the conclusion.
5. The premises are less certain than the conclusion.[22]

Sufficiency. "The premises of an argument may be relevant and precise. Individually, they may be acceptable. Yet together they may be insufficient because they do not supply a sufficient sample of the various kinds of relevant evidence, and they ignore the presence of, or the possibility of, contrary evidence. A good example is the fallacy of 'Hasty Generalization.' "[23]

These are *key terms*, which not only guide and define the use of evaluative terms in the inquiry generally but also guide and define the use of the other value terms that might once have been equal in importance to the key terms. *Precision, consistency*, and *relevance* shape the concepts the inquirers use, the judgments they make, the distinctions they insist on; the whole investigational apparatus comes to be understood as summed up by the understanding we have of the key terms. Once one grasps the characteristic Mozart brio, one hears and understands so much of Mozart's music in *its* terms. It is the same with, say, Wittgensteinian precision, Kantian consistency, and Cartesian

---

[21] Trudy Govier, *A Practical Study of Argument*, 2d ed. (Belmont, Calif.: Wadsworth, 1988).

[22] Ibid.

[23] Ralph H. Johnson and J. Anthony Blair, *Logical Self-Defense* (New York: McGraw-Hill, 1994).

relevance. The values become idiosyncratic, unique, and highly creative. They are no longer the values of critical thinking alone: They are among the values of creative and caring thinking as well.

Still another comment on this point is this: Not only do the key concepts shape and modify all the other applicable concepts, but they come to represent clusters of value terms that are synonymous or otherwise similar to the five key terms. Thus, for example, *precision* is the "front" for many other nouns, such as "accuracy," "exactitude," "correctness," "distinctness," and "scrupulousness."

The following chart considers a number of fallacies selected more or less at random, and their respective subject areas, and indicates the principles that are generally thought to be violated by the faulty reasoning that each fallacy discloses. These situations are not to be confused with those cases in which the fallacy is under certain circumstances no fallacy at all. For example, ad hominem: the fallacy of attacking one's opponent personally, rather than attacking his position. This is often the case but not always. Thus a judge may permit a "character witness" to testify, even though the testimony is unrelated to the opponent's position. It is related only to the opponent as a person.

Using validities to establish standards of reasonableness

What are the chief regulative ideas of an inquiry-driven society? There are at least two. The first has to do with the sociopolitical character of the society, or with procedures in that society, while the second has to do with the character of the individual citizen. The first is *democracy* and the second is *reasonableness*.

Over and over again, when there are disputes to be settled and no clear legal principle to which to appeal, the parties to the dispute will be urged from all sides to seek a *reasonable* settlement. Thus the judge instructs the jury to arrive at a verdict by procedures in which they have confidence "beyond a reasonable doubt." For all those who are in a position of authority or administrative responsibility, reasonableness is the value on which there is a consensus of agreement. It is the *criterion* of ultimate appeal. While this may be vague, there seems to be no alternative to it, except to try to strengthen it by clarifying the *standards* that must be satisfied when that criterion is invoked.

TABLE 10.1.

Name of Fallacy	Description of Fallacy	Thinking Fault	Value-Principle Violated
Ad hominem	An attack on the opponent rather than on the opponent's argument. (e.g., "What would you expect from a woman . . . a kid . . . ?"	Irrelevance	Relevance
Ambiguity	Using a term that has several possible meanings in a particular context, although one cannot tell which meaning is intended.	Vagueness	Precision
Improper appeal to authority	Appeal to an alleged authority who is either not capable of exercising jurisdiction or else is not credible with regard to the matter in question. (Rejoinder: (a) authorities in one field may not be authorities in another; (b) in fields where experts disagree, we need to become experts ourselves; (c) some experts are better than others.)	Irrelevance	Relevance/ acceptability
Appeal to fear	Using threats rather than an argument to obtain agreement.	Violence instead of reasoning	Relevance
Improper appeal to practice	Defending an action on the ground that it is part of a customary or traditional practice. (Rejoinder: The action may not belong to the practice, or the practice may not exist.)	Inadequate or unrelated evidence	Relevance and/or Sufficiency
Faulty argument from analogy	When two things are alleged to be similar, a conclusion applicable to one may be said to be applicable to the other. But if the respect in which the comparison is made lacks similarity, the analogy is faulty and does not support the conclusion.	Unwarranted assumption	Acceptability
Composition	Claiming that what is true of the whole is therefore true of the part.	Doesn't follow necessarily	Relevance
Definition	Defining a word by means of a synonym.	Terms vague and inaccurate	Relevance
Division	Claiming that what is true of the part is therefore true of the whole.	Doesn't follow necessarily	Relevance

Fallacy	Description	Type	Criterion
Begging the question	Assuming or taking for granted the very thing one is trying to prove.	Circular reasoning	Acceptability
Dubious assumption	Employing an assumption that is open to reasonable challenge, or where the assumption is missing a premise.	Unwarranted assumption	Acceptability
Equivocation	Equivocation occurs when a term's meaning shifts from one of its appearances to another in the same context.	Shift of meaning	Consistency
Guilt by association	Attacking the arguer on the ground of an alleged association against which accusations have been made.	Unwarranted assumption	Acceptability
Jumping to conclusions	Presenting an argument with an insufficient sample of relevant evidence, while ignoring the presence of contrary evidence.	Hasty generalization	Sufficiency
Inconsistency	Asserting two propositions that cannot both be true at the same time, or supporting a conclusion with contradictory reasons.	Self-contradiction	Consistency
Non sequitur	Giving a reason that is not relevant, with the result that the argument is invalid.	Irrelevance	Relevance
Red herring	Citing unrelated or phantom issues, thereby distracting attention from the merits of the argument.	Irrelevance	Relevance
Straw person	Falsely attributing a position to an opponent, and then criticizing that rather than the opponent's actual position. Attacking a weaker position than the real one.	Misrepresentation	Relevance
Post hoc, ergo propter hoc	Asserting that the cause of something must be an event that occurred just prior to the thing in question.	Jumping to the conclusion that the two events are causally related	Sufficiency
Two wrongs don't make a right	Exonerating an action solely on the grounds that an allegedly similar action in the past was not blamed or criticized.	Faulty argument from analogy/ Inconsistency	Acceptability/ Consistency
Vagueness	Offering an argument at least one of whose premises is so indeterminate as to be virtually meaningless, thereby rendering the premise useless.	Lack of cut-off points in definition of terms	Acceptability/ Precision

At this point it is important to keep in mind that criteria need cut-off points below which the criteria are not satisfied; these cut-off points are in fact standards. It is my contention that these standards do exist and are well-known. This is not to say that there is general agreement as to their applicability. They are always subject to further consideration. They are continually open to a reexamination that will probe the circumstances under which they can or cannot be utilized. That means that they work together with the value-principles of sensitivity to context and self-correction. Some of the standards I have in mind are known, as we have seen, by the unsatisfactory and misleading title of *informal fallacies*. (They are "informal" only by contrast with "formal" logic. Otherwise they spell out some of the things that are wrong with faulty thinking. That they are fallacious may be of less importance than that they suggest, by inversion, what is right about right reasoning.)

Informal fallacies express the concern with the appropriateness or inappropriateness of particular logical performances. Should this particular instance of analogical reasoning be judged proportionate and equitable, or should it not? Under what circumstances are ambiguity and equivocation permissible, and under what circumstances are they not?

Informal fallacies represent standards of the criteria to distinguish better from worse reasoning. Traditionally, these criteria are precision, relevance, consistency, sufficiency, and acceptability. Those criteria are guidelines to establish the reasonableness of our judgments. Critical thinking aims at reasonableness. This means that it is not just rational, in the sense of a thinking that is rule- and criterion-governed, but that it is also a thinking that accepts the fallibility of its procedures, that engages in self-corrective practice, that takes the contextual differences into account, and that is equitable, in the sense that respects the rights of others as well as its own. Reasonableness thus entails the cultivation of multidimensional thinking.

A table of validities

It is desirable that education for democracy portray the concept of reasonableness with as little arbirtrariness as possible. This is one of the values of the so-called informal fallacies or, preferably, of the basic informal validities, together with their summative formulations as value-principles.

For example, it should be possible to explain to young children that most inconsistencies are undesirable because they lead to self-contradiction. As for what is wrong with self-contradiction, it should be possible to provide the children with ample illustrations of its undesirability, such as that it commits one to arguing against oneself, it undermines any plans one may make for the future, and it destroys any agreements people might make with one another. It is not so much, therefore, that inconsistency is to be rejected because it rests on an ultimate foundation of logical antecedents (the so-called Laws of Thought) as that its consequences are liable to be undesirable.

Fallacies (like torts) are cases of impropriety or wrongdoing, with no mention of the corresponding practices that are considered logically or legally correct. Nevertheless, it would be useful to identify the logically correct practices that match the fallacies – I suggest calling them "validities" – if only to give them a more positive spin. It would be ambiguous and confusing to call these matching practices "rights," just as rights do not correspond to torts. But there is a sense in which the Table of Validities represents an insistence upon sound critical thinking procedures. One usually cannot contradict them, on pain of contradicting oneself, although their correct formulation is certainly subject to debate, just as the Bill of Rights is of fundamental constitutional importance for the Rule of Law, even though its particular formulations are in most cases controversial. The citizens in a democracy need a table of validities just as they need rules of parliamentary order or guidelines of fair play.

In a democratic society, then, it would be desirable that children study the Table of Validities (and the various fallacies that correspond to them) so that they might have some reassurance of just what it is that their intellectual rights consist in, just what it is that makes for intellectual fair play, and just what it is that they can appeal to when they feel that correct critical thinking practices have been violated. Students need to realize, with regard to legal matters, that the fact that there are a thousand ways to violate a law does not mean that the law is ambiguous – it simply covers a host of cases. Similarly, by studying the Table of Validities and its many ways of being violated, they can discover the shield that protects them from the multiverse of

Table of Validities

Traditional Name of Fallacy	Name of Corresponding Basic Validity
Ad hominem	Attacking the argument, not the opponent
Ambiguity	Contextual consistency
Appeal to improper authority	Appeal to proper authority
Appeal to fear	Appeal to courage
Appeal to improper practice	Appeal to proper practice
Argument from faulty analogy	Argument from sound analogy
Fallacy of composition	Proper whole–part reasoning
Violation of rule or rules of definition	Abiding by rules of definition
Fallacy of division	Proper part–whole reasoning
Begging the question	Non-circular reasoning
Dubious assumption	Reasoning from acceptable assumptions
Fallacy of equivocation	Consistent maintenance of meaning
Guilt by association	Propriety of personal associations
Hasty conclusion	Sufficiency of relevant evidence
Inconsistency	Consistency
Non sequitur	Appeal to relevant reasons
Red herring	Sticking to the point
Straw person	Focusing on opponent's actual position
Post hoc, ergo propter hoc	Insistence upon evidence of causal connection
Two wrongs don't make a right	Demanding judgment be made based on rightful evidence, not on a wrongly judged similar case
Vagueness	Precision in reasoning

fallacious informal reasonings. If formal logic provides us with standards of rational inference, the Table of Validities provides us with an important cluster of the standards of reasonableness.

The role of value-principle exercises in teaching for critical thinking

It would be ridiculous to infer from what has just been said that since the value-principles more or less summarize the standards of reasonable thinking, one could arrive at proficiency in thinking critically by doing nothing more than studying the value-principles. On the other hand, the facilitation of critical thinking might very well involve becoming adept with these principles, by means of specially constructed exercises to be discussed in an inquiry environment. Such exercises would foster exactitude in comparing and contrasting mental acts and states, so that they may strengthen student thinking and reasonableness. Here are some illustrations:

Exercise: Identifying similarities and differences among mental acts
STANDARD: Precision
Part One: Are there differences within the following pairs of mental acts, mental states, or speech acts? What are they?

1. (a) John *admitted* the theft.
    (b) John *confessed* to the theft.
2. (a) Denise *knows* French.
    (b) Denise *understands* French.
3. (a) Edgar *knows* that the winter is over.
    (b) Edgar *believes* that the winter is over.
4. (a) Tanya has *asserted* her loyalty to this country.
    (b) Tanya has *affirmed* her loyalty to this country.
5. (a) Fred has *declared* his innocence with regard to the crime.
    (b) Fred has *maintained* his innocence with regard to the crime.
6. (a) The weather announcer has *forecast* rain for tomorrow.
    (b) The weather announcer has *predicted* rain for tomorrow.
7. (a) She *vowed* that she would never again ride in a submarine.
    (b) She *swore* that she would never again ride in a submarine.

8. (a) They claim that they *endorse* the candidate.
   (b) They claim that they *vouch for* the candidate.
9. (a) We *anticipate* a large crowd this evening.
   (b) We *expect* a large crowd this evening.
10. (a) They engaged in *deliberation* about the tax cut all night.
    (b) They engaged in *dialogue* about the tax cut all night.

Part Two: Construct an Item 11 for this exercise.

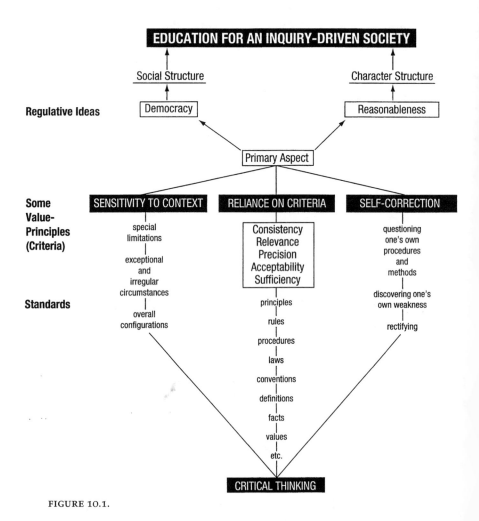

FIGURE 10.1.

11

Education for Creative Thinking

THE PRIMARY ASPECT OF THE WORK OF ART AS
THE STANDARD OF THE WORK

To a certain extent, when we consider an alleged instance of creativity, we bring familiar or traditional criteria to bear upon it. Of a work of art, we may ask about the use of color, or the use of representation, or the quality of line drawing. Of a seemingly excellent student term paper, we may ask traditional questions having to do with coherence and consistency. To this extent, the assessment of creative thinking does not itself require the invention of new criteria. On the other hand, traditional criteria may fail to come to grips with that which is original, unique, and distinctive in the work of art or in the student's performance. Under such circumstances, new criteria are needed, but we must still employ criteria that are relevant. It is necessary that the new criteria be drawn from the work itself, or from the student, or from whatever it is we are attempting to judge. Thus, in grading a student, we conventionally employ certain traditional criteria, such as class participation, doing the work assignments, and so on. But we also are concerned with the individualistic aspect of the student and the extent to which the tasks performed contribute to or detract from that individuality. In judging a painting, likewise, we do not fault the artist for what he or she has attempted (as far as the use of the individualistic criterion is concerned). Instead, we consider which set of parts of the painting help to make it succeed as a whole. This is what George Yoos calls the "primary aspect" of a work.[1] We do not attempt to assess the *primary aspect* of the work, but extract it as a criterion by means of which to judge how well the artist has integrated other aspects (such as colour, texture, line, etc.) with the primary aspect.

Traditional criteria can be employed to assess the task the artist has assigned herself or himself, but only an invented criterion, drawn from the primary aspect of the work itself, can be employed to determine how well the secondary aspects work to bring out the primary aspect.

CREATIVE THINKING IN CRITICAL PERSPECTIVE

A museum director planning an exhibit of paintings is going to have to think accurately and precisely about the spatial requirements of the works, the necessary lighting conditions, storage facilities, security precautions, publicity arrangements, and so on. Even if the paintings were to have been made by mentally disturbed patients, the director's thinking about the exhibit would have to be consistent, coherent, and reasonable. She will have to anticipate what the various art critics who will visit the exhibition are likely to say about the appropriateness of the timing of the display, the historical impact of the works, the relationships of the paintings shown to the life of the artist, and the chronology of the works. These are only a few of the relevant considerations that will have to be taken into account. Most of them involve critical thinking, but some deal with more subjective factors, such as the taste of the director, the underlying layers of meaning to be discerned in the works, and the impact the exhibition is likely to have upon the values of the art world. Insofar as the director deals with these issues by means of reasoned judgments, acknowledging the assumptions she is making, proceeding self-correctively, and taking the context into account wherever possible, her planning can be considered an instance of critical thinking, even though she may be keeping in mind the way the works dramatically express the artist's feelings and emotions.

[1] Ibid., 81–9.

On the other hand, the director may approach the work with criteria or categories more typical of creative than of critical thinking. Or she may employ novel criteria that she has extemporaneously invented, or traditional creativity criteria applied in a new way, and this would be a matter of thinking creatively about creative thinking. What would be some examples of critical and creative characterizations of creative thinking? Consider these:

a. *Originality*. Thinking for which there are no clear precedents. Originality alone is not sufficient to establish the merit of a passage of creative thinking. Some such passages may be highly original but otherwise eccentric or irrational. This is one reason why a quorum of criteria generally needs to be invoked.

b. *Productivity*. Productive thinking is thinking that, when applied in problematic situations, generally brings forth successful results. This is a value-concept that is heavily reliant upon consequentialist considerations.

c. *Imagination*. To imagine is to envisage a possible world, or the details of such a world, or the journey one may take to reach such a world. To have other worlds in which to dwell – and to make them available to others to dwell in also – is no mean feat. What matters is that those who explore the realms of possibility must retain as much as possible their sense of fact, just as those who explore the perceivable world must keep their imagination about them.

d. *Independence*. Creative thinkers are those who, as we say, "think for themselves," and who are not stampeded into thinking the way the crowd thinks. Independent thinkers are inclined to ask questions where others are content to proceed without further reflection. And independent thinkers, when it is their turn to answer, do not do so mechanically and thoughtlessly, but study the question thoroughly before they respond to it.

e. *Experimentation*. Creative thinking is hypothesis-guided rather than rule-guided thinking. The hypotheses, moreover, need not be fully formed: They may be inchoate or rudimentary. There are trial plans, provisional schemes for proceeding; there are "trial facts." Creative thinking involves a constant trying out, or testing, as well as a searching for firm support, which makes it probative.

f. *Holism.* The emerging character of the whole, in creative think- ing, plays an important role in determining the progressive selection of additional parts. The finished product is therefore always a texture of part–whole relationships and means–end relationships that provide the product with its idiosyncratic meanings. What is not immediately given is the extent to which the "whole" is identical with the "primary aspect."

g. *Expression.* Creative thinking is expressive of the thinker as well as of that which is thought about. To think creatively about a tree that one perceives reveals the character of the tree and that of the thinker. This is because creative thinking wrings the expression out of the experience in which the tree is perceived.

h. *Self-transcendance.* The restlessness of creative thinking reveals itself in a striving to go beyond its previous level. Every artist is aware that each successive work is a response to all those that were produced earlier. Not to endeavor to go beyond previous achievements is to risk engaging in a form of inquiry that lacks integrity.

i. *Surprise.* The meaning of originality lies in its consequences, and surprise is one of those consequences, when the original- ity is not merely novel but fresh. Although theoretical thinking seeks understanding, creative thinking defies it, thereby gen- erating astonishment and wonder.

j. *Generativity.* Creative thinking not only is a stimulus to sat- isfaction, pleasure, joy, and delight in others, but it in some cases stimulates other's creativity. This must be construed cau- tiously, however, since it may sometimes inhibit creativity in others. For example, the teacher who thinks creatively is a pre- cious model for her students. However, brilliant lecturers can provide their audiences with very few clues as to how this pro- fusion of glittering ideas came into being. But if a teacher is concerned with encouraging students to think for themselves, she will seek to create the problem conditions that the students will have to think through themselves if they are to become independent and creative thinkers.

k. *Maieuticity* (from "maieutic"). Maieutic persons think and act in a manner calculated to bring forth the best in the world. Such persons are like midwives, bringing human or intellectual offspring to birth, or helping nature in its efforts to do so. Maieuticity is a way of characterizing the thinking of the teacher concerned to bring out the thought and expression of her students.

l. *Inventiveness.* An idea can be understood as a possible solution to a problem, and inventive thought contains many problems and many relevant promising ideas. Such thought can be described as inventive even though the experiments they give rise to are unsuccessful. Thus a contemporary critic (Charles Rosen) can choose to speak of the music of Vivaldi as containing "nothing but ideas," and a philosopher describes the work of Bertrand Russell as "merely brilliant." In other words, a prolific flow of alternatives can be thought of as inventive, but to be considered creative it would have to satisfy other criteria. Inventiveness may be a necessary condition for creativity, but it may not be a sufficient one.

There is nothing magical about the limitation of this list to twelve descriptors; obviously, there could be many more or many less. What would be useful to learn would be the extent to which the items listed here are *summaries* of the values to be found in creative thinking, or are *generic* of more particular and specific values. I suspect they may be both.

FRESHNESS, PROBLEMATICITY, AND INTELLIGIBILITY

At the prospect of having to discourse on creativity, experienced psychologists quail and sophisticated philosophers suddenly discover that they have heavy commitments elsewhere. As well compose an essay on surprise or a disquisition on muddlement!

Philosophy has been said to begin in wonder, but where does wonder begin? A half-educated guess might be that it begins in discovery, for wonder occurs each time we discover nature *afresh* in our perceptions.

It is the wondrousness of the world, then, that commands our wonderment; it is our wonderment that in turn provokes our inquiries. There is nothing strange about this sequence itself. Once we have been challenged to explain what we have discovered, we are at the mercy of our doubts, which sweep us along with them until our inquiries establish certain equilibria.

But physical nature is not the only source of our puzzlement. Our human nature is also perplexing to us, particularly the nonrational aspects of it. And then there is the creative aspect of human nature – talk about perplexing!

Creativity has its roots deep in nature – in nature's diversification and amplification of itself. It also has its roots deep in human nature, where it plays a role in reproduction in addition to its critical role in discovery and invention. But what about *creative thinking* – the thinking that goes beyond our thinking? Even the thought of it is enough to leave us dumbfounded and nonplussed, as Jane Austen (I think it was) suggests when she writes, "We had intended to be surprised, but our astonishment exceeded our expectations!"

Creative thinking is exemplified by the thinking that goes into the making of art, by the idiosyncratic encoding through which each work withholds itself from us. It is the discrimination of or the fabrication of relationships, patterns, and orders producing in us the shock of unfamiliarity. Creative thinking – thinking how to say what merits saying, how to make what merits making, how to do what merits doing – fosters problematicity. Other characteristic features are *freshness* and *intelligibility*.

Let us imagine we ask our students what roles art and education play in human life. Some of them will explain to us that education provides us with knowledge and thereby tells us what the world *is*, while art provides us with standards and values, thereby telling us what the world *can be*.

At this we nod our heads gravely. "And is this the purpose of art, to provide people with meaning?" we ask.

Our students shrug their shoulders at this, as if to say, "What do any of us know about purposes?" But they have wisely told us enough for us to discern what we think to be the assumptions they are making about art and creativity. The world, they seem to be saying, is by itself a well-nigh unintelligible place. Human experience of the world advances us a step toward understanding, because experience is problematic. We then make use of scientific and artistic inquiry to make our experience, and hence the world, intelligible to us.

We can infer from the students' remarks that they conceive art to be a matter of problem solving, and that creative thinking is the moving spirit of that process. When our doubts cause us to suspend our working beliefs, it is our creative thought that reformulates the problematic situation, entertains alternative hypotheses as ways to attack the problem, considers possible consequences, and organizes experiments until the problematic character of the situation is provisionally vanquished and a new set of working beliefs is put into place.

Creative thinking (as contrasted with the psychological disposition to creativity per se) is that minimal element of idiosyncratic judgment in every artist's work. Like all judgment, it is expressive of the person making the judgment and appraisive of that person's world. It represents the artist's individuality even more than does the artist's signature. It is a display of the artist's self, insofar as it is revealed in the work of art, and it is a key to the work. It is by means of a grasp of the *key* that the work as a whole can be unlocked. Nevertheless, it is an idiosyncratic and unique key that we have to study if we are to learn how to use it.

AMPLIFICATIVE THINKING

It is possible to distinguish between implicative and ampliative thinking. The first, as exemplified by deduction, extends our thought without enlarging it. The second, as exemplified by induction and the use of analogy and metaphor, represents cognitive breakthroughs. It goes beyond the given and in the process compels our own thinking to go beyond the given. It stands for evolutionary growth rather than for stability or fixity. Ampliative thinking expands not only our thinking but also our capacity to think expansively.

Generalizations are enlargements or amplifications in the sense that they go beyond the information given, inferring from a group of instances that possess a similar character and that have in common a particular feature that all instances of that character have that particular feature in common. Generalizations, then, presume a certain *uniformity* in the evidence. Hypotheses are also representative of amplified thinking. Hypotheses may emerge in the presence of pieces of evidence that are highly *diversified*: here some apparently unrelated facts, here some inferences, here some generalizations, here some principles, and so on. Hypotheses also go beyond the information given, but they do so in order to explain or predict with regard to highly complex states of affairs rather than uniform phenomena.

Analogical reasoning presumes that things in nature may exhibit a certain *proportionality*, a proportionality that can best be expressed through similarities of relationships rather than through similarity of terms. Thus, we say that the relationship between A and B "is like" the relationship between C and D. Given this understanding, we can, if given A, B, and C, go beyond the information available to us and suppose D, which is to C as B is to A.

What must be kept in mind is that proportionalities (unless they are strict ratios) are based upon resemblances and hence are matters of judgment. It is for this reason that the strengthening of judgment in students generally involves extensive practice in the evaluation of analogies. This is why Plato thought music and mathematics so essential to education – because they embodied systems of proportion. This is also why Aristotle insisted that judgment rested not so much on strict equality (e.g., in equations) as on the approximation of equity.

Metaphorical thinking – and indeed, figurative discourse generally – is ampliative rather than implicative. It represents a mixing of categories or schemata – a mixing that, from a literal or prosaic point of view, seems to be sheer impudence but from which issues a fresh and vigorous confluence of thought incomparably richer than more conventional ways of thinking. Metaphorical thinking is thus a synthesis of incompatibles that yields, like binocularity, a far greater depth of vision by the mere act of juxtaposition. It is thinking that, from the perspective of either of the categories it bridges over, is bound to seem false – a "category-mistake,"[2] just as thinking among the disciplines often seems false by the standards that exist within the disciplines.

---

[2] Cf. Nelson Goodman, *Languages of Art* (Indianapolis, Ind.: Bobbs-Merrill, 1968), p. 73: "Indeed a metaphor might be regarded as a calculated category-mistake – or rather as a happy and revitalizing, even if bigamous, second marriage."

DEFIANT THINKING

It is sometimes thought that creative thinkers are rule-defiant and criterion-defiant. One cannot deny that this has often been the case. To Romanesque architects, for example, the new Gothic architects must have seemed to have a special penchant for breaking the rules merely for the sake of breaking the rules. Some traditional criteria were dropped and others were introduced, with the result that the Gothic architect, when all was said and done, may not have been more defiant than his predecessors. Similarly with the new sculpture: People were of mixed minds about it, and Saint Bernard could be found muttering, "These monstrous beauties, these beautiful monstrosities." Gothic sculpture palpably defied the canons of acceptability to which Bernard had been accustomed.

While we need not go so far as to assert that one must know the rules in order to defy them (since it is possible to violate the rules out of ignorance rather than defiance), it would be useful to consider the relationship between artistic defiance and artistic creativity. An analogy that might be useful would involve considerations of the way games are played. Athletes and managers do make provision for athletic creativity, even in games that are highly regulated, down to minute details. But the public contexts in which games are played usually make it foolhardy to engage in or to encourage deliberate rule breaking. Even if one should get away with doing so, it is seldom classified as a creative move. But there are tactics and strategies, plays and performances, whose execution may be so expert that one feels one has just witnessed a work of art. Thus a team's manager may be considered creative if he or she persistently defies not the rules but the "odds" or percentages that represent the cumulative experience of those who have played the game or observed it being played.

To be sure, the manager does not defy the odds simply to *épater le bourgeois*: Success in sports is more carefully measured than by noting whether or not the spectators that day were left in amazement. But many a manager would gladly sacrifice the otherwise unremarkable player who occasionally makes a remarkable play for the player who regularly swings the bat with a swing so "sweet," as the phrase goes, that it represents an exemplary bonding of beauty and efficiency.

MAIEUTIC THINKING

We can take our cue with respect to creative thinking by turning also to *maieutic thinking*. This is the kind of thinking characteristic of voice coaches, orchestra conductors, painting teachers, writing teachers, and so on. These are people who think *caringly* about the creative thinking of their students. Maieutic thinking is intellectual midwifery. It is extractive, eductive, seeking to elicit the best thinking possible from one's charges. Although the maieutic would normally be classified with other types of caring thinking, it in fact straddles the boundary between the caring and the creative, since its success hinges upon the ability of the practitioner to understand and identify with the creative process from within. Just as the midwife empathizes with both the mother and the child, the voice coach empathizes with the singer struggling to sing and with the song struggling to be sung.

Of course there is a difference between the voice coach endeavoring to help the singer begin a piece of music that is already complete and the writing coach trying to assist a writer to produce a story that has yet to find the shape and identity that belong to it. In the first instance, the coach must empathize with the composer who is different from the singer; in the second instance, the writing coach must empathize with the writer who is also the author.

An objection to the foregoing account would be that midwives, nurses, and doctors must repress their sympathies and antipathies in the course of an operation. The clinical attitude, it will be said, is not empathic but analytical and detached, being much more a case of critical than of caring thinking. But this objection is not well-founded. The emotional responses of medical practitioners are suppressed, remaining in a latent state that is sufficient to assure the patient of the practitioners' care and concern.

The suppression – or at least partial suppression – of one's disposition to engage in caring thinking should alert us to the possibility that analogous tendencies toward suppression might also be found with respect to critical and creative thinking. Thus a nurse engaged in a stipulated medical procedure must inhibit any tendency she might have to engage in an imaginative and innovative but medically unjustified variation of the procedure. This would be an example of the partial suppression of creative thinking. On the other hand, an architect who has been given a commission that entails a highly expressive and decorative construction may be tempted by stylistic treatments that are much more mechanical, but he or she will have to inhibit such temptations. We can conclude that the actual proportion of the amount of thinking of various kinds to be devoted to a single project has to be situationally determined rather than determined by the needs of the particular thinker.

CREATIVE AND CARING THINKING

There is more to be learned about each dimension of thinking by considering it in relationship with the others than by thinking about it in isolation. The relationship between creative and caring thinking is particularly instructive. For example, we may be told of an artist who was renowned for being antisocial, and such an artist is said to be creative but uncaring. Obviously, however, if a person merely prefers one social group to another, that does not make her uncaring, and presumably her paintings are addressed to those with whom she dearly wishes to communicate.

It is not unusual for an intensely creative person to also be intensely affectionate, and to engage intensely in both types of thinking. Thus, for example, Van Gogh's letters to his brother reveal how the artist's deeply caring nature helped him to modulate his style of writing, just as his profoundly creative nature did also. It was for this reason that Meyer Schapiro could contend that Van Gogh's letters were the *literary* equal of anything in nineteenth-century Russian fiction.[3] To be sure, Van Gogh's critical literary abilities are displayed in his letters as well, in the form of countless exquisitely telling artistic judgments, but I am talking now of the critical judgments that help shape the letters themselves and are not simply contained *in* the letters. Had Vincent thought less caringly for his brother, the literary quality of his correspondence with Theo might have been less, just as, had he been less appreciative of the color and shape relationships of the fields and villages of Provence, the artistic quality of the paintings he painted there might have been less.

[3] Meyer Schapiro, *Vincent Van Gogh* (New York: Abradale Press, 1994).

In an educational context, we can see a constant relationship between caring and creative thinking. One student who does not care
much about the change of seasons will paint the leaves as if they were
one dull color. Another student, more caring, and therefore more perceptive, will see leaves as gold, green, brown, red, and so on. So, the
caring produces more precise perception and more colorful depiction,
in this particular case.

CREATIVE AND CRITICAL THINKING

Inquiry, Peirce tells us, is the struggle to believe once the beliefs we
had previously relied upon have been corroded and dissolved by
doubt. It is doubt that signals to us that we are in a problematic
situation, and it is inquiry that we engage in to get some orientation
within the gloom. So it is, in any event, with the critical thinker.

With the creative thinker, matters are very nearly the reverse.
Doubt of what is conventionally believed is the comfortable state
of affairs, but when things become too comfortable, the problematic
evaporates, and the creative thinker agonizes. These agonies persist
until a new disbelief emerges, bringing about a newly problematic
situation: This jettisoning of the old problematic, product of the previous critical thinking, and its replacement with the new problematic,
freshly and richly permeated by doubt, is what creative thinking consists in. So, inquiry needs also creative thinking.

Let us review the contrast and interdependence between the critical thinker and the creative thinker. The merely critical thinker is
somehow conservative, in the sense that he or she is not content until
finding a belief that dispenses with thinking. On the other hand, the
creative thinker is essentially skeptical and radical. Creative thinkers
are never so happy as when they have been let loose, like bulls in
china shops, to smash to smithereens the bric-a-brac of the world.

What do I infer from the claim I have been making that creative thinking is the fabrication of the problematic? I assume that
there is a relationship between problematicity and inquiry – that
the one provokes and yields the other, much as there is a causal
relationship very often between frustration and aggression. If this
is so, then creative thinking provokes and produces appreciation
and criticism (respectively, forms of caring and critical thinking). It is

therefore highly valuable for improving thinking in possible learning situations.

COGNITIVE MOVES IN THE CREATIVE THOUGHT PROCESS

Any technological instrument calls for a cluster of associated movements that are involved in or required for its utilization. An automobile, for example, involves a matrix of such moves as depressing and releasing the accelerator and brake pedal, turning the steering wheel, turning switches on and off, and so on. This matrix of prescribed moves is of course put into operation by drivers, who materialize, as it were, the moves that otherwise have only a theoretical existence.

Similarly with mental acts: Prior to their being performed, they exist in a theoretical or virtual sense, but it cannot be said that, when they are performed, they are being materialized. In fact, neither physical nor cognitive moves are ever really "materialized," although they may be "actualized." The arc of the swing of the golf club recommended by the coach is actualized by the player swinging his or her club, and the thinker who makes a decision is actualizing a decision-making or deciding move. Thus every mental act actualizes a mental move; every thinking skill actualizes a thinking move; every connection of mental acts has already been made possible as a mental association or bridging. In other words, any particular thinker is the site of an enormous number of paths, roadways, avenues, and boulevards that crisscross the terrain that is already familiar through constant use, and that suggest hitherto unrelated connections or clusters of connections to those adventurous thinkers who are looking to explore new terrains. Due to ignorance or prejudice, certain connections are deemed unachievable or improbable, but often it is just these that the inventive or creative or imaginative mind will select for a breakthrough.

All moves are complex; that is to say, they are capable of being broken into smaller moves indefinitely: There are no atomic moves.

CREATIVITY AND DIALOGUE IN THE COMMUNITY OF INQUIRY

A community of inquiry is a deliberative society engaged in multidimensional thinking. This means that its deliberations are not

merely chats or conversations: they are logically disciplined dialogues. The fact that they are logically structured, however, does not
preclude their providing a stage for creative performance.

Take Joan. In the lecture courses she attends, she is normally a
detached observer. The lecturers impress her with their erudition,
and she is seldom so troubled by what any of them say as to think
of asking a question, let alone making a comment or developing a
thesis. But now she attends a seminar in which the instructor acts
only as a facilitator of the dialogue, although at times she pauses to
press individual students about what they may be taking for granted
in their comments. And now the dialogue intensifies, and Joan comes
to realize that there is another side to the issue that she had formerly
understood from just a single point of view. And still the dialogue
continues to intensify; soon Joan realizes there may be many sides, not
just one or two. She leans forward, listening intently, and suddenly
there bursts from her a comment that surprises her as much as it
does the others. It does not settle the discussion, which sweeps on
to the end of the period. Perhaps it made an important contribution;
perhaps it made only a minor one. But as Joan goes home, what she
takes with her and dwells upon is the comment she made, how she
might have made it better, and how wonderful it was that she made
it at all. She had been swept up in the dialogue, had overcome her
normal reticence and self-consciousness, and had been brought to
utterance. And it was she who spoke, she herself, in the first person;
nor did it escape her, as she spoke, that the others were listening
raptly to her – an intoxicating experience for one who has never had
it before. She told them her thoughts and she made them think – this
is what goes through her mind as she walks along, still trying to figure
out what happened to have so intensely moved her. Once again she
rehearses what she said and savors it, even while reproaching herself
for not having made the comment still more trenchantly. But as to
how it happened, all she knows is that *it* – the situation – drew her
utterance out of her. It did not teach her what to say, but it created an
environment in which she found it important to say what she wanted
to say. To do so, she had to teach herself how to speak as it were for
the first time.

The community of deliberative inquiry establishes conditions
evocative of critical, caring, and creative thinking, and such thinking

in turn furthers the objectives of both the community and its members. This is a very different set of conditions from the ones found in a classroom that stresses learning and knowledge – the acquisition of erudition. It is not that the lecture is an inferior or obsolete mode of pedagogy. It can be brilliant; it can be a work of art; it can often penetrate deeper into its subject matter from its single point of view than can a discussion from its multiple points of view. But to the extent that it is fascinating and charismatic, it turns its listeners into passive admirers rather than active inquirers. Too often it inhibits rather than encourages creativity, and the same is even true of critical thinking. It appropriates the means of intellectual production instead of turning them over to the students so as to enable them to become productive themselves.

CREATIVITY AND THINKING FOR OURSELVES

It is unprofitable to think of creativity as a process of emergence out of nowhere. It is rather a transformation of the given into something radically different – not a rabbit produced by magic out of a silk hat, but a silk purse produced by art out of a sow's ear.

Socrates and Kant are both severely critical of those who betray their own creativity by letting other people do their thinking for them. We should think for ourselves, and we should help other people think for themselves. Gilbert Ryle, in his work "Thinking and Self-Teaching,"[4] describes good teachers in these ways:

1. They do not repeat themselves; when they must tell us the same things, they do so in different ways
2. They expect us to do things on our own with what they teach us, "applying it, re-phrasing it, accelerating it, drawing conclusions from it, marrying it with earlier lessons, etc. . . . "
3. They don't tell us, they *show* us what they want done and then get us to move or utter in similar ways
4. They tease us with questions and then question us about our answers

---

4 "Thinking and Self-Teaching," in Konstantin Kolenda (ed.), *Symposium on Gilbert Ryle,* Rice University Studies 58:3 (Summer 1972), as reprinted in *Thinking: The Journal of Philosophy for Children* 1:3–4 (n.d.), 18–23.

5. They make us practice and repractice our exercises, such as our conversions and syllogisms
6. They lead us by the hand along a half-familiar track and leave us in the lurch to get ourselves over its final stretch
7. They cite blatantly erroneous solutions, expecting us to pinpoint what is wrong in them or how to improve on them
8. They draw our attention to partly analogous, but easier, problems and leave us to use these analogies as banisters
9. They break up complex problems into simpler ingredients and then leave us to resolve the simpler problems and reunite the solutions
10. When we have hit upon a solution, they set us subsidiary or parallel problems

Having specified what good teachers in any subject do with their students, Ryle proceeds to argue that these are precisely the things we do with ourselves when we are trying to get ourselves to think. It is not exactly that we shuttle back and forth between the role of teacher and the role of learner when we are trying to think for ourselves. It is rather that we try to get ourselves to do what a good teacher would try to get us to do.

When we ponder, Ryle says, we are trying to make up for the fact that we are not being taught, and so we impose upon ourselves the sorts of tasks a teacher might impose on us. Ryle denies that he is affirming an identity here between being taught and thinking, but there is, he insists, an important connection between the two.

What I particularly want to emphasize about Ryle's analysis is that he begins by identifying the inquiry procedures or search operations that are characteristic of teacher–student dialogue. He then argues that, in our own private deliberations, we internalize the identical procedures. He helps us institute, as it were, a dialogue with ourselves.

Thinking for ourselves is, then, dialogical. And if it is the case, as I suspect it is, that thinking for ourselves is the most appropriate paradigm of creative thought, then Ryle's suggestions would hold good in any workshop, studio, atelier, coaching session, or laboratory in which a teacher is trying to stimulate students to "be creative."

Indeed, it seems to me that this is precisely the hypothesis that needs to be verified, that an individual's creative thinking resembles the dialogical interchange between good teachers and their students as exemplified by the operations Ryle has specified. Is this how would-be artists can be encouraged to be creative? Would-be physicians and physicists? Would-be poets, lawyers, and biologists? For wherever we are taught a craft and somehow learn to transcend that craft, we find encouragement to think for ourselves. To learn a craft is to learn how others think and have thought – knowledge and expertise not to be scoffed at. To acquire an art, however, is to enter into dialogue with those others, parrying their thinking here, building on it there, rejecting it here, modifying it there, until we have discovered our own way of making, saying, or doing, which is to say we have discovered our own creativity.

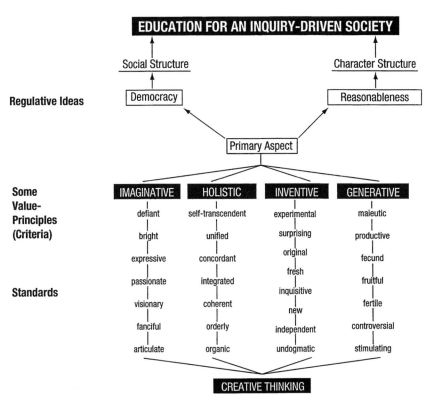

FIGURE 11.1.

The search techniques and inquiry procedures Ryle has mentioned are among those characteristic of the community of inquiry. These techniques and procedures are precisely those internalized by students, with the result that the methodical deliberations of the community are translated into the methodical deliberations and ponderings of the individual.

12

Education for Caring Thinking

Any collection of the world's great sonnets would contain, critics apparently agree, mostly those of Shakespeare. And if anyone were to look for the best illustrations of multidimensional thinking, one would turn again to the "Metaphysical Poets," especially Shakespeare and Donne, whose works express a balance of critical, creative, and caring thinking. Shakespeare, for example, does not hesitate to begin a sonnet with a critical question as to how he should begin – with what sort of simile: "Shall I compare thee to a summer's day?" His figures of speech are highly inventive: Every sonnet contains highly imaginative metaphors. And at the same time, his feeling for the person to whom the sonnet is addressed is usually an intense love and admiration that guides his choice of words and images. Likewise, Heloise's love letters to Abelard rise to the level of great literature because they interfuse critical and creative thinking with the tender passion that permeates her writing.

It is this matter of passion that is most controversial in the proposal to explain thinking as a combination of critical, creative, and caring thinking. We tend to identify critical thinking with reasoning and argumentation, with deduction and induction, with form, structure, and composition. We fail to see how profoundly our emotions shape and direct our thoughts, provide them with a framework, with a sense of proportion, with a perspective, or better still, with a number of different perspectives. Without emotion, thinking would be flat and uninteresting. Not even the dramatic imagination of the artist would stir us. To care is to focus on that which we respect, to appreciate its worth, to value its value.

Caring thinking involves a double meaning, for on the one hand it means to think solicitously about that which is the subject matter of our thought, and on the other hand it is to be concerned about one's *manner* of thinking. Thus, for example, a man writing a love letter writes *lovingly* to the person to whom the letter is addressed, while at the same time he is anxious about the letter itself.

CARING THINKING AS CONCERN FOR MATTERS OF IMPORTANCE

Gilbert Ryle did just about everything he could to overcome the fallacy of supposing that our thinking is the effect of some unthinking cause, as if our laughing at a ridiculous incident could be analyzed into there first being an emotionless observation of the occurrence and then a spasm of feeling and laughing, rather than that the incident was itself, from the beginning, laughable, and we were merely responding to it with appropriate appreciation when we laughed. It would be better, Ryle tells us, simply to say that one found the incident funny:

Nor does the anxious mother first dispassionately consider an unformulated truth about her child's illness and then go on to have a feeling of anxiety and then go on to wring her hands. She thinks anxiously, and she is anxious enough to keep thinking about her child, and to think little of other things, unless as things connected with and colored by her child's danger.[1]

It is more than thirty years since this particular essay of Ryle's was first published, but we are still inclined to make the same epistemological mistake he was here excoriating. Someone will say, "It is because she is concerned *about* her son that she cares *for* him," whereupon someone will reply, "No, it is precisely because she cares *for* him that she is concerned *about* him." But just as we laugh at the incident because it is ridiculous or laughable, she cares for her son

---

[1] Gilbert Ryle, "A Rational Animal," in *Dilemmas*, p. 182.

because he matters, and her caring is the judgment that he does matter. We continue to debate how the ethical emerges from the nonethical and how the aesthetic emerges from the nonaesthetic, completely ignoring the inference to be drawn from Ryle, that the nonethical and the nonaesthetic are myths stemming from totally antiquated epistemological ideas. People wonder, incredibly, how music with aesthetic properties can emerge from "mere sounds" and how paintings with aesthetic properties can emerge from "mere paints," while forgetting (if they ever knew it) that mere sounds and mere paints are intensely imbued with aesthetic qualities already. Creation is not an extraction of the aesthetic out of the wholly nonaesthetic, but a transformation of one kind of aesthetic quality into another. Likewise, education is not the extraction of a reasonable adult out of an unreasonable child, but a development of the child's impulses to be reasonable. Indeed, what passes as education is often the damping down of the child's wholesome philosophical impulses, so that the philosophically inclined child becomes an unphilosophically inclined adult.

This brings us back to Ryle's point – that we laugh at the joke because it is funny, at the scene because it is comical, at the incident because it is ridiculous, and so on. Likewise, we care about things that matter, even though how much they matter is a matter of degree, depending upon how much we care. Rare stones, in themselves, are not more precious than common stones, nor are they less precious; what decides whether they are more or less precious is our caring, that is, our careful discrimination of their worth.

One type of caring turns readily into another, as in *Through the Looking Glass* the cook's baby turns into a pig and back into a baby. X reads Y's paper carefully, from beginning to end. But X may begin the reading because she cares for Y personally, continues reading because she feels she has an editorial responsibility to do so, and completes her reading because she finds the paper genuinely appealing and likable. Each is a form of caring that provides a rationale for her reading, but they are three different rationales for the same act. As a rationale, each caring represents a "why she thinks she is reading the paper," and it is therefore a thinking, even though one might prima facie identify it as a "mere feeling."

SOME KINDS OF CARING THINKING

I have been emphasizing that caring is not merely a causal condition
of thinking – or need not be, in any case – but can, instead, be a mode
or dimension or aspect of thinking itself.[2] Thus, caring is a kind of
thinking when it performs such cognitive operations as scanning for
alternatives, discovering or inventing relationships, instituting connections among connections, and gauging differences. And yet, it is
of the very nature of caring to obliterate distinctions and rankings
when they threaten to become invidious and, thereby, outlive their
usefulness. Thus, caring parents, recognizing that "being human" is
not a matter of degree, just as "being natural" is not a matter of hierarchy, do not attempt to assign rankings to their children; yet at
the same time they recognize that there are significant differences of
perspective so that things have different proportions in one perspective than they have in another. Those who care, therefore, struggle
continually to strike a balance between that ontological parity that
sees all beings as standing on the same footing and those perspectival differences of proportion and nuances of perception that flow
from our emotional discriminations.

I do not feel, however, that I am in a position to offer a definition
of caring thinking in the sense that I might contend that the criteria
I offered for critical thinking could be combined to form a definition
of that aspect of cognition. What I can offer, instead, is an inventory of a number of varieties of caring thinking that I sense to be
neither nonoverlapping nor exhaustive. They are, however, promi-
nent features of the terrain, and we would do well to take note of
them.

Appreciative thinking

John Dewey has pointed out that we must distinguish between prizing and appraising, between esteeming and estimating, between
valuing and evaluating.[3] To value is to appreciate, to cherish, to hold

[2] This selection appeared originally as "Caring as Thinking" in *Inquiry: Critical
Thinking across the Disciplines*, vol. 15, no. 1 (autumn 1995), 1–13.
[3] John Dewey, "Theory of Valuation," *International Encyclopedia of Unified Science*
(Chicago: University of Chicago Press, 1939), p. 5. Dewey suggests that *prizing* means

dear; to evaluate is to calculate the worth of. The difference between prizing and appraising, as well as between pairs of similar terms, is a difference of degree: there is no prizing that does not contain at least a germ of appraisal and no appraisal that does not contain at least a germ of prizing.

In any event, when we prize, admire, cherish, and appreciate, we are engaged in valuing something for the relationships it sustains. To value a gift is to value the thing given for the feelings it expresses toward us from the donor of the gift. The gift is valuable because it establishes connections between our attitudes, dispositions, and emotions and those of the donor, connections that might be difficult to establish in any other fashion.

Thus, to appreciate a work of art is to find joy in observing the relationships of the parts of the work to one another and to the primary aspect of which the work is comprised. To appreciate the cinematography of a film is to enjoy the pictorial relationships that the camera makes available to the viewer, as well as the relationships between the camera work and the acting, directing, music, and other aspects of the film. Likewise, to find a face interesting or beautiful is to admire and enjoy the relationships among the features as well as the relationships within the features. If pressed, we can always cite these relationships within the features, just as we can always cite these internal relationships as the reasons for the admiration we experience.

To appreciate is to pay attention to what matters, to what is of importance. Never mind the seeming circularity: that what matters is of importance precisely because we pay attention to it. It is only partially true. Things in nature are neither better nor worse than other things, but when we compare and contrast them in particular perspectives, we pay attention to and, therefore, value their similarities and differences. In itself, a lake is neither better nor worse than an ocean, and a hill is neither better nor worse than a mountain. It is only in particular contexts that we experience them relationally, hence, valuationally. It is in this sense that curators care for works of art, doctors care for health, and curates care for souls: These people are caring people in

a holding precious or holding dear, while *appraising* means assigning a value to. Prizing has a definite *personal* reference and "an aspectual quality called emotional." In appraising, on the other hand, the intellectual aspect is uppermost.

that they attend to what matters to them, and their doing so is no "merely emotional" display, but has genuine cognitive worth.[4]

Affective thinking

Affective thinking is a conception that cuts like a laser across the reason versus emotion dichotomy. Instead of assuming that emotions are psychological storms that disrupt the clear daylight of reason, one can conceive of the emotions as themselves forms of judgment or, more broadly, forms of thought. Martha Nussbaum writes:

> Emotion is a kind of thought. Like any thought, it can go wrong: even Aristotle and Rousseau will insist that one can have misplaced emotions, such as excessive concern for one's property or reputation . . . [O]ne will have to grant that if emotion is not there, neither is that judgment fully there . . . It means that in order to represent certain sorts of truths one must represent emotions. It also means that to communicate certain truths to one's reader one will have to write so as to arouse the reader's emotions."[5]

Once again, the point being insisted upon is that at least some emotions are not merely the physiological consequences of human judgments: They are those judgments themselves. The very indignation one feels when one reads of some unspeakable indignity committed upon a stranger *is* one's judgment of the shamefulness of that event. Schemes to improve thinking can hardly flourish so long as the only kind of thinking thought worthy of the name is deductive thinking or some other austere form of rationality. The educational approach to the teaching of thinking has to include affective thinking, not simply out of deference to some vague allegiance to democratic pluralism, but because underemphasis upon the other varieties simply results in the superficiality of the treatment of the one intellectual variety that is acknowledged.

---

4 Harry Frankfort writes, "How is it possible, then, for anything to be genuinely unimportant? It can only be because the difference such a thing makes is itself of no importance. Thus, it is evidently essential to include, in the analysis of the concept of importance, a proviso to the effect that nothing is important unless the difference it makes is an important one." From *The Importance of What We Care About* (New York: Cambridge University Press, 1988), p. 82. I have reservations, however, about Frankfort's contention that caring has to do with what matters to one personally in contrast to what concerns one interpersonally and, hence, ethically.

5 M. Nussbaum, "Emotions as Judgments of Value," *Yale J. of Criticism* 5, no. 2. (1992), 209–10.

Consider this example. You observe an innocent child being abused and you are indignant. Does your indignation qualify as thinking? Surely your indignation involves an awareness that the abuse of someone innocent is improper, and it involves the additional awareness that the indignation you feel is warranted. Indignation is unlikely to be produced by an isolated causal event: It needs a reason. The reason may not be a strong one or a good one, but it is a reason, not a cause, and it is *part of the indignation itself.*

Thus, the indignation one feels is the development of one's initial realization that someone innocent is being hurt, as well as one's realization that such behavior is *inappropriate.* What is inappropriate in a given context is lacking in warrant, lacking in justification. The abuse is felt to be inappropriate; the indignation is felt to be appropriate. And appropriateness is just as much a cognitive criterion as is, say, coherence or relevance.

This is a matter whose importance for moral education cannot be underestimated. Frequently, our actions follow directly upon our emotions. One hates, one behaves destructively, one loves, one behaves amicably, and so on. Consequently, if we can temper the antisocial emotions, we are likely to be able to temper the antisocial conduct.

Active thinking

From what has just been said about emotions being cognitive, it should hardly be surprising to find actions being sometimes described as cognitive. There are languages of gesture and other bodily movements, such as facial expressions. And even an act that does not have a standard assignable meaning may take one on when performed in a suitable context.

Few discussions of caring fail to note the ambiguity between the use of the term to mean *caring for* or *about* (in the sense of having an affectionate feeling for) and *caring for* (in the sense of taking care of or looking after). We might want to distinguish these senses by classifying the first with affective thinking and the second with active thinking. I am using the term 'active' in this context to refer to actions that are at the same time ways of thinking.

Thus, one type of active thinking is curatorial – a conserving of what one cherishes. People try to preserve their looks or their youth; they take steps to save the things they value from the maw of time.

Others seek to preserve abstract values, as logicians seek to preserve the truth of the premises of an argument in its conclusion and as translators seek to preserve the meaning of a statement from one language to another.

Another type of active thinking is illustrated by such professional activities as sport. Thus, a game such as baseball is meticulously rule-guided in certain respects but open and criterion-guided in other respects. Some situations call for merely mechanical behavior, such as moving away from the plate after having struck out. Other situations call for creative judgments, such as trying for a triple play. We call such activities cognitive because, like most professional conduct, they are shot through with judgments.

This requires a fresh look at the notion of judgment, such as that provided by Buchler. Every judgment, according to Buchler, is expressive of the person who performs it and is appraisive of that person's world.[6] Throw a baseball and the way you throw it will be expressive of you, while the way you throw it will also take into account such considerations as the velocity of the wind, the readiness of the catcher, and the proficiency of the batter. Every act is an intervention that tests one's circumstances.

There is, thus, a language of acts as there are languages of words, and if the meanings of words are to be found in their connections with the sentences that incorporate them, so the meanings of acts are to be found in their relationships to the projects and scenarios that embody them. Their meanings are also to be found in their relationships with the consequences that flow from them, as well as in their contextual relationships.

Normative thinking

A word is in order here with regard to the thinking in tandem that yokes thinking about what is with thinking about what ought to be. To some extent, this is a matter of moral upbringing in the home and in the schools. We insist that the child consider, with every instance of desiring, what ought to be desired and, thereby, link the desired

---

[6] Michael Lewis and Linda Michalson develop this fugal theory in *Children's Emotions and Moods* (New York: Plenum Press, 1983), pp. 87–93.

always with the desirable. The desirable is one example of the result of reflection upon actual practice, for inquiry into what *is* done should be able to come up with a sketch or blueprint for what *ought to be* done, if the inquiry is sufficiently sustained.

This conjunction of the normative with the actual intensifies the reflective component of both action and caring. One who cares is concerned always with the ideal possibilities of caring conduct, so that reflection upon the ideal becomes part and parcel of the attention one pays to what is actually going on. Since the normative element is always cognitive, its inseparability from other aspects of caring simply adds further to their claim to cognitive status.

Those who are able to reflect upon who they are need to be able to take into account, as well, the sort of persons they want to be and ought to want to be. Those able to consider the world as it is should be helped to consider the sort of world they want to live in and the sort of world they ought to want to live in. Such an agenda may well occupy them for the larger parts of their lives, but it will be time well spent.

Empathic thinking

The term "empathy" has a wide range of meanings, but for my purposes here it has to do solely with what happens when we put ourselves into another's situation and experience that person's emotions as if they were our own. As such, the importance of the term is primarily ethical. That is, one way of caring is to step out of our own feelings, perspective, and horizon and imagine ourselves instead as having the feelings, perspective, and horizon of another. As Mark Johnson says, "We need not worry that empathic imagination is a private, personal, or utterly subjective activity. Rather, it is the chief activity by which we are able to inhabit a more or less common world – a world of shared gestures, actions, perceptions, experiences, meanings, symbols and narratives."[7] Given the important role that our feelings play in our own understanding of our situation, it is not difficult to see that the substitution of someone else's feelings would enable us to understand much better how that other person views his or her situation.

[7] Mark Johnson, *Moral Imagination* (Chicago: University of Chicago Press, 1993), p. 201.

Indeed, what often causes a breakdown of understanding is that the parties involved are able to appreciate only the linguistic or the cognitive factors involved in their interaction with one another but fail to achieve that exchange of emotions that would make their mutual understanding a reality.

Moral imagination is sometimes treated as though it were a merely playful dealing with fictions. On the contrary, it is a procedure that makes moral seriousness possible. It is when we do *not* put ourselves in the other person's place that we are merely playing at being ethical. To be sure, the empathic act does not require that we accept the other's evaluation: We still have a judgment to make. But now we have better reasons, and the judgment we make can be a stronger one.

I have been insisting on the addition of caring thinking to critical and creative thinking in any factoring out of the major aspects for the improvement of thinking in education for two major reasons: (1) Caring has ample credentials as a cognitive enterprise, even though it often consists of hardly discernible mental acts like screening, filtering, gauging, weighing, and so on, rather than pronouncedly discernible acts like inferring and defining. But the cognitive is not restricted to acts of high visibility alone, just as the vital bodily organs are not limited to those that are engaged in dramatic pumping activities such as the heart and the lungs. The liver and the kidneys are vital organs too, for the screening or discriminations they perform are essential to our lives. (2) Without caring, thinking is devoid of a values component. If thinking does not contain valuing or valuation, it is liable to approach its subject matters apathetically, indifferently, and uncaringly, and this means it would be diffident even about inquiry itself. In attempting to make a case for caring thinking I in no way intend to disparage critical and creative thinking, just as in making a case for applied thinking, I would not aim to disparage theoretical thinking. I am aware, however, that the almost Manichean dualism of rationalism/irrationalism is one to which many people are profoundly committed, so that a reorientation to reasonableness would be, for them, far more easily said than done.

I suspect we feel emotions when we have choices and decisions to make, and these choices and decisions are the leading edges of judgment. Indeed, so important is the role of the emotion in the thinking that leads up to the judgment and in the thinking that leads down from and away from it that we would be hard put to tell the one from the other. In fact, they may very well be indistinguishable; they may very well be identical, in which case it would make perfect sense to say that the emotion *is* the choice, it *is* the decision, it *is* the judgment. And it is this kind of thinking that we may well call caring thinking when it has to do with matters of importance.

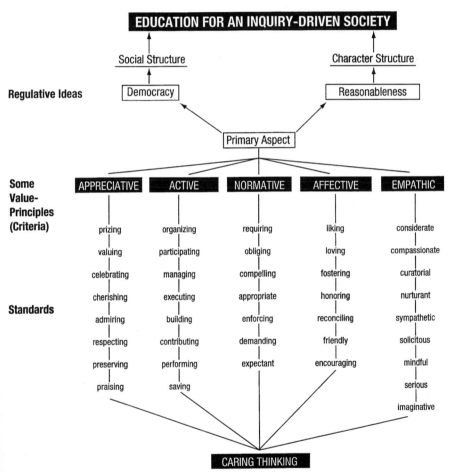

FIGURE 12.1.

13

Strengthening the Power of Judgment

Expertness in judgment is generally thought to be the result of principle or of practice. Principled judgments are those guided by standards, criteria, and reasons. Teaching students to make principled judgments therefore focuses upon having them learn the principles by which their judgments are to be regulated. Judgments of practice, on the other hand, are the products of experience, and students are expected to arrive at expertness by profiting from their experience as they gradually make their judgments better and better.

Now, both of these approaches are on target. True, in theoretical fields the emphasis will be on the acquisition of principles; in fields populated by craftpersons and artists, the emphasis will be on practice; and in professional and technological fields the emphasis will be approximately equal. Obviously, both approaches are necessary. The question is – and here what I have primarily in mind is the formation of judgment in *educational* contexts – are they sufficient?

Before proceeding to deal at some length with this question, I am aware of another that interposes itself. It is a question many educators would feel inclined to ask, and the reasoning would run something like this: "Why are we spending all this time talking about judgment? Judgment is in no way a recognized area of educational responsibility. It has never been. Children come to us to learn – to acquire knowledge. How well or badly they apply that knowledge is up to them.

Granted, we have neglected the teaching of reasoning. But we need not apologize for failing to teach judgment. No one has offered to show us how to do it in a school context, and it is doubtful that anyone ever will."

Parents have been inclined to accept this argument, although not without a little grumbling. To the extent that they are aware of their children's poor judgment, they are likely to think that it is they, the parents, who have failed and not the schools. Are the children impulsive, irresponsible, prejudiced toward others? These frailties, it has been intimated, are defects of character, and defects of character are attributable to home upbringing rather than to schooling. But this explanation leaves the parents frustrated. Even if they accept the responsibility that has been thrust upon them, they see no way out except with the school's help. The school, whether it likes it or not, has become a surrogate home, and the development of judgment is now a task for which there must be shared accountability.

Some parents are inclined to think that the improvement of children's judgment can be achieved by more effectively implanting in them strict codes of traditional values. But others shake their heads and say, "Perhaps, but the nub of the matter is judgment, and this is where we have to do better. Our youngsters have to learn to distinguish the authentic from the phony, the profound from the superficial, the justified from the unwarranted. They have to learn that the world they inhabit is not always candid with itself, so that violence against the innocent and helpless is only reluctantly defined as injustice, while victims are routinely told that they and those with whom they associate are the authors of their own suffering. If the schools could do more to teach children to exercise better judgment, it would protect them against those who would inflame them with prejudice and manipulate them through indoctrination. It would make them better producers and consumers, better citizens, and better future parents. So why not education for better judgment?"

To many, this question will seem a plaintive one, similar to the one posed by Henry Higgins: "Why can't a woman be more like a man?" But the problem children have – of making sense of the world, making judgments about it, and acting accordingly – is a profoundly serious one. We like to think of ourselves as "firm" when we retort that the schools have never taught for judgment and are not going to start doing it now – until we recall Bertrand Russell's mocking comment, "I am firm, you are stubborn, he is pig-headed." Like it or not, we are going to have to teach for better judgment. We had better set about figuring out how to do it.

JUDGMENT AS CRITICAL, CREATIVE, AND CARING

We should not assume, to begin with, that the improvement of children's reasoning will necessarily result in their exercising better judgment, just as it cannot be assumed that better judgments will necessarily be followed by better actions. We are in the area of likelihood here, not necessity.

The reasonablenss we want to cultivate in students is, to be sure, the result of a combination of reasoning and judgment, but the relationship between the two is highly complex. Probably – we are not quite sure how – there is a kind of osmosis by means of which they flow into each other, so that at least some judgment informs all reasonings and at least some reasoning informs all judgments. Or, as Santayana might have put it, all judgments have a kernel of reasoning and all reasonings have judgment as their natural fruition.

Creative, caring, and critical judgment together enable us to get a grip on things. An example (for third and fourth graders) would be doing an exercise in the assessment of analogies, where the students are asked to rank or grade a series of figurative expressions. The analogies range from shallow to insightful and so represent a range of judgments whose creativity is controversial. The students' evaluative judgments, for which they are asked to provide reasons, represent the critical aspect of the exercise. The valuative and the emotive aspects are present in the content of some of the analogies, which deal with ethical, aesthetic and emotive values. These are some of the items:

1. Thoughts are to thinkers as shoes are to shoemakers
2. Giggling is to laughter as whimpering is to crying
3. Words are to stories as seeds are to flowerbeds
4. Value is to price as quality is to size
5. Ideas are to children as memories are to adults
6. Taking home a report card is like removing a Band-Aid from an open wound

7. Putting sauerkraut over your pizza is like putting chow mein in your milkshake.
8. Joking is to ridiculing as caressing is to scratching
9. Trying to teach someone by means of a test is like trying to put air in a bicycle tire by means of a pressure gauge
10. Respect is to a good neighbor as love is to a good friend

Students of nine or ten years of age welcome such opportunities to assess figures of speech that are presented to them, but in addition they are prolific inventors of fresh analogies, metaphors, and similes. They must learn to employ this newfound creative initiative judiciously. Carried to an extreme, it can result in the atrophy of critical judgment, in an outpouring of inventiveness that lacks a sense of direction or responsibility.

These extremes are not at all hard to find; they are quite prevalent. Critical thinking often moves in the direction of the construction of algorithms that eliminate the need for judgment, while creative thinking may move in the direction of heuristics such that all that counts is success and not the means by which it is achieved. Algorithms, in the extreme, represent reasoning without judgment, while heuristics, in the extreme, represent judgment without reasoning.

If educators concede that the schools must cultivate both reasoning and judgment, then they must grant the importance of three pedagogical moves. The first is that students encountering discrepancies that perplex them should be encouraged to find principles from which these puzzling events would follow as unsurprising and a matter of course. For example, the students are puzzled by the fact that litmus paper, when placed in some unknown liquid, turns red. They then learn that litmus paper will behave this way if and only if it is placed in acid. The students now see that the behavior of the litmus paper is no longer an anomaly: It follows *as a matter of course* from the general principle they have now acquired.

The second pedagogical move is one that stimulates creativity by encouraging students to preserve the element of surprise. The surprising fact opens the door to new discoveries and still further surprises. If critical thinking tends to eliminate surprise by seeing the perplexing event as something that happens quite as a matter of course, creative thinking tends to escalate surprise by seeing the surprising event as merely the first in a rapidly expanding series of surprises. For example, the Matruschka doll when opened by a child contains within itself a smaller doll that turns out also to be a Matruschka doll and so on.

The third pedagogical move stimulates valuative thinking regarding things that matter by encouraging students to think contextually and to be aware of the implicit and explicit values that go along with our critical and creative judgments. For example, if a small child discovers a hermit crab in a shell it may be sufficeint to trigger her perception of many other kinds of shells and other kinds of crabs.

The critical judgment therefore contrasts with the creative judgment in a way that can perhaps be best summarized by considering the questions to which they are typically the answers. The characteristic discourse of critical thinkers aims at the articulation of judgments that respond to the query "What, precisely, is the question?" The characteristic conduct of creative thinkers, on the other hand, seems to be guided by the query "Now that this surprising thing has been invented, to what surprising but previously unasked question is it the answer?" The element of caring is in both fields. Thus, the critical thinker looks for answers in the form of questions that will point the way to the elimination of inquiry. The creative thinker looks for questions in the form of answers that will lead to the perpetuation of inquiry. And both are concerned with the preservation of what matters. Therefore, both care about questions that are important. Teachers who wish to strengthen judgment must encourage the three forms of thinking and their convergence.

THE JUNCTURE OF THE UNIVERSAL AND THE PARTICULAR

If a group of college students were to be asked what instances come to mind when they hear such phrases as "logical reasoning" and "logical judgments," they might well reply by citing such examples as these:

1. All Greeks are human.
    All humans are mortal.
    Therefore, all Greeks are mortal.

2. If someone is a man, then he's mortal.
   Socrates is a man.
   Therefore, Socrates is mortal.

Now, formal judgments are only one kind of judgment; there are countless other kinds. And formal reasoning is only one kind of reasoning. There are part–whole reasoning and means–end reasoning, for example. And indeed, whenever we perform work on what we know, whenever we seek to extend it or defend it or coordinate it, or order it, we are involved in reasoning.

If we are concerned to strengthen reasoning and judgment in education, it has to involve, it seems to me, this enlarged sense of reasoning and this diversified sense of judgment as creative, caring, and critical, as particular and as universal. I have not sought to conceal my own preference for the formation of classroom communities of inquiry that reflect on intrinsically interesting materials, such as conceptually rich stories, when the communities then try to construct such stories themselves. This provides an outlet both for the students' impulse to analyze for the sake of understanding and for their impulse to emulate the thinking people they encounter in their reading by thinking like them. The critical thinker cares about solving problems because she or he cares for the people who suffer as a result of those problems. The creative thinker is looking for an imaginative solution to the problem; the critical thinker is looking for any solution.

We have until now been holding to the notion that reading and writing should be taught in the context of language and literature – and rightly so. But if we are to stress the analytical as well as the creative and the caring, if we are to stress the universal as well as the particular, then it seems to me we have to teach reading and writing – along with reasoning, speaking, and listening – in the context of the humanities generally and in the context especially of language and philosophy.

Philosophy contains, along with many other things, a core of concepts. These concepts are embodied or illustrated in all of the humanities, but it is in philosophy that they are analyzed, discussed, interpreted, and clarified. Many of these concepts represent profoundly important and profoundly general human values, such as truth and meaning and community. In fact, it can be argued that philosophy is the conceptualizable, teachable aspect of human values generally, just as craft is the conceptualizable, teachable aspect of art. Without philosophy, there is a tendency for the behaviors these concepts represent to remain unarticulated and mute. One reads Homer and accepts Agamemnon as just. But what is justice? Only a philosophical discussion can provide the process of dialogical inquiry that properly deals with this question.

Now, there is no reason why such concepts as those just referred to cannot be presented first in literary form, embodied and concrete, and then get taken up in more abstract form for discussion and analysis. Indeed, if we want to get students to confront the relationship between the universal and the particular, we must have them examine both a particular friendship – say, between Achilles and Patroclus or between David and Jonathan – and friendship in general. Likewise, they must not be allowed to rest content with this or that particular instance or variety of truth. We must get them to push on and consider if there is such a thing as truth in general, or "the Truth."

Elementary school philosophy provides a forum that enables children to reflect upon their values as well as upon their actions. Thanks to these reflections, children can begin to see ways of rejecting those values that do not measure up to their standards and of retaining those that do. Philosophy offers a forum in which values can be subjected to criticism. This is perhaps a major reason for its exclusion, until now, from the elementary school classroom, and a major reason for its now, at last, being included. Consider, for example, the value of *toleration*. As long as one group in a society is in an authoritarian position, other groups will plead with it to be tolerant, and tolerance in this instance is put forth as an unambiguous virtue. But if no one group is in the ascendancy, as in a pluralist society, it becomes condescending or hypocritical for one group to claim that it tolerates the others. It is for this reason that toleration as a value has gone out of vogue, in contrast with the time of John Locke and Spinoza, when it was a value of crucial importance. Students have to be able to discuss and recognize differences of context, just as they have to be able to ask themselves when loyalty turns into blind fanaticism or when moderation is merely a label for indifference. It is hard to see how we can strengthen children's judgment without encouraging them to examine carefully the values upon which that judgment must rest.

THREE ORDERS OF JUDGMENT

A child comes to see a doctor, and tells the doctor he has been bitten by a bumble bee. The doctor may make several judgments, such as (1) bumble bee bites and mosquito bites are very different; (2) this bite was caused by a mosquito; and (3) it is the doctor's professional opinion that this bite requires only a topical anesthetic.

On the other hand, if we consider what is involved in attempting to strengthen judgment in an educational context, we might want to view these judgments as exemplifying three different orders whose differences are related to the roles they play in the teaching/learning process and in the subsequent life of the child. I want to emphasize that my aim is not to propose a general hierarchy of judgments but simply to suggest some functional distinctions that can be found operative in the pedagogical process.

Take the illustration I have just used, the doctor observing the child with the bite. The first is a judgment of difference, the second a causal judgment, and the third a professional judgment. These judgment types in turn express a still broader set of distinctions. Judgments of difference belong to an order that also comprises judgments of similarity and judgments of identity; causal judgments belong to an order that also comprises analogical judgments, hypothetical judgments, and numerous others; and professional judgments belong to an order that encompasses social judgments, aesthetic judgments, ethical judgments, technological judgments, and many others. I shall call these the order of generic judgments, the order of mediating judgments, and the order of culminating judgments, not to suggest that some judgments are intrinsically more fundamental than others, but to suggest that for the purposes of strengthening judgment in a school setting all three types are needed.

In ordinary discourse, what people generally seem to mean when they speak of judgment are ethical, social, political, and aesthetic judgments and the like – in short, culminating judgments, judgments applied directly to life situations. People engaged in ordinary discourse are apt to view judgments of similarity, difference, and identity as highly abstract and remote from life situations. They are not likely to recognize the pertinence that considerations of comparison and contrast have for every effort we make to reach a determination or settlement. Nor are they likely to recognize the mediating role that still other judgments play in the making of decisions or the solving of problems.

What we see, then, is that practice in the making of culminating judgments can be strengthened by giving students practice in the making of generic and mediating judgments (in addition to giving them practice in making culminating judgments directly). It is thanks to generic judgments that we find it possible to connect and relate or to distinguish and differentiate, and these make it possible for us to generalize and individuate. Nevertheless, important as generic judgments may be, they are for the most part too formal to be of much use in making culminating judgments *directly*. Too many other considerations have to be taken into account in those exquisitely subtle and complex situations in which we have to make an ethical or aesthetic or professional judgment. We may, for example, be clear enough in our minds that all murders belong to the class of morally wrong and legally punishable actions, on the ground that murders are acts that have many things in common with those other acts. But "having things in common" is not the same as "belong to the class of," which is a judgment of membership. And even if we introduce this latter judgment, we are still a long way from being in a position to assert that what X did to Y was wrong. In addition to problems of membership, there will be problems of relevance, problems of instrumentality, problems of inference, and so on. Relevance surfaces when the question is asked "But was this murder or self-defense?" Instrumentality surfaces with the question "Was Y's death a consequence of what X did?" And inference is inescapable if the conclusion that what X did was wrong is to be drawn from the premises "All murder is wrong" and "What X did was murder."

What I am arguing, then, is that in the preparation of a curriculum aimed at strengthening children's reasoning and judgment, continual practice should be given in the making of generic and mediating judgments. This is not to say that very young children should be discouraged from making culminating judgments. However, their culminating judgments are likely to be more sagacious if they have been given practice in the making of generic and mediating judgments earlier on. Judgments express relationships such as difference, similarity, identity, causality, interdependency . . .

If I offer at this point characterization of the judgments in each of these orders, it is not because I think such brevity is what they deserve. Many volumes have been written about each of them, and much more needs to be said. As for the domain of culminating judgments, it is so vast and far-reaching that I shall make no effort at all at characterizing its contents.

One way of visualizing the relationships among these different types of judgments is to see them as comprising a wheel connecting to its hub by a large number of spokes. One can even see the wheel as forming a cone with culminating judgments forming the apex and generic judgments forming the base.

Generic judgments

Judgments of identity. As similarities increase, they approach the condition of identity. Identity is therefore the limiting condition of increasing similarity. In natural language, identity is expressed by such phrases as "is equal to" or "is the same as." All mathematical equations take the principle of identity for granted. We do the same when we express ourselves in tautologies, definitions, and even synonyms. Whether two things can nevertheless be said to be identical with one another and whether one thing can be said to be identical with itself are matters of philosophical dispute.

Judgments of difference. This is one of the few types of judgment that have their own name ("distinctions"). Subsumed under it are discriminations of every possible sort: perceptual (to observe is to distinguish), conceptual, and logical. Distinctions are judgments of elementary unlikeness, or mere difference. When combined with judgments of membership (i.e., of inclusion or exclusion), they gravitate toward such categorical propositions as "No S are P" or "Some S are not P." When they are expressed relationally, they issue in such phrases as "is unlike," "is different from," and "is not the same as," but they can

THE WHEEL OF JUDGMENT

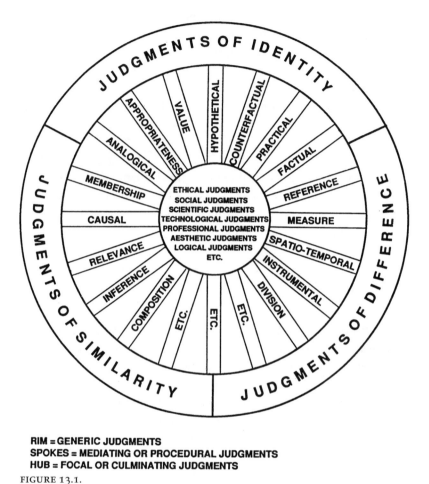

RIM = GENERIC JUDGMENTS
SPOKES = MEDIATING OR PROCEDURAL JUDGMENTS
HUB = FOCAL OR CULMINATING JUDGMENTS
FIGURE 13.1.

also express more explicit comparatives, such as "is happier than," "is longer than," or "is less safe than."

Judgments of similarity. These are judgments of simple, primitive likeness or resemblance. When working in tandem with judgments of membership, they facilitate the making of such categorical propositions as "All *S* are *P*" and "Some *S* are *P*." An act of comparison that leads to a determination of similarity is generally expressed by such phrases as "is like," "resembles," and "is similar to."

Mediating or procedural judgments

Judgments of composition. These are simply pronouncements that something is (or is not) a part of something else. They may use such phrases as "is a part of," "belongs to," "is a component of," and so on. When combined with an invalid inference, these part–whole judgments give rise to the so-called Fallacy of Composition, as in "Since his individual features are handsome, it follows that he has a handsome face." What is in question is not that his face comprises its individual features but that its quality can be logically inferred from theirs.

Judgments of inference. When we reason, we attempt to coordinate our knowledge, to defend it, or to extend it. Inference is counted on very heavily when it comes to *extending* knowledge. When we are certain that no loss of truth will occur in moving from what we know to what we do not know, the inferential judgment is considered a *deduction*. When we cannot be sure that the truth is being preserved, the inferential judgment is considered an *induction*. Moreover, deductive inference is governed by rules, whereas inductive inference is, at best, merely guided by rules. Judgments of inference are often expressed in such locutions as "It follows that" and "It means that." That these phrases are not synonymous has been a source of vexation to a number of logicians.

Judgments of relevance. Relevance is a fairly fuzzy notion but an extremely useful one for all that. This is so because much thinking is wasted upon what later turn out to have been irrelevant considerations. No wonder, then, that many "informal fallacies" of reasoning turn out to be "fallacies of relevance." (This is true even with formal fallacies, such as the "assertion of the antecedent." Let it be true that "If my cat is sick, it meows." But if it is now asserted that my cat is *not* sick, nothing follows, because what the cat does when sick tells us nothing about what it does when well.) Judgments of relevance evidently involve the number of connections between the entities in question and the importance of those connections.

Causal judgments. These range from simple statements of cause–effect relationships, such as "The stone broke the window," to full-blown explanations. The judgment that a causal process has taken place may be conveyed by any of a vast number of verbs, such as "produced," "created," "generated," "affected," "effected," and the like.

Judgments of membership. These are classificatory judgments and are expressed in statements to the effect that a given thing or class of things is a member of some other class. (It is obvious that judgments of membership are not easily distinguished from judgments of composition.) Judgments of membership are guided by distinguishing criteria, and such criteria in turn make up generic definitions. Thus, whenever we cite an instance or example of a family or class, we are making a judgment of membership. Both "Mary is a girl" and "Mary is a Watson" are judgments of membership.

Analogical judgments. This family of judgments is both vast and important. There are exact analogies, like ratios ("Three is to five as six is to ten"), and there are inexact analogies, such as "Thumbs are to hands as big toes are to feet." Examples like these lead us to think of analogies as based on judgments of identity ($3/5 = 3/5$) or on judgments of similarity. In any event, analogical judgments form a category of utmost importance in every field of inquiry. Analogical judgments are central to inductive inference. We are reasoning by analogy when we infer that, a number of similar cases having been observed to possess a certain characteristic, it is likely that a forthcoming case, also similar in other respects, will likewise possess this particular characteristic. And when it comes to sheer invention, whether artistic, scientific, or technological, it is unlikely that there is any mode of judgment that has greater utility than analogical judgment.

Judgments of appropriateness. Judgments of appropriateness range from determinations of what is *fit* to determinations of what is *equitable*. What guides us in the making of such judgments is not a particular rule or criterion but the whole context of the inquiry in which we are engaged, as revealed by our tact, taste, or sensibility. We make judgments of appropriateness when we shape, fashion, or proportion the act to fit the context. When people are accused of "lack of judgment" it is often the failure of this kind of judgment that the accusers have in mind.

Judgments of value. When things or matters are contrasted with one another with respect to value (e.g., "is better than," "is nicer than," "is more lovely than," "is more noble than," "is better made than"), using such criteria as originality, authenticity, perfection, coherence, and the like, the resulting expressions are judgments of value. When one judges the same things or matters by other criteria, the resulting expressions may be judgments of fact, of membership, and so on. The study of the making of judgments of value, as well as of the criteria to be employed in arriving at such determinations, is what is known as *criticism*.

Hypothetical judgments. These are not judgments of mere possibility, but judgments of the consequences of possible happenings. Thus, "It may rain tomorrow" is not a hypothetical judgment, but "If it rains tomorrow, the farmers will be happy" is. Hypothetical judgments, which take the form "If . . . , then . . . ," are therefore assertions subject to explicit conditions. They may alternatively be called conditional judgments.

Counterfactual judgments. If hypothetical judgments tell us what consequences will ensue if certain conditions do prevail, counterfactual judgments purport to enlighten us about what would have happened had matters been otherwise. Thus someone who asserts, "If the Nazis had won World War II, they would have dominated the world for a thousand years" is making a counterfactual judgment. Counterfactual judgments are especially relevant in the formulation of scientific laws, since they demonstrate that such laws would prevail even if certain circumstances now existing were not the case. If there were inhabitants of Mercury, the gravitational force they would experience could be calculated as we calculate the force we experience on Earth.

Practical judgments. Judgments of practice are made in accordance with received understanding as to what constitutes standard operating procedure in a given activity, field, or discipline. Farmers make judgments of practice when they decide to harvest, as do district attorneys when they decide to prosecute alleged wrongdoers, or as clergymen do when they decide on a particular sermon for a particular day. Judgments of practice are not mechanical but are guided by routines, precedents, customs, and traditions that allow for discretion but circumscribe it narrowly. There are times when judgments of practice and judgments of appropriateness complement each other and work, as it were, hand in hand; on other occasions, however, we may substitute the one for the other. We may turn our backs on established practice and try to deal with the case before us on its own merits, or we may deny that the case before us is unique and proceed to deal with it as others it resembles have been dealt with.

Judgments of fact. Judgments of fact are judgments that there is or is not sufficient evidence to warrant the assertion that something is the case. This is intricate, because it involves, among other things, being sure what counts for *evidence* (as opposed, for example, to mere testimony), and it involves being able to judge just when that evidence is *sufficient*. Anyone claiming something to be a fact must be concerned about just how much evidence is needed in order to justify making that claim.

Judgments of reference. Many judgments of identity or similarity are the result of acts of comparison, in which the conclusion has been reached that the entities under consideration *correspond* to or are correlated with one another. Other acts of comparison disclose that some things (e.g., signs) refer to or stand for other things. There are overlaps: A map of Japan stands for Japan and corresponds to it, whereas the word "Japan" merely stands for it. And two congruent geometrical constructions will correspond with one another without standing for one another.

Judgments of measure. Very often we make distinctions based on readily observable differences. Thus, we distinguish between hot and cold or night and day. But we may want a more precise way of differentiating degrees or gradation in sharply contrasting differences, so we construct a range of temperatures or we divide a night-day period into hours, minutes, and seconds. Now we can treat the degrees or gradations as units and superimpose a quantitative template over the qualitative texture of things. It is quantification of the world that makes judgments of measure and proportion possible.

Judgments of translation. As judgments of inference preserve, in the conclusion of an argument, the *truth* of its premises, so judgments of translation preserve, in a shift of contexts, a particular burden of *meaning*. We may write an expository paragraph and then conclude that our meaning could be conveyed at least as well by a cartoon as by a graph. "The cat is on the table" (in English) preserves the meaning of *"Le chat est sur le table"* (in French). Some judgments of translation are scrupulously rule-governed, as is the case with the standardization of natural-language sentences into the canonical forms of statements in classical logic. And so meaning, like capital, is an exchange value, and judgments of translation are judgments of the soundness of such exchanges in the overall economy of meaning.

Instrumental judgments. These judgments govern the adjustment of means to ends and of ends to means. Such adjustment is sometimes assigned a very lofty status, and it is seen as an essential component of rationality. Be that as it may, it may nevertheless be contended that instrumental judgments are settlements or determinations that play some role in the heightening of the consummatory or culminating aspects of experience.

Judgments of division. My glimpse of the order of mediating judgments began with mention of judgments of composition and concludes with mention of their counterpart – judgments of division. In making judgments of division, we pronounce whether or not a property of a given whole is also a property of the parts of that whole. (The fallacy of division is committed by those who assume that what is a property of the whole *must* be a property of its parts. Chicago may be a windy city, but it does not follow that the city's inhabitants are therefore windy. Blood is red, but it does not follow that the particles that compose it, viewed through a microscope, are red. Water is wet, but this does not imply that it is constituted of wet hydrogen and wet oxygen.)

Absurd as the reasoning may be of those who commit fallacies of composition and division, it is not more absurd than the reasoning of those who assume that whatever has aesthetic quality must be composed of nonaesthetic ingredients and that whatever is moral must be constructed out of nonmoral elements. The domain of unsound judgments of composition and division is a very large one indeed.

There may be many other categories in the order of mediating judgments. I am not concerned to spell them out. I want merely to suggest that they have enormous preparatory value if we are looking ahead to the strengthening of student judgment in the various walks of life in which students are likely to tread. It seems to me we are bound to be foiled if we think that a given form of culminating judgment, such as the ethical, can be strengthened either by (1) consideration of ethical principles alone with no excursions into practice or by (2) giving practice only in the making of ethical judgments without providing practice in the making of generic or mediating judgments.

Focal or culminating judgments

Focal or culminating judgments are performed when the generic and mediating judgments are applied to a specific situation. This is where expertise comes in; it is where professionalism comes in; it is the category of judgment at its most astute: the surgeon engaged in a spinal operation; a parliament deciding on war; the publisher deciding to publish a book that will rewrite history. This is where emotions can be most helpful in providing guidance, emphasis, or perspective. This is where mental acts swarm about, sometimes sustaining, sometimes interfering with the making of the decisions that have got to be made primarily and procedurally. It is where the context, the cognitive environment, must be recognized and given its due, as when a community of inquiry becomes involved and seeks a reasonable conclusion. It is where reasons are sifted and screened, to try to find those that are most reasonable, or least irrational. It is where alternative arguments are marshaled, just to see if there are arguments more persuasive or more enticing than what is being decided upon.

As professionals, teachers are in the forefront of those who are chiefly known by the judgments they make. At every moment, a teacher must make decisions that are not exactly like the previous year's so that there are few algorithms to be followed. Nevertheless, teachers are given heavy responsibility for the development of several groups of students in ways commended by the larger community. The success of the culminating judgments performed by the teacher becomes a major factor in the reputation of that teacher, making it all the more important that the strengthening of the prospective teachers' judicative capability be keenly emphasized in the college of education they attend.

THE BALANCE WHEEL OF JUDGMENT IN EDUCATIONAL SETTINGS

If history is sometimes characterized as a history of struggle, it can also be seen as a history of mediation. Often, indeed, the combatants themselves experience a fission in which half of them mediate while the other half continue the struggle. This balance of conflict and mediation will even be found internalized in individual participants so that, however many the directions in which they are pulled, it is judgment that works within them to redirect them toward wholeness and proportion and equity.

Judgment is called for whenever there are conflicting passions or conflicting goods or competing arguments. It is needed when the demands of the body must be weighed against the demands of the mind or when critical thinking is matched against creative or caring thinking. As we wobble like tops through the vicissitudes of life, it is to judgment that we turn for equilibrium. Like the balance wheel of a gyroscope, it helps maintain our stability despite the crazy angles at which we sometimes find ourselves. A life with little judgment can be a glorious thing, but it is likely to be short; with a little more judgment, we might yet be able to prevail.

Still, I would not have it thought that the only role of judgment is in restoring stability, however important a role this may be. For there are other times when we come to see the central direction of our lives as bleak and unprofitable, when our better judgment concludes that things must be otherwise, and the sooner the better. On such an occasion, judgment may play the role of *agent provocateur* – an unsettling, disturbing force tipping the balance one way or another so as to clear the way for a new equilibrium. In the intellectual life, it is philosophical judgment that has often played this role.

In our working lives, judgment is certainly of much importance, and in the professions it is vital. It is for this reason that the education of professionals so often centers on the honing of professional judgment. The preparation of future lawyers and doctors includes considerable simulation of practice: moot courts, internships, and the like. The professors who conduct such training are fully prepared to have their students use them as models, with the result that doctors emerge from the tutelage of doctors, lawyers from the tutelage of lawyers, and so on. Professionalism and judgment are so closely associated as to be almost synonymous.

The centrality of judgment is not so clearly visible in the preparation of future teachers – neither in the work of the instructors in the colleges of education nor in the day-to-day work of the teachers themselves nor in the lives of the end recipients of all this preparation, the children. All too often the work of the teacher is seen as a series of questions, answers, and commands, of rewardings and punishings, wheedlings and cajolings. Once it is admitted that the cultivation of judgment is the pivot upon which the education of a child must turn, an inescapable logic will compel schools of education to make such cultivation central to the preparation of teachers. This will help, in turn, to bring about that recognition of the professional status of teachers to which so much lip service is paid but that is still so far from becoming a reality.

I am not saying that the teaching of content is useless and that we are in danger of turning children into idiot savants. But I do contend that the stress on their acquisition of information has been exaggerated and should be complemented with the sharpening of their thinking and judgment.

There is at present a widespread recognition that something is amiss, but efforts at improvement often turn out to be merely cosmetic. There is nothing wrong with attempting to remodel lesson plans so as to make them more likely to encourage critical reflection and to strengthen judgment within and among the disciplines. But these efforts at "infusion" are bound to be fumbling, haphazard, and unavailing as long as students are not permitted to examine directly and for themselves the standards, criteria, concepts, and values that are needed to evaluate whatever it is they are talking and thinking about. Merely to encourage differences of opinion, open discussion, and debate will not provide a comfortable escalator to the improvement of thinking. This will happen only if students are given access to the tools of inquiry, the methods and principles of reasoning, practice in concept analysis, experience in critical reading and writing, opportunities for creative description and narration as well as in the formulation of arguments and explanations, and a community setting in which ideas and intellectual contexts can be fluently and openly exchanged. These are educational conditions that provide an infrastructure upon which a sound superstructure of good judgment can be erected.

To withhold from children access to ideas and reasons and criteria for judgment and yet to expect them to judge well is about like withholding air from them and expecting them not to suffocate. But how else are we to make these intellectual tools available to them if not through a series of courses in philosophy, redesigned so as to be accessible to children? If they are afforded no opportunity to compare and contrast the reasons people have for calling things true and good, how can they be expected to know what they are talking about when they are asked to decide which statements are true and which are not or which things are good and which are not?

Philosophy is ready to be made a required part of the elementary and secondary school curriculum. This happens infrequently at present because the existing curriculum is so bloated as to exclude all "outsiders." But when the existing curriculum has been suitably slimmed down, philosophy will no longer have to masquerade, as it is often required to do nowadays, as a course in language arts or reading or social studies.

People sometimes remark that philosophy is too much for children, but this seems merely to be a euphemistic way of saying that teaching teachers to teach children philosophy is just too much trouble. Nevertheless, schools of education should recognize the central role of the strengthening of judgment in the education of children and the need to prepare teachers to perform this task.

JUDGMENTS AS EXPRESSIVE OF PERSONS

One cannot say that a judgment is a microcosmic version of a person, or that a person is a judgment writ large, without taxing the credulity of the listener or reader: It seems like such a gross synecdoche. And yet, clearly, if there is anywhere that *the style that is the person* gets to be expressed, it is in that person's judgments. Perhaps it would be better to say that to take a judgment as the minimal *unit* of person-hood is metaphorical, but to take it as broadly representative of an individual's personhood is to understand it almost literally.

Not everyone agrees, of course, that one puts oneself into one's judgments. Thus Simone Weil, for whom personality is a curse and an affliction, contends that "Truth and beauty are impersonal.... If a child is doing a sum and does it wrong, the mistake bears the stamp of his personality. If he does the sum exactly right, his personality does not enter into it at all.... Perfection is impersonal. Our personality is the part of us that belongs to error and sin."[1] If we were to follow this reasoning it would evidently mean that only *bad* judgments are expressive. Apparently Weil is suggesting that only universal ideals are perfect and impersonal, and that, consequently, these are incompatible with whatever displays individuality. But this is implausible. The Renaissance celebrated the unity of the universal and the individual, as did the classic world the Renaissance sought to reawaken. When we judge rightly, we express who we are no less than when we judge wrongly. Instances can be as perfect as types, parts can be as perfect as wholes, particulars can be as perfect as universals. These are some of the reasons that can be put forth in support of the notion that each new judgment is projected upon and added to a composite image formed of all previous judicative projections. We are not like trees, whose cross-sections reveal the mere addition each year of a new circumference; we are *cumulative* beings, and each increment forces its way into our summed-up self and causes all the other parts to readjust their relationships with one another, even while the increment is itself altered as we seek to compel it to adapt to its new environment.

[1] From *Selected Essays, 1934–1943*, translated from the French by Sir Richard Rees, published by Oxford University Press, pp. 10–11, 22–34. Reprinted by permission of A. D. Peters & Co. Ltd.

Those who wish to devote themselves to a thoroughgoing reworking of the design of education should take very seriously this understanding of judgment as expressive of one's person. For if freedom, as Dewey conceives it, involves both the freedom to choose among alternatives and the freedom to carry out those alternatives that are selected, then the enhancement of the first – what might be called judicative freedom – necessarily entails the spelling out of alternatives to be taken into consideration. Educators therefore have this obligation – to assist students in finding the alternatives that are open to them, to help them discover the means needed to achieve those objectives, and to get them to see the consequences that might possibly flow from their realization. To be sure, freedom of the person entails much, much more than the liberation of judgment, but this cannot conceal the fact that the liberation of judgment is an indispensable component of that larger freedom.

The teacher, whose professional life is given over to making judgments of how best to prepare students to make judgments (unlike a judge, whose professional life involves passing judgment upon someone else's past judgments), exemplifies judgment in its forward-looking aspect. This is what is so fulfilling and liberating about the life of the teacher, and helps make up for the drudgery that such a career often entails.

Bibliography

Aristotle. *The Basic Works of Aristotle.* Edited by Richard McKeon. New York: Random House, 1941.

Austin, J. L. *How to Do Things with Words.* Cambridge, Mass.: Harvard University Press, 1962.

　Philosophical Papers. Edited by J. O. Urmson and G. J. Warnock. 3d ed. Oxford: Oxford University Press, 1979.

Bloom, Benjamin S., Max D. Engelhart, Edward J. Furst, Walker H. Hill, and David R. Krathwohl, eds. *Taxonomy of Educational Objectives.* Vol. 1; *Cognitive Domain.* New York: McKay, 1956.

Brown, John Seely, Allan Collins, and Paul Duguid. "Situated Cognition and the Culture of Learning." *Educational Researcher* (January–February 1989).

Bruner, J. S. *Processes of Cognitive Growth.* Worcester, Mass.: Clark University with Barre, 1968.

　Actual Minds, Possible Worlds. Cambridge, Mass.: Harvard University Press, 1990.

Bruner, J. S., and K. Connolly, eds. *The Growth of Competence.* London: Academic Press, 1974.

Buchler, Justus. *Toward a General Theory of Human Judgment.* New York: Columbia University Press, 1951.

　The Philosophy of Peirce: Selected Writings. New York: Harcourt Brace, 1940.

Coles, M. J., and W. D. Robinson. *Teaching Thinking: A Survey of Programmes in Education.* London: Duckworth, 1989.

Costello, Patrick. *Thinking Skills and Early Childhood Education.* London: David Fulton (U.K.), 2000.

de Sousa, Ronald. "Emotions, Education and Time," *Metaphilosophy,* 21, no. 4 (October, 1990).

　The Rationality of Emotions. Cambridge, Mass.: MIT Press, 1986.

Dewey, John. *The Child and the Curriculum.* Chicago: University of Chicago Press, 1902.

Democracy and Education. 1916. New York: Macmillan, 1944.

Experience and Education. 1938. New York: Collier, 1963.

Logic: The Theory of Inquiry. New York: Holt, 1938.

Elgin, Catherine Z. *Considered Judgment.* Princeton: Princeton University Press, 1996.

Frischman, Bärbel. "Philosophieren mit Kindern. Theoretische Grundlagen, Konzepte, Defizite." In *Deutsche Zeitschrift für Philosophie* 46, Jg., Heft 2. Berlin, 1998.

Gadamer, Hans-Georg. "Hermeneutics as Practical Philosophy." *Reason in the Age of Science.* Cambridge, Mass.: MIT Press, 1983.

Philosophical Apprenticeships. Cambridge, Mass.: MiT Press, 1985.

Gal'perin, P. Y. "Stages in the Development of Mental Acts." In Michael Cole and Irving Maltzman, eds., *A Handbook of Contemporary Soviet Psychology.* New York: Basic Books, 1969.

Geach, P. T. l, and M. Black, eds. *Translations from the Philosophical Writings of Gottlob Frege.* Oxford: Blackwell Publisher, 1966.

Gewirth, Alan. "The Rationality of Reasonableness." *Synthèse* 57 (1983).

Gibbard, Allan. *Wise Choices, Apt Feelings.* Cambridge, Mass.: Harvard University Press, 1990.

Hahn, Carl. "Should Fallacies Be Used to Teach Critical Thinking?" In Wendy Oxman, Mark Weinstein, and Nicholas M. Michelli, eds., *Critical Thinking Implications for Teaching and Teachers.* Upper Montclair, N.J.: Institute for Critical Thinking, Montclair State University, 1992.

Hamlyn, D. W. "Epistemology and Conceptual Development." In T. Mischel, ed., *Cognitive Development and Epistemology.* London: Academic Press, 1971.

Experience and the Growth of Understanding. London: Routledge and Kegan Paul, 1978.

Hirst, Paul H., ed. *Knowledge and the Curriculum.* London: Routledge and Kegan Paul, 1974.

Husserl, Edmund. *Experience and Judgment: Investigations in a Genealogy of Logic.* Evanston, Ill.: Northwestern University Press, 1973.

Inhelder, Barbel, and Jean Piaget. *The Early Growth of Logic in the Child.* New York: Norton, 1964.

Kapp, Ernst. *Greek Foundations of Traditional Logic.* New York: AMS Press, 1967.

Kuhn, Thomas S. *The Essential Tension.* Chicago: University of Chicago Press, 1977.

La Charité, Raymond C. *The Concept of Judgment in Montaigne.* The Hague: Martinus Nijhoff, 1968.

Lewis, C. I. *An Analysis of Knowledge and Valuation.* La Salle, Ill.: Open Court, 1971.

Link, Frances R., ed. *Essays on the Intellect*. Alexandria, Va.: ASCD, 1985.

Lipman, Matthew. "Critical Thinking – What Can It Be?" *Educational Leadership* 16:1 (September 1988).

"Philosophy for Children." *Metaphilosophy* 7:1 (January 1976).

Philosophy Goes to School. Philadelphia: Temple University Press, 1988.

Lipman, Matthew, and Ann Margaret Sharp. *Growing Up With Philosophy*. Philadelphia: Temple University Press, 1978.

Lipman, Matthew, Ann Margaret Sharp, and Frederick S. Oscanyan. *Philosophy in the Classroom*. 2d ed. Philadelphia: Temple University Press, 1980.

Lloyd, G. E. R. *Polarity and Analogy: Two Types of Argumentation in Early Greek Thought*. London: Cambridge University Press, 1971.

Lyotard, Jean-Francois. *The Post-Modern Condition: A Report on Knowledge*. Minneapolis: University of Minnesota Press, 1984.

Martin, Benjamin. *Splitting the Difference: Compromise and Integrity in Ethics and Politics*. Lawrence: University Press of Kansas, 1990.

Matthews, Gareth B. *The Philosophy of Childhood*. Cambridge, Mass.: Harvard University Press, 1994.

McPeck, John E. *Critical Thinking and Education*. New York: St. Martin's, 1981.

Mead, G. H. *Mind, Self and Society*. Chicago: University of Chicago Press, 1934.

Moran, Richard. *Authority and Estrangement: An Essay on Self-knowledge*. Princeton: Princeton University Press, 2001.

Nickerson, Raymond S., David N. Perkins, and Edward E. Smith. *The Teaching of Thinking*. Hillsdale, N.J.: Erlbaum, 1985.

"Why Teach Thinking?" In J. B. Baron and R. J. Sternberg, eds., *Teaching Thinking Skills: Theory and Practice*. New York: W. H. Freeman and Company, 1986.

Peirce, Charles Sanders. *Collected Papers*. Edited by Charles Hartshorne and Paul Weiss. 8 vols. Cambridge, Mass.: Belknap Press of Harvard University Pres, 1965–6.

"Some Consequences of Four Incapacities." In Justus Buchler, ed., *Philosophical Writings of Peirce*. New York: Dover, 1955.

Perkins, David N. *The Mind's Best Work*. Cambridge, Mass.: Harvard University Press, 1981.

Perkins, David N., and Gavriel Salomon. "Are Cognitive Skills Context-Bound?" *Educational Researcher* (January–February 1989).

Peters, R. S., ed. *The Concept of Education*. New York: Humanities Press, 1967.

Piaget, Jean. *Judgment and Reasoning in the Child*. London: Routledge, 1924.

Logic and Psychology. New York: Basic, 1957.

Pines, A. Leon. "Toward a Taxonomy of Conceptual Relations and the Implications for the Evaluation of Cognitive Structures." In Leo H. T. West and A. Leon Pines, eds., *Cognitive Structure and Conceptual Change*. New York: Academic Press, 1985.

Pritchard, Michael S. *Reasonable Children*. Lawrence: University Press of Kansas, 1996.

Rawls, John. *Political Liberalism*. New York: Columbia University Press, 1993.

Rondhis, Thecla, and Karel van der Leeuw. "Performances and Progress in Philosophy: An Attempt at Operationalization of Criteria." *Teaching Philosophy* 23 (2000). (This article discusses some of the most important evaluative reports on the effects of philosophy for children.)

Ryle, Gilbert. *Collected Papers*. 2 vols. New York: Barnes and Noble, 1971.

Scheffler, Israel. *Conditions of Knowledge: An Introduction to Epistemology and Education*. Chicago: Scott, Foresman, 1965.

Schleifer, Michel, ed. *La Formation du Jugement*. Montréal: Les Editions Logique, 1992.

Smith, Barry, ed. *Practical Knowledge: Outlines of a Theory of Traditions and Skills*. London: Croom Helm, 1988.

Toulmin, Stephen. "Concept-formation in Philosophy and Psychology." In Sidney Hook, ed., *Dimensions of Mind*. New York: Collier Books, 1960.

Turner, Susan M., and Gareth B. Matthews. *The Philosopher's Child: Critical Perspectives in the Western Tradition*. Rochester, N.Y.: University of Rochester Press, 1994.

Vygotsky, Lev. *Thought and Language*. Edited and translated by Eugenia Hanfman and Gertrude Vakar. Cambridge, Mass.: MIT Press, 1962.

Williams, B. A. O. *Ethics and the Limits of Philosophy*. Cambridge, Mass.: Harvard University Press, 1985.

Wittgenstein, Ludwig. *Philosophical Investigations*. Oxford: Blackwell Publisher, 1953.

Remarks on the Foundations of Mathematics. Edited by C. H. von Wright, R. Rhees, and G. E. Anscombe. Cambridge, Mass.: MIT Press, 1983.

Index